CREATIVE TEACHING:
SCIENCE IN THE EARLY YEARS
AND PRIMARY CLASSROOM

Also available:

Science 5–11
A Guide for Teachers
Alan Howe, Dan Davies, Kendra McMahon, Lee Towler and Tonie Scott
1-84312-319-3

The Teaching of Science in Primary Schools 4e
Wynne Harlen and Anne Qualter
1-84312-132-8

Science Knowledge for Primary Teachers
Understanding the Science in the QCA Scheme
Linda Gillard
1-84312-188-3

Science and ICT
A Creative Approach to Big Ideas
John Meadows
1-84312-120-4

CREATIVE TEACHING:
SCIENCE IN THE EARLY YEARS AND PRIMARY CLASSROOM

Ann Oliver

David Fulton Publishers

This edition reprinted 2010 by Routledge
2 Park Square, Milton Park, Abingdon, Oxon, OX14 4RN
Simultaneously published in the USA and Canada
By Routledge
270 Madison Avenue, New York, NY 10016

www.onestopeducation.co.uk

First published in Great Britain in 2006 by David Fulton Publishers

10 9 8 7 6 5 4 3

British Library Cataloguing in Publication Data
A catalogue record for this book is available from the British Library.

ISBN: 1 84312 259 6

EAN: 978 184312 259 3

Typeset by RefineCatch Limited, Bungay, Suffolk
Printed and bound in Great Britain

Contents

Acknowledgements

The writing of this book would not have been possible without the inspiration received from the many primary teachers, trainee teachers and children with whom I have worked over the past few years. Their creative thinking has illustrated how learning science in the context of the classroom can be amazingly imaginative, original and fun.

I would particularly like to thank local primary teachers – Andy McConnell, Denise Grant, Zoë Ladbrooke, Jo Luce, Alan Pagden and Paul Williams – for their courage to teach science with vision. Throughout the project I have been grateful for the critical advice of my colleague Rob Barnes; to Tom Moore for his technical assistance; and to Tracey Alcock of David Fulton for her encouragement and serenity in guiding me to completion. Finally, I would like to thank my family and friends for listening so patiently to me talk about creative science teaching at every opportunity!

I would finally like to thank Alan Howe, Kendra McMahon, Chris Collier and Dan Davies from Bath Spa University for their important contributions to the book as authors of Chapters 6, 7, 8 and 9 respectively. Their assistance was invaluable!

Ann Oliver
2006

About the contributors

Chris Collier is Senior Lecturer in Primary Education at Bath Spa University where he teaches primary science and design and technology on the undergraduate, postgraduate and continuing professional development programmes. He also acts as a PGCE professional tutor. His research interests include the development of thinking skills through science and the different approaches to teaching science in the early years.

Professor Dan Davies is Principal Lecturer in Primary Education and leader of the PGCE Primary Programme in the School of Education at Bath Spa University. He teaches primary science and design and technology, together with learning theory, research methodology and creativity on undergraduate and postgraduate programmes. He has recently directed two funded research projects: 'Creative Teachers for Creative Learners' funded by the TDA, and an evaluation of science learning projects supported by the National Endowment for Science, Technology and the Arts (NESTA). His books include *Primary Design and Technology for the Future* (with Alan Howe and Ron Ritchie 2001), *Teaching Science and Design and Technology in the Early Years* (with Alan Howe 2003) and *Science 5–11: A Guide for Teachers* (with Alan Howe, Kendra McMahon, Lee Towler and Tonie Scott 2005).

Alan Howe is leader of the primary science team within the School of Education at Bath Spa University. He also teaches on undergraduate education modules, acts as a PGCE professional tutor and teaches design and technology education courses. His research interests are related to creativity and science/technology in primary education and teacher education and he is currently involved in a TDA research project, 'Creative Teacher, Creative Learner', which is exploring ways we can help trainee teachers understand and support creativity in their classrooms of the future. Recent publications include *Science 5–11: A Guide for Teachers* (with Dan Davies, Kendra McMahon, Lee Towler and Tonie Scott 2005), *Teaching Science and Design and Technology in the Early Years* (with Dan Davies 2003) and *Primary Design and Technology for the Future* (with Dan Davies and Ron Ritchie 2001).

Kendra McMahon teaches on both the undergraduate education modules and the Primary PGCE, specialising in Primary Science Education, at Bath Spa University. Her research interests include the teaching of science in primary schools, particularly at Key Stage 2, with a focus on how whole-class interactive teaching is used in science, and she is currently undertaking a PhD in this area of research. Recent publications have been in the areas of transition between Key Stages 2 and 3, and the assessment of scientific enquiry, and include *Science 5–11: A Guide for Teachers* (with Alan Howe, Dan Davies, Lee Towler and Tonie Scott 2005).

CHAPTER 1

The importance of teaching science creatively

I've been given this block of work on electricity, I have an idea about an activity but the teacher told me I have to do the one they do every year. I knew the practical bit putting batteries into appliances would be over in ten minutes but I still had to do it. I have been told not to do an investigation as it is not on their plan.

(Trainee teacher on block placement 2004)

She told me that the whisked white of an egg is chemically foam. I've been puzzling all day about why butter is also chemical foam. I think I can work it out, but it has set me thinking how I might explain this to my class. Bread and foam doesn't sound quite right does it?

(Primary teacher 2005)

Though he seems to view his schoolmasters with amused and olympian contempt, the present illusion of a superior mind is usually shattered by a display of abominable ignorance. He is a lazy observer and lazy in acquiring the solid factual foundations of knowledge. He *could* work hard.

Form master's report of John Polanyi (1929–), Nobel Prize winner, Chemistry 1986

(Hurley 2002)

The success of any lesson can be gauged by what the children have learnt and how they have been involved in that process. In reaching this goal a teacher has to decide how to go about the business of teaching and create an environment in which pupils have the opportunity to learn. If pupils are to become fascinated by science, much more is needed than coverage of topics. Some teachers are more creative than others in making decisions which influence both teaching and learning. This chapter will look at the practice of creative teachers. It draws on anecdotal evidence and examples of creative teaching to illustrate the importance placed on teaching science through investigation, making creative connections and discovering more than one answer to scientific problems.

It is clear that there is no single definition which encompasses all views of what it is to be creative or that there is a consistency in how creativity is defined (Boden 2004; Craft 2002). Even when working with prescribed schemes of work every teacher will interpret plans slightly differently. Responding to the needs of individual children involves making choices and adapting ideas. This might only be done in some small way but every lesson will be unique. A creative teacher will plan and organise activities to present a sense of purpose and build on individual talents within the framework of the prescribed curriculum. Creative teachers will see the value of providing a rich variety of experience based on practical activity. Children will be supported in considering connections, making links and finding out information as well as developing process skills.

Good science teaching reflects certain principles which promote learning, such as recognising the tentative nature of scientific results, the value of focused questions and the uncertainty of inquiry. These are evident in everything the science teacher says and does. Children quickly pick up teachers' expectations and attitudes. Children know intuitively if they are required to ask questions, come up with solutions, try alternatives or simply remember facts from a worksheet. If children see their teacher comfortable with being surprised, perplexed or confused by something observed in a science session then they will probably feel that this is an acceptable reaction. If they see their teacher trying to solve a problem, looking at alternative ways of approaching a challenge and listening carefully to several different explanations then this too will be seen as the acceptable ethos of the lesson. If they see their teacher delighted at an unexpected outcome then they too will value the unanticipated.

Creative science

My friend asked me what I was writing a book about. I replied that it was about teaching science. She responded with a single word, 'Boring'. Being a keen and knowledgeable gardener her conversations often refer to scientific processes and descriptions. She is extremely animated when talking about variation and diversity of plants or the particular care needed to germinate different seeds and diverse methods of propagation. Science knowledge and understanding are unmistakably evident in her explanations. In common with some teachers there is a clear mismatch of perception of science as a subject and science as an activity. If experience of school science has been mundane, prescriptive or lacking in purpose then it is understandable that science is seen as boring. What she didn't acknowledge was that she was already talking about scientific processes, not even realising the creative ideas she had sparked.

Children seem to have fewer problems thinking more widely. All we need to do is ask them about their perfect science lesson.

I would get all the equipment out like spatulas and pipettes and mix everything to design new chemicals and investigate suspensions and solutions and find out more about DNA. Mix different DNA extracts.

(Kimberley 10 years)

Go to a zoo and let all the animals go.

(Ruby 7 years)

I would like to dissect different animals. Cut them open and look inside.

(Rajeev 10 years)

Make dinosaur models and put them in the garden and tell people about them, how they killed other animals with their teeth and jaws and feet.

(Daniel 9 years)

Mix chemicals to make explosives and fireworks and try all dangerous stuff.

(Sean 8 years)

I would start by picking a topic out of food hygiene or electricity or dissecting frogs. Then we would go to Las Vegas to study electricity, then an aquarium to study fish: how their bones are like and their body. I would start with options then in groups report back with results and ideas then experiment on our own and research with someone.

(Levi 10 years)

My perfect science lesson would be if we could go round our homes/schools and see what had the most bacteria. I wish though we could do genetic splicing.

(Padma 10 years)

Make a film about a caterpillar and a butterfly.

(Jessica 5 years)

Make electrical circuits all the time.

(Ben 10 years)

A creative approach to teaching delivered in an interesting and fun way does not mean learning is diminished.

Creative teachers:

- provide imaginative activities;
- vary methods of teaching;
- explain in ways to engage thinking, including modelling;
- plan for pupils to use their own initiative;
- are flexible in pursuing ideas;
- respond to unplanned opportunities;
- challenge thinking;
- value the exchange of ideas;

- accept uncertainty;
- raise questions;
- make connections clearer;
- discuss thinking and consider alternatives;
- look at things closely and differently;
- encourage speculation;
- respond to surprise.

Almost everyone remembers a lesson or learning experience which was positive in some way. It might be because they were different from the usual format but those experiences which stick in people's minds often include some of the characteristics mentioned above. In reading the following examples, think about the ways in which a creative stance has been adopted by the teacher.

Creative example 1

In 1961 there was a total eclipse of the Sun. All the children were taken into the playground and warned not to look at the Sun. They were scared about looking at it. It became cold, eerily quiet and dark. Once back in the classroom the teacher drew a diagram on the board showing the spherical bodies of the Earth, Sun and moon and went on to explain what had just been experienced. She then used three children to model the movement of the heavenly bodies. Although the model was crude it had a lasting impression because of the previous physical experience in the playground. She had helped the pupils make a connection between theory and practice. This was before the time of space travel or real-time photo images from satellites. Her creative approach left a lasting impression not only in establishing basic facts but also the importance of modelling to develop scientific understanding. Forty-three years on, this lesson is remembered and discussed. In 1961 there was no National Curriculum and no statutory requirement to put primary science on the timetable. The teacher had successfully used an opportune moment to engage thinking and explain facts.

Creative example 2

More recently, in the year 2000, a football sock was found at the edge of a school pond, sodden, misshapen and covered in weed and grass. On examination, five different plants had successfully germinated and grown on the sock; intertwined roots had established a secure and unbreakable hold between layers of fabric. The sock was retrieved by a 7-year-old boy during a class nature walk looking for evidence of animal habitats. At first it prompted a great deal of disgust as it was soggy and smelly. The sock was taken back to the classroom by the teacher and used to promote discussion on what plants need to grow (NC). Previously, many children had told the teacher that plants need soil to grow. She decided to challenge this belief and suggested that socks were brought in on which a variety of seeds would be placed and various conditions observed. Many socks, large, small, old, new, holey and decidedly ancient, appeared. Ideas progressed from this simple beginning. Children independently set up experiments using a variety of seeds and materials as growing mediums. The plants growing on the original football sock were all identified using keys and the internet as well as reference books. The children were astounded by the strength of the roots and their inability to tear some of them. These were examined using an Intel microscope and observational drawings of the form and structure were completed. This led to a discussion of roots we eat and root adaptation to various climates and soil types. One girl mentioned that her mother grew orchids and they had roots in the air. Another group used a Newton meter to measure the pull they could exert on the roots and to see the force needed to break them. They were amazed at how strong they were. Discussions concerning the difference between germination and growth developed, as did the desire to set up experiments and find things out. Pupils began to use their initiative to follow lines of inquiry. Thinking had been challenged and exploration encouraged.

Identifying a creative approach

Although each example of creative teaching is unique, there is a common underlying principle that teaching is most successful when children are required to be more than receivers of knowledge. Consider the football sock (Creative example 2) as a catalyst for pursuing ideas by promoting inquiry and the eclipse (Creative example 1) as a way of explaining a complex cause and effect model through related personal experience. By comparison, a prescribed worksheet method of teaching has limited potential for helping pupils understand both science subject knowledge and the nature of science. Requiring exact memorisation may well hamper formation of more constructive ideas. The notion that there is only one way of working through a solution and, probably more importantly, that there is always a solution is damaging to the creative process. In a creative approach the outcome will depend on the line of inquiry pursued. The acquisition of process skills to link and test ideas is vital to a creative approach to learning. If these skills are not developed then they will not be used efficiently or with any rigour and ideas will not be properly tested. Time is needed to explore questions and follow ideas; sometimes what is not found out, or found out to be wrong, leads to greater understanding.

Creative example 3

Naresh, aged 10, read in a book how to make crystals by placing a piece of thread in a salt solution suspended on a pencil. He was eager to try this, carefully followed instructions and monitored progress for a week. He was both puzzled and disappointed that he could not see any evidence indicating the formation of a crystal. The teacher encouraged him to consider and identify the factors involved which would influence the formation of a crystal, including the strength of the solution, temperature of the liquid, length of the string, time taken and so on. This discussion led Naresh to research crystal formation and set up a new, improved experiment. This time he used a more concentrated solution and placed it in a cooler box. A crystal formed and Naresh was able not only to explain the procedure but also to recognise and discuss the conditions required. In the original experiment the instructions were flawed as the ratio of salt to water was not sufficient to start the process. If the teacher had explained in a recipe, step-by-step, 'painting by numbers' fashion how a successful formation of a crystal could be achieved the children would probably be able to repeat the process. The outcome would be the same but the journey would be different. In challenging thinking and considering alternatives the responsibility is put on the learner to make sense of what they are doing. Encouraging speculation, raising questions and considering ideas involves a creative approach.

Creative example 4

In a cookery lesson children mixed air with egg white, beating the mixture to form stiff peaks. Charlotte asked the question, 'Is this a physical change or a chemical change?' This was not a science lesson but Charlotte was used to asking questions about things that she found puzzling. Her teacher encouraged her to do so. This was a difficult question to answer and although the teacher made an attempt, she was not happy with her response. She shared this unease with the children, telling them that she thought it was a chemical change because she thought a different substance had been made but she was not sure. This question led to a wider discussion, with the pupils asking different teachers and scientists about their views.

Several of the scientists, mostly secondary schoolteachers, replied that a chemical change had taken place. One response was more informative and speculative:

From the chemistry expert . . .

Egg white (whipped in this way to make meringue) is a foam.

A foam is a colloid – of which there are 4 types:

1. Foam – gas suspended in liquid

2. Emulsion – liquid suspended in liquid

3. Suspension – solid suspended in liquid

4. Gel – liquid suspended in solid

> The type of change doesn't really fit in either chemical or physical categories very comfortably. It's not a chemical change because you haven't really made new substances but by beating in the gas (air) to make the colloid the bonds are changed so it's 'more' than a physical change.
>
> Can you get the egg white back? Well – maybe if you left it for a long time but obviously the enzymes would come into play before that time and it would go off and begin to decompose. Similarly, if you tried to heat it to break the bonds you'd cook it.

Charlotte is 10 years old and a very able, inquisitive child (Browne and Haylock 2004). She realised that her question raised debate. Even experts found it difficult to be certain of a correct answer. Her question was not of a controversial nature but highlighted the precise understanding of molecular change needed to give an accurate response. On this occasion the teacher used the opportunity to set up a debate board. The responses of science teachers and scientists collected by e-mail were displayed as they were received. This information helped pupils recognise the complex nature of a scientifically correct explanation and also that experts explained in different ways. The teacher decided to set homework to extend this idea. Pupils were asked to find evidence of scientific debate in the press. The teacher wanted to raise awareness of alternative views. Chosen headlines were pasted on the board and different opinions were added. Children were encouraged to add their own views over a period of time as new evidence was collected. Two main topics became talking points, obesity and 'designer babies'. As a result of this development a healthy eating topic based on research became the focus of the children's science work for the next month, with the more able pupils debating ethical issues concerning gene manipulation. Methods of creative planning are further examined in Chapter 3.

Predictable routes to known outcomes

By contrast, much school science is centred on teaching and learning banks of knowledge on a *need to know basis* using certain vocabulary, identifying factors and looking at a particular cause and effect. There is huge creative potential to build on this model by following ideas, responding to curiosity and questioning beliefs. The lack of flexibility in a predictable route diminishes choice. Content is restricted and there is little opportunity or scope for following lines of interest. Dealing with problems raised by pupils is fundamental to teaching creatively.

If the answer to a question is already known there is little point to exploring possible results. Investigations with known outcomes following a predictable route do little to hold pupils' attention or advance their learning (Oliver 2001). Too often children are not inspired to want to find out because they already have experience of the activity or some understanding of what will happen. In play they explore materials and have some notion of their properties. Even a very young child will realise that materials behave differently. Any question posed which does not challenge or intrigue will not engage the learner in pursuing inquiry, and although they might enjoy the process science will be routine and mundane.

Predictable example 1

Various kinds of paper, including kitchen roll, laminated paper, cartridge paper, tissue paper and tracing paper, were cut into strips and suspended over a tray of water. The children were asked to predict which one would soak up the most water. Absorbency as a material property was explained (Wenham 1995). Not surprisingly, everyone predicted that the kitchen roll would absorb the most water. Observations were made about the various papers, 'Tissue paper will melt and go sticky if it gets wet', 'Water leaves raindrops on plastic paper', 'Wet slides off tracing paper', 'My mum always uses kitchen roll to wipe up spilt drink'. A test to see if the results matched the prediction was carried out. Children were occupied and enjoyed the activity. Process skills, including observation, measuring, predicting, recording data and testing, were all practised in a collaborative way. Children practised what they knew, including how to carry out a test. Verification that their prediction was right probably satisfied them. Learning about absorbency as a property or developing curiosity to explain the nature of absorbent materials did not happen. Pupils were limited to the predictable; carrying out instructions to find out something they already knew. There are simple adaptations a teacher can make to raise the profile of inquiry in this lesson. For example, limiting the choice of paper to a selection of five different kitchen rolls would encourage speculation, discussion and observation. Theories on absorbency would be tested through disagreement and debate. Refining ideas and explaining reasons for choices demands higher-order thinking if the outcome is unknown. Findings would either verify or dispute manufacturers' claims but the outcome would not be predictable.

The method of teaching using problematic situations or questions to advance thinking and inspire inquiry demands a creative approach. It is not a predictable route to a known outcome. Exploring diverse developments requires a confidence based on the understanding that the process of science is of value and that meaning is often partially constructed. Thoroughly interesting questions are respected as an end in themselves and contradictions are used to stimulate debate. The teacher is responsive to issues raised and adapts subject matter accordingly. It demands a great deal of confidence to encourage awareness of controversial issues as a focus for teaching the curriculum. It is not common practice in primary science teaching. Although many teachers would welcome the opportunity to pursue ideas and follow leads unfamiliar to the prescribed curriculum, they feel a compulsion to stick to the requirements of imparting factual knowledge and understanding of process skills. Teachers' reflections on their own practice indicate that they often feel restricted and unable to teach creatively.

Limitations on outcomes

A significant proportion of school science does not fit well with creative teaching. There is no doubt that in the climate of OfSTED, SATs and QCA many teachers feel not only are they being told what to teach but also how to teach. The pressure to perform well in league tables and achieve even better SATs results drives decisions about how to teach. Doing what OfSTED likes is seen by some as a safe option. Although science does not develop in a linear way any more than learning does, the pressure is on teachers to deliver an outcome-driven curriculum no more evident than in following the QCA and preparing children for SATs testing.

> We are cramming for SATs this term. It is boring. When I say we are doing science the children groan. They used to love it, now they are turned off. All they do is learn the answers and they hate it. Whatever are we doing to them?
>
> (Year 6 teacher 2004)
>
> If I have to watch another 20 ice cubes on a piece of cling film melt I will scream. There must be better ways to teach the water cycle.
>
> (KS2 teacher 2006)
>
> Why can't the National Curriculum be taught without using the rather dry experiments recommended by prescriptive schemes?
>
> (KS2 teacher 2005)
>
> I am going to have a staff meeting and get the teachers to come up with their own activities for addressing the units of work more creatively. I am interested in exploring how the National Curriculum can be taught without using the rather dry experiments suggested by schemes.
>
> (Science co-ordinator 2004)
>
> Prescriptive schemes are killing school science.
>
> (Science co-ordinator 2005)

In referring to recommended schemes of work some teachers actually believe that the QCA is a statutory document and that they have to follow it prescriptively. Others realise that it is not statutory but feel a need to conform. More enlightened teachers use schemes constructively and adapt plans to the needs of their pupils. Some teachers devise their own plans in line with National Curriculum requirements and use opportunities which present themselves to make science relate to experience. More creative teachers look for opportunities to challenge thinking and teach science in a way that enables pupils also to be creative. When teachers use schemes they do so in a variety of ways.

- Prescriptively including only suggested activities in a closed time frame. 'We always do this in Year 6 at this time of the year as it says in the scheme we have to.'

- Following the structure to ensure coverage and adapting some suggested activities. 'We feel that we are covering all we need to do if we follow the scheme but sometimes we add other activities because they are boring to teach.'

- Identifying objectives and using them as a framework for planning. 'We thought that we could start with the learning objectives and devise our own activities.'

- Using parts of the document selectively. 'If we think the unit fits in well with the National Curriculum and we can't think of a better way we use it.'

- Using the framework as a starting point. 'We like the idea of how the scheme covers the curriculum but we then work out our own plan by taking one aspect and having a brainstorming session to see what we can come up with.'

Nowhere, perhaps, does a teacher feel more frustrated than when they are unable to use their professional judgement. When a lesson does not go well, teachers reflect on the influence they had on the outcome with the aim to improve the quality of their teaching. If they feel powerless or restricted in changing their practice or unable to work effectively with the guidelines presented, teaching becomes a chore. Science taught didactically is primarily concerned with following instructions and is creatively counter-productive. It does little to help engender questioning, engage speculation or teach children about the nature of science. Sadly but not surprisingly, some teachers take this route and feel prevented from teaching science with flair and creativity. They are missing out and so are their pupils. Children want to explore ideas, ask questions and search for answers. They are naturally inquisitive. A holistic approach related to experience will make science meaningful for children. They do not see the world in terms of adult-conceived disciplines but as a whole, and wonder at how things are connected, happen and affect other things. Creative science teaching is about the process of both teaching and learning. They cannot be separate. The following examples clearly show how some teachers have brought creativity into their teaching despite current restrictions and the trend of delivering science as a bank of knowledge to be learnt.

Unpredictable routes to unknown outcomes

How much does it matter that an outcome is predictable? This seems to many teachers to be the essential feature of good science teaching. Experiments are proved by repeating them and predicting outcomes. This fits well with assessment and memorising scientific facts. Yet this is to miss the point. Scientists do not succeed by knowing exactly the outcomes of their experiments. Creative teachers will promote acceptance of unpredictable findings and recognise the value of chance. It could be said that modern antibiotics resulted from an untidy laboratory. If Fleming had not left a dish of agar-jelly uncovered, or if the window had been closed, spores would not have settled on the nutrient. Penicillin, so widely used today to combat infection, might never have been discovered. More importantly, other scientists might not have recognised the importance of what Fleming observed. Seeing differently, making connections and valuing coincidence all play a part in creative thinking. Such techniques can be utilised in the classroom by setting challenges, providing information – but not a route to be taken – and encouraging individual methods of exploration.

Creative example 5

Andy, a teacher with five years' experience, had become increasingly frustrated with the idea of prescriptively following the science scheme of work. He no longer looked forward to teaching science. A lesson on separating solids, looking at filtering with the objective and suggested task in Unit 6C 'More about dissolving', was planned. At lunchtime he made a decision: 'I'm bored with this scheme. In 10 minutes I've got to think of something more meaningful and interesting to do.' What he came up with was a problem to solve.

He set the scene of a village in Africa where resources were limited and the people were used to being creative about recycling objects and finding different ways and methods of using materials. He called them inventive thinkers. The children were then set the task of separating salt water from large cans filled with millet. He knew he could quickly gather these resources together. Andy was amazed at the way the lesson progressed. Discussions focused on methods of sieving, putting holes at certain levels in the cans, heating the cans and even comparing the temperature in Africa and the effect it would have on the speed of evaporation. Andy felt the lesson had been productive and was pleased with the results. The children were highly motivated and developed science understanding in context. They made notes and reported findings. He felt that there had been a purpose which helped pupils become critically involved in the activity. Skills to follow science exploration, refining and testing ideas, looking carefully at the process and experimental aspects of science were all used. He felt they were *doing science* and he was able to tour the room, assessing progress, guiding thinking and raising questions to challenge understanding.

He recognised that to promote a climate conducive to inquiry in which ideas are shared and valued is for him a top priority. An atmosphere which is sympathetic to debate to encourage involvement and promote higher-order thinking was clearly evident in this lesson. He was pleased with the outcome because pupils worked collaboratively, discussed information, tried out ideas, designed and tested prototypes as well as covering all obligatory objectives. Importantly, he felt that the pupils had gone further than the expected *need to know* requirements stated in the pre-scribed scheme. They had become engrossed in solving the challenge and in the process had progressed in their thinking beyond the low-level follow-instruction type of activity. Scientific thinking was evident in connections made between temperature and evaporation. Science subject knowledge was used and developed in a practical way; purpose, knowledge, methods of inquiry and procedures were all apparent.

Creative example 6

Alan is another creative teacher. He set his class of 8- and 9-year-olds a challenge to build sails for a wind turbine which would generate electricity. There is a wind turbine in the playground which generates the electricity needed for the school. Alan asked the children to think about how the structure enabled the force exerted by the wind to be used effectively. Pupils were given CDs with holes drilled in them and a variety of materials, including wood, cardboard, plastic and tin foil, to make the blades. In designing and building the structure they had to consider the position, size, shape, form and direction of the blades. The children worked independently but were expected to share their ideas and explain their thinking. An electronic data-logging system to check the prototypes with a fan to simulate the wind was set up. Power generated was logged on a graph. A whiteboard was used to display the information in real time to enable the whole class to view the results. One of the children made a sail which was slightly too large to fit the testing equipment. Many of the sails needed adapting to work at all and only a few managed to produce a reading on the screen. When they did there were whoops of delight and there was an immediate inquisition as to how the design was made.

What was especially creative about this lesson was the way in which failure was viewed. Ideas were valued and mistakes were seen as productive. Alan finished the lesson by saying that he would have to change his model to accommodate the larger sail and that science was about trying things out, changing them and using new ideas. The atmosphere was certainly conducive to inquiry. Children were keen and thoughtful in explaining why they thought their model did not work. Often in science lessons pupils are far from keen to discuss failure. This was not true in this lesson because ideas were valued and failure was seen as part of a process. It is not easy for a teacher to achieve an atmosphere conducive to inquiry. Children will respond to teachers' expectations and if discussion of why things don't work is high on the agenda they will respond. Consider the two following conversations, both excellent examples of a dialogic process in which alternatives are considered and new meanings are negotiated. T is the teacher, H and S are pupils.

Conversation 1

H. I bent both sides of my blades and it would be better if I just did one side.

T. Why did you bend both?

H. I thought it would catch more wind.

T. But it didn't?

H. No, well it did but it didn't work.

T. Why do you think that was?

H. The wind gets trapped and it needs to push.

T. So what do you think might work better?

H. Cut them in half?

T. Do you want to try that?

H. Yes.

T. Brilliant, you are working it out.

Conversation 2

S. I put some of my blades one way and one in the middle the other way.

T. Why did you do that?

S. I don't really know.

T. What did you think would happen?

S. Well, I thought it was a good idea but now I don't.

T. Why have you changed your mind?

S. Well, it stops and if they are the same way it wouldn't stop.

T. What made you think of that?

S. The way it moved it sort of stopped, I'm going to put them all the same way.

T. Excellent thinking, give it a try.

Although both examples fundamentally deal with failure, the outcome is positive. Pupils were praised for their deductive thinking and considerations of alternatives linked to scientific understanding. Crucially, it was all right to have a model that was not working. The important message received was that trial and error helped make sense of things. The children were keen to refine their models. They wanted to make it work and used the failed attempt to inform their thinking. Rewarding thinking as well as the outcome is part of a creative approach. Rewards are very powerful. Children seek to gain rewards. Creative teachers will reward those willing to take a risk, have a go at trying something, considering alternatives and thinking through surprises and discussing things that have 'gone wrong'. It is not always easy to work things out, so why not reward recognition of this. Alan was pleased with the outcome because he felt that the desire to find a good solution continued after the lesson. Discussions continued throughout the week at playtime and out of school. Some pupils tried to make a successful model at home. Others adapted the idea and used commercial kits to build models and brought them to school. This indicated clearly that the problem posed had engaged thinking and the worlds of family and friends had become congruent with the worlds of school and science.

Encouraging autonomy

Allowing and encouraging children to make decisions is crucial to a creative approach; a degree of autonomy is necessary to allow for creative thinking. Understandably, some teachers find the idea of *letting go* and giving children control a daunting prospect. Zoë worked as a scientist for some years before becoming a primary teacher. Her expert science knowledge and clear view of how children learn is evident in her confident, creative manner of teaching. She is keen to encourage decision making in her pupils; giving them opportunities to make choices and decisions is part of her teaching style. She also runs an after-school science club. Twenty-two children attend and there is a waiting list of thirty more. From start to finish it is a hive of activity; involvement is continuous, some children work independently, some collaboratively, interesting questions are raised and everyone reports findings. So why are children queuing up to do extra science after school? Pupils' responses included:

- 'After school is better than normal school because you get to work faster and do more things, you are not held up by other people.'
- 'I like after-school science because you get more choice, in normal lessons equipment is limited and you don't get to choose it.'
- 'You get to find out stuff for yourself, not just what the teacher tells you. You get to write your own notes, not just what the teacher writes.'
- 'I like the club better than normal lessons because you get to go outside and not follow a plan.'

The after-school science club is obviously a great success, not just in the way it is received but most importantly in the learning which takes place. Each week a different aspect of the National Curriculum is studied. This is chosen by the teacher and several work stations with resources, equipment and reference material are set up. At each work station there is a question to guide thinking. Does light travel in straight lines? Can you make a shadow smaller? How does a photocopier work? Can you make a camera? Which pair of sunglasses let the most light through? Can you explain how a prism splits white light? Which surface reflects the most light? All suggested activities are based on the National Curriculum programme of study for Key Stage 2, Sc4 'Physical processes', everyday effects of light: but many aspects of Key Stage 3 were touched on because pupils made decisions to follow lines of inquiry and experiment with ideas beyond the expectations of the KS2 curriculum, including: (3b–3f) *That non-luminous objects are seen because light scattered from them enters our eyes; How light is reflected from plane surfaces; How light is refracted at the boundary between two different materials; That white light can be dispersed to give a range of colours; The effect of colour filters on white light and how coloured objects appear in white light and in other colours of light.*

Zoë explained how she organised the sessions:

I set out several research questions around the room. The children decide which question they are going to take as a starting point; they might have their own ideas to pursue. If they do, that's OK and I try to find the resources they need. I also try to do as little formal teaching as possible. Adam is colour blind and he has been asking questions about it so I have included some information at the research table for him. They take their own notes and they decide how to do this, they decide what is important to write down. They know that they will be expected to report back and explain what they have done and present at least one interesting fact.

By giving children a degree of autonomy within a well-organised structure they often feel more responsible for their learning. The pace of individual learning is catered for. Even though the rules for reporting back to the group are demanding, there is purpose in this form of reporting. Minimising laborious and time-consuming writing tasks is necessary if an intriguing and creative approach is to be followed. Younger children find writing to a specific format difficult and often have problems in making sense of charts produced. A good rule is to ask a child to explain the information set out on any chosen method of recording. If they can explain the data presented and interpret findings then the method is appropriate. If children choose how they record data it has purpose for them; they are not producing something the teacher wants but rather something which will help them in explaining to others what they have found out. This information can be used both summatively and formatively to assess progress and understanding of science process skills and levels of subject knowledge. Creative assessment strategies are discussed further in Chapter 10.

By requiring at least one interesting fact from each pupil there is no pressure on individuals to produce pages of correct or acceptable answers. Each fact builds on the findings of others. The strong conviction that choice is essential to creative development is a focus of autonomous teaching. Knowledge is constructed in a developmental manner by considering and accepting new ideas which replace naïve understanding. If this process takes place in a way that engages the learner in a context familiar to their experience then the tension created by *having to know* can be lessened or even eliminated. Children feel secure in reporting *one interesting fact* but the body of knowledge gained goes beyond individual expectations. Scientists often work in this way and this method should be considered a worthy enterprise in the classroom. Recognising the value of collaboration, sharing ideas and views promotes an emphasis on how to do science. This is a creative approach to learning and transcends individual recall of facts as an effective way of testing and challenging existing understanding. Teachers face the dilemma of matching attainment of understanding designated by the curriculum and providing opportunities for self-directed learning that has the characteristics of authentic scientific activity. The model of teaching presented by Zoë clearly indicates a match between the two, with subject knowledge attainment going beyond the expected.

Summary of main points

Creative science teachers plan beyond the prescribed, not only in the content of the lesson but also in methods of working. Pedagogy clearly relates to interest and significance, prioritising questions to be explored and testing ideas in a sensitive way. They know that learning science is not just a matter of acquiring a few specialist terms. It involves gaining familiarity with the way in which concepts and ideas are related. Understanding concepts is a developmental process and cannot be about answering questions in a tick-box fashion. Teaching creatively is not concerned with coverage or ease.

Creative science teachers:

- provide challenging activities;
- give children time to talk;
- share and generate ideas;
- encourage independent exploration and discovery;
- value speculation and original thinking;
- help pupils make useful connections;
- give permission to try something new, take risks;
- encourage wonder, curiosity and spontaneity;
- follow children's ideas purposefully;

- accept individual routes to learning;
- show flexibility in their thinking;
- opt for alternative non-routine approaches;
- encourage complexity as a way of stimulating interest.

Creative science teachers do not:

- follow schemes of work without adaptation;
- teach to the test;
- focus on pupils producing written work;
- stifle lateral thinking;
- expect predictable outcomes;
- use resources restrictively;
- teach didactically;
- ignore pupils' ideas;
- discourage interaction;
- support an ethos of prescription.

Issues for reflection

- Think about the science you have taught and which sessions come readily to mind. How have you responded to children's ideas and questions to initiate inquiry? Do you encourage individual contributions or do you consider them a hindrance to teaching?

- If there was no statutory requirement or prescribed schemes of work for primary science, how would you plan and teach science?

- If you were given a block of time, say a week, to do science, would you welcome the opportunity to organise activities which acted as starting points without prescribed outcomes?

- In your experience of learning science, do you think you were taught in a creative way? Did you have a teacher who made science interesting, relevant and fun? Did you feel that you had the opportunity to develop your ideas and make decisions?

- Make a list of ways in which you would like to teach science. Check the points on your list against the bullet points referring to creative teaching and creative teachers. If you have identified several similarities then consider how easy you find it to adopt a creative approach to teaching.

Discussion points

- How do you define creativity? Are there different kinds of creativity? Is it possible to be creative and be a scientist?

- Are teachers comfortable teaching the National Curriculum using suggested schemes of work or would they prefer to devise their own programme of study? Is there middle ground?

- Some people find it harder to be creative than others. Is it possible to develop a more creative approach to science teaching if you consider yourself to be one of these people?

Recommended reading

Boden, M. (2004) *The Creative Mind: Myths and Mechanisms*. London: Open University Press

Boo, M.D. (1999) *Enquiring Children, Challenging Teaching*. Buckingham: Open University Press

Frost, J. (1997) *Creativity in Primary Science*. Buckingham: Open University Press

Johnston, J. (1996) *Early Explorations in Science*. Buckingham: Open University Press

References

Boden, M. (2004) *The Creative Mind: Myths and Mechanisms*. London: Open University Press

Browne, A. and Haylock, D. (2004) *Professional Issues for Primary Teachers*. London: Paul Chapman

Craft, A. (2002) *Creativity across the Primary Curriculum: Framing and Developing Practice*. London: Routledge Falmer

Hurley, C. (2002) *Could Do Better*. London: Pocket Books

Oliver, A. (2001) 'Teaching Science', in A. Cockburn (ed.) *Teaching Children 3–11: A Student's Guide*. London: Paul Chapman

Wenham, M. (1995) *Understanding Primary Science*. London: Paul Chapman

CHAPTER 2

Creative science teaching

Creativity should not be considered a separate mental faculty but a characteristic of our way of thinking, knowing and making choices.

(Edwards, Gandini and Forman 1998)

There is hardly a better example of this way of thinking and knowing than the work of Miriam Rothschild (1908–2005). She considered herself no scientist, yet had published over 350 research papers, 150 of them about fleas. She held several honorary degrees. In a Radio 4 interview (1997), she commented, 'I get so interested in everything; I've always been free to play.' At the age of 4 she had a ladybird collection, as well as quails and worms. As the only applicant she won a research scholarship to Naples: 'The sea fauna were so beautiful, incredible jellyfish.' 'The next thing I got obsessed with was fleas; you could forget everything observing fleas.' If this was play, where did it lead? Miriam Rothschild discovered some amazing connections in nature: heart poisons collected by butterflies, oestrogen of the doe rabbit needed by the mixi flea (giving us some idea of how the contraceptive pill works), and her 'Eureka moment' was to discover how fleas jump by the release of a force, click mechanism. 'I saw it in my mind's eye ... that's how it happened. Everyone can be a naturalist, all you need is interest.'

The creative process involved here is one of playing and making connections, something many teachers do every day in their lessons. Even with the same starting point, objectives and resources, teachers will interpret, plan and deliver lessons differently. This is because teaching is not just a job to be done. Every lesson is created. In this process the degree of creative expectation and experience will relate to the value placed on creativity as an aid to learning. Creativity is not measurable and consequently it is difficult to define. It is possible, however, to recognise features of a creative approach to teaching science. Despite sometimes being able to predict outcomes, creative science teaching is full of unexpected responses to what is happening. There are yet more unexpected responses to what children think is happening rather than what actually is.

A creative approach to teaching science

You probably take the same route each day unless something happens to alter the routine. It might be that the road is difficult to negotiate because there has been a build-up of traffic and ahead you can see a line of vehicles snaking to the horizon. Deciding to turn off, you take a route along country lanes. You have a very different, less predictable journey, seeing many unfamiliar scenes, dappled shadows, autumn colours on trees, pheasants in a field and steam rising from a dung heap, lacy frosted spiders' webs and fewer cars. Concentration is necessary as the road is twisting and narrow. The journey is longer but the experience is different and often richer for having deviated from the expected route.

Creative teaching is about offering a rich experience. Unlike the route along a narrow country lane, it need take no longer but is a better learning experience because it makes children think. Essentially it involves:

- recognising that learning is a process and that attainment is not an end in itself;
- striving for meaning and understanding;
- remaining open to possible outcomes;
- trusting natural inquisitiveness to explore;
- not necessarily taking the safe option;
- considering and evaluating different consequences, including dead ends;
- rejecting, refining and redefining findings;
- playing with results;
- raising questions.

These characteristics are not new to education, but for some teachers they seem the antithesis of scientific activity. Surely science has to be precise and is all about knowledge of how things work and why? Nobody wants children to learn science that is plainly wrong. Creative science teachers would not disagree with any of this. They can play with scientific results and raise questions because their basic knowledge of science is actually very sound. They play that old philosopher's trick of not giving away answers but actively encouraging understanding and discovery. Creative teachers know how to listen to children, how to encourage them to take the initiative in pursuing ideas and guide them in industrious ways to understand. Work of quality and meaning is the desired outcome, not simply arriving at right answers by the fastest means. Methods of achieving such aims are flexible and grounded in the belief that children have the ability to discover for themselves, debate issues and sometimes struggle to achieve success.

How children learn

It is widely recognised that children learn subject knowledge in context and through practical application (Craft 2002; Hodson 1998; Wood 1988). The choice to develop understanding in a particular way which is different from the formalised fits well with how children learn. However, this approach is not as common as it might be.

> Mostly teachers anticipate a specific outcome related to a set of objectives. They talk about autonomy and choice but it is rarely evident in primary science other than choices made within controlled conditions. I think some reasons for this lie in the way that evolving science tasks are a bit difficult to manage and organise. They don't fit with coverage of an accepted route, do they?
>
> (Lecturer in Education 2005)

Understandably, teachers are concerned about achieving particular targets and not with something which does not relate to an expected outcome. This is all very reasonable but misguided and too often assessment driven. The best creative teaching counters this attitude by achieving both high standards and coverage through effective pupil participation. If pupils participate, you can be sure this involves questions, leading to misconceptions, leading to debate and a good deal of rigour. It is surprising, for example, how many answers children will give to the following three questions:

- How do demolition experts get buildings to fall inwards (implode) and not fall outwards?
- Why are skyscrapers designed to sway in the wind?
- Why was there only a small amount of rubble when the Twin Towers collapsed?

Finding answers to these questions can make children question their assumptions and the assumptions implied by the questions themselves. A skilful teacher will recognise that children cannot be inquisitive without also being critical of the results of their investigation. Science, presented as a puzzle, a curiosity with quizzical questions, does not just test existing knowledge. It can promote understanding in a meaningful context of peer-group discussion, competition, co-operation, misconception and the search for some agreement.

Progress and requirements

Progress in science and technology accelerates at a rapid rate. On 26 June 2000 the 'working draft' of the human genome sequence was announced. The technology advanced so quickly that it took four years to sequence the first billion letters, but only four months to sequence the second billion (Tallack 2001). When the National Curriculum became statutory in 1988 there was no internet facility and e-mail communication was something of the future. Today, both are used competently by 5-year-olds. The next generation will be dealing with advances, decisions and opportunities which we can only guess at. Teaching that is limited to the acquisition of knowledge and assessment of existing knowledge will not prepare children to make well-informed decisions, question beliefs or challenge thinking. The teacher has a responsibility to equip pupils to make decisions and interpret data. This can be done successfully in the context of the National Curriculum but not if schemes of work are followed didactically, without imagination or creative interpretation. Taking advantage of key moments to make science meaningful is crucial in helping children be critical, just as accepting disagreement as a mechanism for developing understanding is necessary for consideration of evidence. Fundamental questions a teacher might ask include:

- What science are children learning?
- Why are they learning this science?
- How can teachers be dynamic in extending communication and understanding of science?
- How can a creative approach to science aid learning?

In England the National Curriculum is the only statutory requirement placed on primary teachers. The entitlement to this in science begins at Year 1 when children are 5 years old. At this age an aim is to teach by developing children's understanding of science as a process (Sc1) and increasing their subject knowledge (Sc2, Sc3, Sc4). Much good practice, including provoking instances of scientific interest, encouraging scepticism and rational thought, fits well with the content of the National Curriculum. This is not a problem. What appears to be problematic is the application of suggested prescribed activities and routine methods of delivery. The National Curriculum offers freedom of interpretation, which schemes of work do not. In following a scheme, choices made are rarely made by the child. Usually a tight control is placed on content and methods of working. Children learn best if they can relate findings to experience and make links with familiar objects and events. Teachers can and do help pupils make connections in scientific understanding through everyday experience.

So far, examples have included questions, but science teaching involves a great deal of purposeful observation made by children. If children are to make connections, they need to raise their own questions through observing. For example:

- thinking about the changes experienced moving from strong sunlight to shadow;
- comparing the length of individual children's shadows when walking;
- observing how shadows change during the year;
- looking at shadows which cross over each other.

The connections children make do not stop at science. There is scope to enhance scientific understanding throughout the primary phase by encouraging exploration through other disciplines. This is of course limited if a subject-based curriculum does not accommodate it. In an art lesson children paint pictures of shadows, reflections in water and images refracted all the way through a goldfish bowl. By close examination of the subject linked to scientific knowledge their understanding of how light travels can be increased. The creative teacher can use this opportunity to refer to observations made in the art session in a science lesson on light. Ideas can be linked through informal relaxed discussion or formalised to include accepted scientific explanations and comparisons.

Science teaching

In science certain principles apply. Planning, organising, classifying, reflecting and evaluating are all generic cognitive skills which children need to practise and assimilate. There is scientific vocabulary and technical knowledge to be learnt. Rigour and accuracy in measuring are essential if children are to validate their findings. All these processes can be taught didactically, without placing any expectation of higher-order thinking on the child. For example, it might be that pupils are required to check the progress of a plant's growth and record the height at daily intervals on graph paper, or copy a diagram of the heart and label parts with arrows drawn to indicate the direction of blood flow. What has the teacher done? Once achieved, very little more is expected of the learner. By contrast, children can be encouraged to notice and control how different beans are growing. They can carry out a simple practical experiment, pouring coloured red water into a bucket to try to match the speed at which the heart pumps blood around the body. There is no guarantee that they will be required to think at a higher level, but the opportunities to do so are maximised. They will almost certainly remember more about the circulatory system in the human body than from a diagram alone.

It is no surprise that the QCA, on the National Curriculum Gifted and Talented website, recognises that characteristics of pupils who are gifted in science go beyond expectations of didactic teaching and that they would most probably approach undemanding work indifferently and carelessly. The following is taken from a more comprehensive list identifying characteristics of pupils who are recognised as being gifted in science. The guidance states that gifted children are likely to:

- be extremely interested in finding out more about themselves and things around them;
- be inquisitive about how things work and why things happen;
- ask many questions, suggesting that they are willing to hypothesise and speculate;
- use different strategies for finding things out;
- put forward objective arguments, using combinations of evidence and creative ideas, and question other people's conclusions;
- consider alternative suggestions and strategies for investigations.

I suspect that if science teaching is creatively challenging then this list is in direct keeping with the majority of children's behaviour and is not mutually exclusive to gifted children. If teaching follows a path in which questions are valued, speculation is encouraged and alternatives are considered then all children will have the experience of being involved in the process. It will be possible to create a sense of ownership.

Valuing naïve ideas

Although young children know some science, they hold naïve ideas and are often unaware that their understanding is scientifically incorrect. This is often of little concern to them as they are willing to reassess their understanding or hold a tight grip on it depending on the plausibility of changing their view. The teacher has to be prepared for naïve ideas and partial knowledge and not regard them as a hindrance to learning. Misconception can be used as a starting point to explain complex concepts and have a direct impact on supporting the progression of understanding. Children, after all, are not the first scientists to hold naïve views. History is littered with examples of scientific belief which are quite wrong. Science is full of uncertainties. From alchemy to medicine, for example, there have been cures for diseases which turn out to have contributed to a patient's death. Two Nobel prize-winners won their prize for quite different answers to the question 'How does light travel?' Both of them, it turned out, were right, but in different ways of understanding light.

By careful attention to pupils' naïve comments, explanations and questions a great deal of information can be gleaned. This information can then be used to direct discussion to encourage a more accurate scientific understanding. The question for creative teachers is not 'Is this right?', but 'How can I use this to build understanding which is more accurate?' Appreciating facts, realising that people give rise to ideas and that theories are based on cultural understanding and observation are all important considerations which shed light on the uncertain nature of science. If children's understanding of science grew in a linear, logical way, then basing the content of school science within a programme of progressive assessment would work. The supposition that linear progression supports the way children learn is misguided.

Figure 2.1   Playground

Children learn according to their capability and strengths, experience and inclination, all of which are influenced by their experience of learning. Of course, this poses quite a challenge for teachers who want to work more creatively.

Ten ways to make science teaching creative

1. Turning predictable outcomes into something better

Making the commonplace intriguing often creates the spark needed to fascinate. Science lessons which follow a predictable route on a regular basis will do little to raise curiosity or inspire wonder. The time to worry about quality in science teaching is when predictable knowledge and outcomes surface. If pupils are turned on to the *how* of science, the *what* will follow. For example, setting a challenge to find the best fabric to make curtains to help *baby bear* go to sleep will introduce the idea of fair testing. Data-logging equipment, including a light sensor, can be used by young children. Providing resources including a variety of curtain fabric chosen for similar properties will help make testing less predictable. Although children may recognise that a high number reading indicates a less efficient curtain material, they cannot recognise this by simple observation. The outcome is surprising. Another example might be deciding which objects might float and which might sink. Holding an air ball (plastic ball with holes in) and considering if it will float demands speculation. Sorting things into floating or sinking sets may not intrigue if objects are familiar.

> We know polystyrene floats because when we go swimming we use polystyrene boards.

Teachers can use a variety of methods to ban the predictable systematic approach to fair testing and worksheet ethos often followed to achieve certain objectives. It should be noted that no one method is more effective than another in gaining interest or sustaining participation. More importantly, no one strategy, however successful, is sufficient to maintain enthusiasm if used repeatedly. To engage the learner the creative teacher uses a raft of approaches which are interlinked and relevant to a particular aspect of science and the needs of the children. They might include:

- using questions to which there are several answers;
- providing demonstrations specifically to raise curiosity;
- using analogies and models to promote understanding;
- varying methods of recording;
- studying the approach of different scientists;
- ensuring research has purpose and application;
- addressing complex scientific ideas in a practical and relevant way;
- using resources imaginatively;
- comparing different viewpoints;
- making cross-curricular connections, such as through drama, art and music;
- valuing play and exploration;
- giving children thinking time;
- focusing on the quality of ideas, comments and observations.

2. Making the ordinary fascinating

The teacher's ability to make the ordinary fascinating is a key skill in developing a curious approach to science. Young children often do not realise that science is about everything. Everyday objects and phenomena can be used creatively to stimulate interest. For example,

A swede was left on the Year 4 classroom windowsill for an entire school year. Once a week it was measured and weighed. A year later a Year 5 boy came into the room and asked, 'Where's our swede?'

Clearly for that child, examining the life of the swede had not been boring. The teacher had used a tangible and weighable object from life. Children tend to see the world subjectively and have not yet developed analytical skills to be objective. They do not readily make abstract connections. It is the here and now, first-hand experience and connections in their own lives that will have meaning.

Swamped with media hype about scientific inventions, it is easy to become blasé about the wonder of everyday things. I remember well the comment of a colleague just before I taught a science lesson about changing materials. We were going to consider both physical and chemical changes by burning toast. 'What is so interesting about a piece of burnt toast, the children will find that boring,' she said. 'I can't see why you find that so interesting.' There are plenty of people who would agree that this commonplace event is not rocket-science. The fact remains that burning toast is a complete chemical and molecular change which occurs in front of children's eyes. During the lesson, we used night lights (candles) in sand trays, and test tube holders for safety. The children carefully observed the changes which occurred as the bread was toasted, something they may never have done before with such a level of concentration.

The investigation was structured so that the children worked in pairs or small groups. Pupils decided about timing observations at 10-second intervals, comparing different types of bread and altering the thickness of slices. They also added butter to see how it melted. All of this resulted from pupil discussion about how to observe a chemical and physical change. One group decided to see which was the easiest toast to scrape once it was carbonised, and another group looked at the ingredients and additives and the speed of change. Simple cause and effect statements were made as a result of observation:

> The white processed bread goes black really quickly if it is near the flame.
>
> The wholemeal bread only gets burnt on the very top, inside it is still soft.

Another group became totally absorbed in presenting their findings in a very systematic way, placing each example in a polythene bag and stapling it to a chart on which they wrote their predictions and findings. Pupils carried on testing toasted bread independently and brought in many samples from home, including a variety of wrappers. They began to make a simple hypothesis based on their observation.

> Bread which has lots of chemicals added burns quicker.

Wanting to find out more is a good indicator of children's involvement. Freedom from prescriptive teaching methods is a necessary precursor of creativity. If a teacher can accommodate this degree of freedom in a session then the chances are that motivation to explore science is increased. As teachers we have a very powerful influence on pupils' perceptions and values. How we present information will greatly influence their attitude and understanding of everyday things. Children who are encouraged to pursue their own lines of inquiry within a set topic can develop the process skills of science in context. In putting a familiar everyday commodity like toast under the scientific spotlight, children can plan experiments with growing confidence. If the project focused on a less common enterprise outside of the experience of most pupils, what might happen? In my experience, children would be more dependent on the teacher for directing planning of activities, and less inclined to suggest scientific hypotheses or give reasons. Over time, whatever we use as examples builds attitudes and dispositions towards learning. Ask anyone who hated a school subject such as music, maths or science and the chances are their reaction is strongly emotional. Ask anyone who loves science and is burning with curiosity to tell you about their experience. That too is often strongly emotional.

3. Sharing a sense of wonder

Few teachers would disagree that by sharing their amazement they can convey a sense of wonder to their pupils. An interesting twist to this is to consider things that were once amazing and have become accepted as rather commonplace. In this way views about the changing nature of scientific discovery, understanding and application can be introduced through comparison and discussion. Pupils can view their own contributions as being useful and open to change if they are already used to considering change. For example, there is a large metal object moving through the air, another moves through space, faxes arrive in America, there are pictures of babies 12 weeks after conception, X-rays are sent by a computer in seconds from one hospital department to another. There is satellite navigation which both gives and corrects directions to a car driver. These phenomena would not have been understood by people living a hundred years ago. Importantly, these things are currently accepted as commonplace.

Although generations of children have been born in the UK where a television is in almost every household, misconceptions about the power of television persisted in the early 1950s. There are stories of great-grandmother's fear of 'not getting ready for bed in front of a moving image on the television in case the people on the screen could see her'. This seems as laughable now as does the notion that the world is flat, although at one time it was widely believed that anyone going too near the edge of the world would fall off. Microwave ovens arrived amidst fears of radiation hazards and we now think they are safe. We once thought that asbestos was a safe substance and it is actually highly toxic. It was once thought safe to smoke cigarettes and X-ray our feet in shoe shops to examine our shoe fittings. Technological wonders change as progress is made and no longer hold for the observer the sense of wonder initially felt, although they were once considered marvellous, unbelievable and amazing. Technological wonders also prove to be scientific disasters. For grannies and children, belief and disbelief are often based on personal fears and erroneous observations. If children were taught that the Sun moved around the Earth, this would coincide quite nicely with their experience of sunrise and sunset.

An historical slant on changing attitudes to science can help pupils appreciate the shift of focus, advances and acceptance of scientific ideas. By comparison, the natural world endures as a source of wonder and interest and children can be alerted to this in many ways. A starfish regenerating lost limbs or turning over, the intricacy of a well-woven bird's nest, vines putting down their roots ten metres to find water, a flower identified by a grain of pollen all indicate the process of adaptation and survival. These are fundamental to living things. Without instruction or discussion in the classroom the complexities and characteristics of such examples may never be questioned or recognised as significant. Science cannot be taught well or received well without feeling some magic in everyday occurrences in nature and the natural world. For example, sprouts are for eating, but they can also be used to develop observational skills, raise questions and stimulate inquiry.

4. Seeing differently

I can remember my very first experience of looking at cheese under a microscope. It was years before I dared to eat blue cheese like that sampled under the lens, but the sense of wonder remains. If a child jumps up and down with excitement at a first attempt to make sense of what they see under a microscope, what an opportunity this is. Here we have a revelation of things not seen by the naked eye. The value of such activity is understood; the reaction of pupil involvement is clear. The microscope is one way of changing perception but what of shifts in thinking which depend much more on seeing a different aspect of the same event? Stimulating interest in the learner often results from looking at things from various viewpoints not previously considered.

As part of a science INSET session head teachers were engrossed in the activity of trying to make two helium-filled balloons float equidistant from the floor. They had limited success. When it was suggested to them that they might experiment with the position and mass of the Blu-tack stuck to the balloons, the balloons behaved themselves. The look of absolute pleasure on the teachers' faces was not very different from that seen on a 5-year-old doing the same experiment. As they put it,

> We thought that was wonderful, we really enjoyed it, we hadn't thought of those things before, there is so much to think about.

They found value in the activity because it made them consider the complex behind the apparently '*simple*'. This inspired interest and raised questions.

Seeing differently is necessary for the successful study of science. It is just as necessary for eminent, professional, '*white coat*' scientists as it is for the teachers and young children. Great scientific discoveries have been made by people seeing differently, challenging accepted ideas and making sense of phenomena observed by many but not yet interpreted in a way that advances understanding. There is much scope for teachers to use stories from scientific history to support the idea of seeing differently. For example, it could be said that if Pasteur had done his washing up before leaving the laboratory he would not have returned to a mouldy set of Petri dishes. More importantly, if he had washed them up on his return he would not have looked closely at the growing organisms and noticed the unexplainable changes which puzzled him. Looking more closely, he noticed transformations not previously understood as significant and by *seeing differently* he discovered vaccines for various diseases. Seeing differently is a hallmark of genius, but it just might begin by inspiring children to think that seeing differently is not only acceptable but an admirable quality for a scientist to have.

5. Maximising opportune moments

It was not until Victorian times that the population moved to cities and we had our drainage system created, hence collapsing constructions that have stood the test of time. Who in the city these days will find frog spawn? How far do children need to walk to observe their countryside and life as it has gone on for centuries? On a recent rural walk a group of Year 6 children came across some frog spawn in a pool of stagnant water. The group were enthralled and asked many questions and made on-the-spot observations:

'Look how many there are.' 'What are they doing?' 'Look at all the holes like bubble wrap in it.' 'Did one frog lay all these eggs?' 'Is that because not many will survive?'

The same children watched a woodlouse give birth to several minute woodlice. Neither of these activities was planned into the walk, but the conversations that were generated showed a genuine desire to know more. Such questions would form a strong base for research as well as on-the-spot discussion. What, though, does a teacher do if the idyll of a walk in the country is just fantasy?

Opportunities do not always depend on being there. Topical issues and daily reports in the press can also be used in an opportune way. The benefits are great, as children will see that science is not just something learnt in school but a big part of our lives. Examples abound, such as the discovery of a new star, giant crabs advancing from Siberia, climate change having an effect on habitats and conditions needed for growth. New clothing materials synthesised by recycling plastic bottles and designer babies readily come to mind. As well as the big ideas debated, reported and discussed in the media, teachers can use small instances of experience at opportune moments to help children make connections between scientific theory and practice.

Minute by minute scientific connections can be made with everyday events. Teachers can use fleeting moments to focus thinking; making connections between unrelated ideas is crucial to creativity. Making connections is also vital to recognising science. Sunlight making it difficult to see, for example, is a function of the pupil's eyes. Sweating after running a race is a function of the body's cooling system; shadows lengthening in the afternoon is actually a result of the revolving movement of the Earth. Putting on coats to keep warm is the science of insulation to retain body heat. Litter in the playground is an example of environmental irresponsibility. These and similar examples could be used to link everyday experience to develop conceptual understanding. They are all the better for being concrete examples.

6. Humanising science

Imagine a 'bad-hair day', a white coat and someone who never displays a sense of humour because life is, of course, totally serious, isn't it? Better still: imagine an ageing, bald-headed male scientist who is brilliantly intelligent and absorbed with research into the small hours. This male scientist cannot remember what day of the week it is or when he ate his last meal but this does not matter because his discovery will change the world for ever. I have always wondered who washed his white coat and why it is white in the first place. Here we have a caricature. Here we have the stuff of cartoons and the word 'boffin' springs to mind. The 'mad', 'eccentric' world of the scientist suggests a crazy approach rather than an ordered one, a social outcast who lives in a world of things rather than people.

Recent research from Roni Malek and Fani Stylianidou would echo this:

Researchers Roni Malek and Fani Stylianidou are completing their research in April but have analysed around half the responses so far. They found around 80% of pupils thought scientists did 'very important work' and 70% thought they worked 'creatively and imaginatively'. Only 40% said they agreed that scientists did 'boring and repetitive work'. Over three-quarters of the respondents thought scientists were 'really brainy people'. The research is being undertaken as part of Einstein Year. Among those who said they would not like to be scientists, reasons included: 'Because you would constantly be depressed and tired and not have time for family', and 'because they all wear big glasses and white coats and I am female'.

(BBC 2006)

Is the true scientist a loony loner? Children might not realise that scientists often work in teams. In humanising science there is a role-model here. Working in teams could be used as a strategy in the classroom with *teams of scientists* working on a solution for a big company. Role-play can define the image of the scientist. Three useful tasks include: finding the stretchiest pair of tights, the most effective washing-up liquid, or the strongest carrier bag. If children are expected to plan, carry out a fair test, and report back findings, this can be a good way to assess their understanding of the process skills required by the National Curriculum in Science (assessment of this will be discussed in Chapter 10).

The humanity of scientists has already been mentioned at the start of this chapter. We have the example of Miriam Rothschild, never formally trained. There are many other examples of the wide diversity of eminent scientists and their methods of working.

If teachers suggest children study the lives of scientists they are usually concerned with humanising science as well as exploring the purpose and nature of science. I see this as no bad thing to do. Children can be encouraged to consider certain characteristics, noting attitude, risks taken and the nebulous nature of creative thought. Science discovery is not an easy journey; it is never certain and creative thinking is needed to make connections, see possibilities and accept failure. By looking at the lives of scientists pupils will be helped to recognise science as a human endeavour, not the activity of caricatured stereotypes. The community of teachers and community of scientists do collaborate in several areas by belonging to groups such as the Teacher Scientist Network, www.TSN.org (TSN 2006). Realising the potential of such an arrangement, practising scientists go into schools and work alongside the pupils in the classroom. It was through this route that Zoë became a teacher (see Chapter 1).

7. Valuing questions

If children believe that questions have value and that an answer is not necessarily the end of debate, they will be willing to ask more sophisticated and productive questions. Setting up lessons where the only requirement is to raise questions may take courage. The outcome of such a session is not known as the learning will be focused on raising good scientific questions. Confronted with candles burning, the children might ask: Why is one flame bigger than another? Why are some flames moving about and others going straight up? How long will the candle burn? Why does a candle smoke when you blow it out? Why are flames different colours? Why does wax melt? What is burning? Why does the candle run out and disappear? Unravelling a host of random questions into categories can enable pupils to identify those which can be investigated, answered or researched. It may also enable the teacher to identify what it is that the children actually want to know and can be used as an effective planning tool (Elstgeest 1985).

8. Modelling explanations

Explanations are important in supporting the development of scientific understanding. The dilemma which all primary school teachers face is to give an explanation which is accurate and will not confuse the learner. Accuracy demands expert science knowledge coupled with the ability to present information at an appropriate level. This means using real-life examples and language children will understand. Young children find it difficult to respond to explanations which are not part of their experience of reality or fantasy. Putting a picture in their heads will go some way to enable connections between theory and practice. Rather like trying to describe the taste of apple pie, some scientific concepts are by nature difficult to explain. Friction, the force which opposes movement, is typical of concepts that are not easy. What can be done to help understand?

As a starting point pupils need to consider friction between two solid surfaces; rubbing hands together and noticing the increase in heat is an example often used. This is easy to demonstrate and results are dramatic. How straightforward the link of conceptual understanding between theory and practice is made is debatable. Children need a simple model within their experience, and the action of a toothbrush might do. In thinking about how a toothbrush is used they will explore the relationship between the movement of the brush and the surface of the tooth, noticing if it is easy or difficult. This model can be extended to use a toothbrush in ways it is not designed for, including drawing using paint, noticing the gaps left on various surfaces; moving it across the bristles of another brush, then turning it over to move the back of the brush against the bristles or even back to back; comparing these effects using a variety of brushes and looking for patterns. All this activity is intended to provide a simple hypothesis, which in this case might be:

brushes with stiff bristles do not move so easily.

In any modelling strategy the creative use of familiar objects will not advance learning any more than the hand-rubbing model unless pupils are encouraged to notice certain relationships. After becoming familiar with friction between two solid surfaces, progression of learning would move towards friction between liquids (imagine trying to swim in syrup or cooking oil) and gas; at primary level this would be concerned with air resistance (describe and compare the way a parachute and stone fall through the air). The child's mind needs to be trained to accept new schemas and patterns of thought. Modelling is one way that creative teachers use to achieve this. A child might ask, for example, 'Why can I see myself in a mirror?' The scientific answer – that light is reflected from all surfaces and back into the eyes – may have little meaning. However, if a tennis ball is bounced against a wall and the direction of the bounce is noticed, this can be compared to how light travels. Children seem to have a great problem understanding enormous distances and sizes. One way of modelling this is to create comparison models such as those planned to create the relative sizes and distances of planets in the solar system. Wenham (2001: 259) describes 'modelling the Solar System (Scale: 1 to 5,000 million). At this scale the Sun is 28cm in diameter and can be represented by a beach ball. Earth 2.5mm can be represented by a peppercorn.' By comparison, a model with a torch and a tennis ball to simulate day and night will have little relevance. Perhaps this simulation is no longer used, but it is one that many primary science teachers will remember from their school days.

9. Encouraging autonomy

One way to nurture individual ideas is to offer a degree of autonomy to the learner. If children make choices then they are beginning to take ownership and experience an openness to practice not offered by a closed or prescribed route. A simple beginning might be to present an 'either or' scenario to encourage decision making by controlling outcomes. For example, a parachute made from a plastic bag and string and then dropped from a height will behave differently from one made from silk and fishing wire. By encouraging children to make decisions about materials used, the size of the canopy and the height of the drop, without restriction, various lines of inquiry will be pursued. Creative thinking is linked to the ability to explore and play. The actual learning that occurs will depend on the sense made of the play and the evaluation of that play.

The degree of autonomy fostered will depend on the confidence and ability of the child to pursue ideas. It is very rare to find pupils being innovative without an element of personal control of their destinies. Conceptual space, free of teacher intervention, is needed for independent thinking. Interventions can actually deter the learner from pursuing ideas and taking ownership. Time is needed for children to explore issues and experiment by themselves. Creating the psychological space for interactions and dialogue which seek the child's point of view is a significant feature of quality teaching, listening and learning alongside the child. For example, a child might invent a siphon to make moving a tray of water more manageable by siphoning off the bulk of the water. The thinking behind the design will most likely be valued much more than following an instruction sheet, or being told of a good solution to the problem. If confidence is needed, then pursuing ideas needs to be not only allowable in the classroom, but actively encouraged whatever the initial outcomes might be.

10. Allowing for flexible beginnings

Rather like the tributaries of a tidal river flowing towards a much bigger mass of water, children's meandering beginnings are not wrong. They may not look much of a starting point, but the professionalism of a skilful teacher can make something of them. An example of this was when children were asked to build a tower as high as they could. They were to do this using a set of various irregular building blocks of different materials. The intended aim of the lesson was to encourage children to recognise that if the base of a structure is wider then the structure will be more stable. The activity progressed and the teacher noticed that some children had begun to knock down their towers; they were not so concerned with stability or thinking about the construction but were seeing which one could be knocked down more easily. In this situation it would be tempting to bring them back on task to guide their thinking towards the intended outcome. The teacher, in this example, recognised the learning potential of following their lead and helped them devise a demolition site. They made a demolition ball with play dough and string, through which the basic principles of a pendulum swing were learnt.

The lesson now took a new slant, with considerations of fair testing, measurement and predicting all being evident. Through trial and error ideas were refined and the stability and construction of the structure were considered in detail. At the end of the activity they wanted to use a bigger and heavier ball and build a wall from real bricks. This was planned by the children and took place after following lines of inquiry as to how to make cement, how to place bricks and how to build foundations. The whole project covered many aspects of science and took a few weeks to complete. The beginnings were not promising, but the outcomes were rich in scientific thought.

Having fun

In addition to the above ten ways to make science teaching creative could be considered the idea of 'having fun'. Some lessons are not fun by any means, but most can be made so. Having fun and being creative will not only make the experience of learning memorable but can also demand higher-order thinking. For instance, children might need to consider the physical property of brittleness. If a material has low values of toughness it will break in a certain way without plastic deformation. That much we know is true, but how do we convince children? This is a concept which will need experiment to understand just what brittle and plastic mean. How do we put these ideas across to children yet let them speculate, predict and consider alternatives? We could of course use a piece of china, but there may be more fun to be had with that comical and well-known substance, jelly. There are boiled sweets and Turkish delight, erasers and Kendal Mint Cake to test. If science becomes fun, the difficult concepts can be tackled because pupils have not dulled their emotional response. The question to ask is not so much 'How can I put this concept of brittleness across?', but 'What variety of substances can I enjoyably use to test out brittleness?'

Encouraging pupil's creativity

The desire to investigate reality is an innate part of a child's persona (Dewey 1933; Elstgeest and Harlen 1990; Piaget 2003; Popper 1968); this is evident in play, behaviour and response. In summary, the important professional teaching skill is knowing how to identify and harness significant events as they appear. Teacher intervention should be well thought out to support the desire to know without hindering children's natural curiosity. The quality of any learning experience is directly related to the involvement of the learner. Words, actions, images and expectations will encourage or discourage participation and development. The child is the builder or 'constructionist' of their learning (Bruner 1996). If being alive to significant events in a lesson is a teaching skill, then leaving children alone to think is another. Creativity is often diminished by pressure to produce a correct answer. Habit is a blocking mechanism of creative thought. Children enter school with their own agenda, not always one that sits easily with the teacher's agenda. Creative teachers enable and encourage children to be creative, both by example and design. The ethos set promotes an atmosphere in which children interact and collaborate, or drop out and do the minimum. Meaning is made relevant to the child, sometimes before any formal scientific vocabulary is used. Questions are actually answers of a kind because of the creative track they carve out.

Summary of main points

Creative teaching will provide:

- a stimulating secure learning environment;
- the opportunity to make choices;
- time to follow ideas;
- space to alter minds;
- an awareness of possibilities;
- the belief that the process of learning is to be valued;
- a sense of wonder.

Issues for reflection

- Think about how you intervene to support learning. Do you find it difficult to stand back and allow children to take the lead in their learning? What effect do you feel your interventions have on creative thinking?

- In explaining scientific phenomena and accepted facts, which analogies, models and simulations do you use to help pupils make connections between theory and practice?

- What do you personally understand by the term 'teaching creatively' within the context of the primary classroom? How easily in your opinion does a creative approach to teaching match with the requirements of National Curriculum science?

- Consider how you responded to misconceptions or inaccurate statements. Have you used these as starting points to challenge existing ideas and consider alternative possibilities?

- Some teachers find it difficult to trust children's judgement and give them little opportunity for ownership and independence. Some teachers hold a different view and encourage autonomy. Which category do you feel most comfortable with?

Discussion points

- How do creative teachers teach within the statutory requirements to achieve expected targets and results?

- It is widely recognised that there is value in giving young children time to play. Does this apply in the teaching of science across Key Stages 1 and 2?

- Creative science teaching encourages the pursuit of ideas. Why might this be to the detriment of developing scientific understanding?

Answers from p. 21

1. There is no other way for them to go but down. They are too big. There is nothing that can exert a big enough force to push a skyscraper sideways.

2. The wind load is trying to bend it, it sways back and forth. Skyscrapers are designed to be flexible so that they bend rather than break. The action of a willow tree bending in the wind is a good analogy.

3. The construction of the Twin Towers was mostly air; the walls were a very small fraction of the total mass. Consequently the rubble generated would be about 5% of the total mass.

Recommended reading

Burke, C. and Grosvenor, I. (2003) *The School I'd Like*. London: Routledge Falmer

Craft, A. (2002) *Creativity across the Primary Curriculum: Framing and Developing Practice*. London: Routledge Falmer

Edwards, C., Gandini, L. and Forman, G. (1998) *The Hundred Languages of Children, The Reggio Emilia Approach – Advanced Reflections* (2nd edn). Westport and London: Ablex

References

BBC (2006) *Science 'not for normal people'*. Available: http://news.bbc.co.uk/1/hi/education/4630808.stm

Bruner, J. (1996) *The Culture of Education*. Cambridge: Harvard University Press

Craft, A. (2002) *Creativity across the Primary Curriculum: Framing and Developing Practice*. London: Routledge Falmer

Dewey, J. (1933) *How We Think: A Restatement of the Relation of Reflective Thinking to the Educative Process* (2nd edn). Boston: D. C. Heath

Edwards, C., Gandini, L. and Forman, G. (1998) *The Hundred Languages of Children, The Reggio Emilia Approach – Advanced Reflections* (2nd edn). Westport and London: Ablex

Elstgeest, J. (1985) *The Right Question at the Right Time*. London: Heinemann

Elstgeest, J. and Harlen, W. (1990) *Environmental Science in the Primary Curriculum*. London: Paul Chapman

Hodson, D. (1998) *Teaching and Learning Science*. Buckingham: Open University Press

Piaget, J. (2003) *The Language and Thought of the Child.* London: Routledge

Popper, K. (1968) *The Logic of Scientific Discovery.* London: Routledge

Tallack, P. (2001) *The Science Book.* London: Cassell and Co

TSN (2006) *Teacher Scientist Network.* Available: http://www.tsn.org.uk/22/09/2005

Wenham, M. (2001) *200 Science Investigations for Young Students.* London: Paul Chapman

Wood, D. (1988) *How Children Think and Learn: The Social Contexts of Cognitive Development.* Oxford: Blackwell

CHAPTER 3

Planning for a creative approach

> If we value flexibility then we must be willing to live, at least temporarily, with strange and conflicting ideas. They may be totally unrealistic yet ultimately prove to be a stepping stone to something else more credible.
>
> (Barnes 1989)

Teachers might say that planning for creativity is a paradox, in that planning is the very activity that stifles creativity. Most teachers will be acquainted with planning as a premeditated process, sometimes one that lacks spontaneity. But what many teachers want to do is be flexible in their planning so they can respond and interact in a creative way. Creative planning for science teaching is not just a matter of making the occasional swerve from a fixed plan. It needs an understanding of how a flexible framework for creative planning can be constructed, used and developed.

Creative planning

Consider the way in which primary school teachers used the following experiences to plan a series of lessons. Although the two examples that follow are very different in application, they both link science with experience to promote subject knowledge. They do this by making connections to open up dialogue with children about their understanding. A creative approach to planning for science is one where learning is significantly more personal. The pupil is at the centre of the learning and the creative teacher seizes the moment to adapt plans and encourage involvement. This is quite different from science teaching where knowledge is regarded as something to be transmitted with a predetermined outcome and logical steps to achieve it.

Example 1

A group of 7-year-old children standing on a bridge were fascinated watching ducklings in the water below. The distinct protective quack from the mother kept the babies in check if they strayed too far. Nearby on a concrete slope, used for putting boats into the river, a well-camouflaged rat was spotted nibbling at some corn meal. Two of the nine baby ducks also saw the chance of easy food and circled the pile of meal; the rat carried on eating but appeared protective and the ducks backed off. The other baby ducks at intervals jumped flapping onto the concrete over a small ridge which they had to navigate to take an easy path to the food. One remaining duckling found the challenge of the ridge very problematic and swam frantically backwards and forwards looking for a place to go over; several unsuccessful attempts were made before he managed to join the others who were now nibbling on the edge of the pile. The rat had backed off but was also feeding on the other side of the pile. Only when the large, quacking mother duck appeared did the rat make a quick exit.

Lessons looking at life cycles, predator and prey, food chains, habitats and adaptation were planned around this incident. The differences between ducks and rats in a particular habitat, interdependence and survival strategies were discussed and the children could relate theory to the experience. At one point simple explanations were given that ducks do not feed their young, so the flightless chicks must leave the nest after just one day to find food; the discussion moved to mummy and daddy ducks and ended with some children drawing the eclipse plumage of males at the end of the summer. The questions and answers as to why the drakes' plumage alters after mating is at a high level, understandably not totally understood by all the young children in this class. As with many such examples, the dialogue was initiated by the pupils and not planned in advance by the teacher. The resourceful teacher would have to think carefully about responding to the quite logical question, 'Does this mean that the ones with bright shiny heads are virgins?' (Helen age 8).

Example 2

Another teacher took the theme of live baby chicks to look at growth and plan lessons. She organised the delivery of ten fertile eggs and an incubator to the classroom. The pupils learnt about conditions needed for germination and incubation as well as the control necessary for successful hatching and rearing. They watched the eggs cracking and one chick emerge. A digital camera was used by the pupils to record the event. Not all eggs hatched whilst the school was in session but one did and a series of time lapse images recorded the event. The chicks were measured and weighed every day for a month, as was the food and water they were given, and then they were returned to the farm. Each chick was a different breed and could be easily identified by colouring, size and shape; not surprisingly, they were given names. Heredity and genetic engineering and selective breeding were all discussed at a simple level. A branching database was presented to show the breeding line of the chicks. Data-logging equipment was used to keep a record of progress and photographs were used as evidence to observe change.

It is difficult to imagine a more stimulating way of learning about living things. Not surprisingly, the work generated from this event was remarkable in detail and content. The wide range and high level of science covered reflected genuine interest. Children with special needs participated alongside others with enthusiasm. Many of them achieved a higher standard of work than ever before. There were links made with several areas of the curriculum, including probability, *what is the chance of picking up a white chick?*, speaking and listening, chronological writing and non-chronological writing, *accounts of the progress recorded weighing and measuring*, and *observational drawing*. These links evolved as a result of lines of inquiry opened up by the pupils. Without planning for a shared atmosphere conducive to inquiry and dialogue this level of commitment and variety from the learner would not happen.

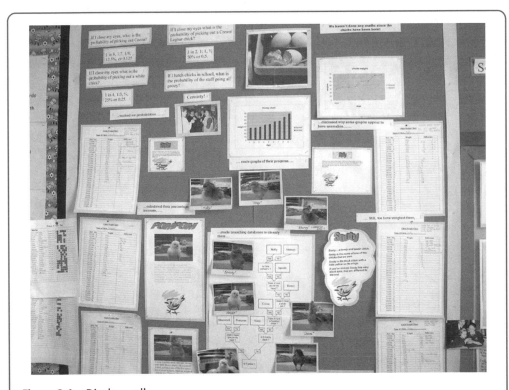

Figure 3.1 Display wall

Figure 3.2a, b & c   Brown chick, shaggy chick and yellow chick

What is happening here? Both examples show a creative approach to planning. Imaginative and practical components of each lesson interlink not by chance but by design. It is this design which supports both pupils and teachers in being creative. Carefully designed planning goes beyond an outcome-based approach limited to set activities which are easily managed. To create effective plans to accommodate children's ideas and help them develop scientific knowledge and understanding the teacher needs to know:

- the existing level of children's science subject knowledge;
- how confident they are in using process skills;
- how they view science;
- that different outcomes can lead to better scientific understanding;
- how they will assess these different outcomes.

Assessment of scientific understanding is usually the item in this list that causes teachers to plan for prescribed outcomes. After all, a predictable outcome is much easier to cope with than the unknown. Assessment of different outcomes is not straightforward, but possible through negotiation with the learner. This is different from assessment limited to a prescribed outcome. It is far from being a vague way to assess because it eventually reinforces understanding and unravels misconceptions. Assessment by negotiation with the learner will need further explanation, and this topic is discussed in detail in Chapter 10.

Planning by design

In the first example an opportune moment is used as the catalyst to develop scientific knowledge through a shared experience. The teacher skilfully links observations made with aspects of the curriculum to interest the children. Much work is done through discussion and dialogue, empathy and simulation. Questions raised form the basis of exploration of ideas and subsequent explanations. In the second example planning is not so free and a systematic approach to observation and measurement is taken. However, in both cases the children are encouraged to think creatively and outcomes are not limited to *what the teacher wanted* or *the answers the teacher was looking for*. This is not so much that any old outcome will do. The dilemma faced by teachers who believe in creative learning is to design a plan that encourages a democratic approach yet still fits a framework of prescribed content and assessment. As Barnes (1989) points out,

To make interesting connections and leave the matter there cannot be the same thing as sifting through the many ideas which have come to mind, then evaluating, developing and adapting them.

Good planning can create a climate of inquiry, so that the questions raised by children become catalysts for learning far more. There is mystery, problem solving and a number of ingredients that make science creative. Teachers who plan creatively include:

- negotiated learning;
- collaboration with a sense of purpose;
- ways of opening up dialogue;
- opportunities to listen to dialogue;
- group identification of questions to follow;
- democratic decisions as to the next step;
- following unknown routes;
- playing with ideas;
- opportunities to make connections;
- supporting imaginative thinking;
- using surprises;
- promoting inquiry;
- linking science with experience;
- shared verification of outcomes;
- assessment as part of learning;
- an holistic approach.

Planning to encourage negotiated learning

Planning is needed to communicate expectations, just as negotiation is needed to open dialogue and interaction. Structure is always necessary to cover the curriculum. In creative planning the structure will support participation. Establishing a culture in which children are confident to explore resources and ideas and raise their own questions to investigate will not happen without a great deal of preparation. Negotiation does not happen by chance but is part of a democratic process of decision making. If the teacher's aim is to offer a democratic process of decision making then confidence is needed to give children autonomy and flexibility in making choices.

The structure offered here for an investigation for primary science is not limited to a science time slot. Different stages can be addressed at different times. For example, a PE lesson might be a good time to guide thinking about friction, a windy day would raise questions regarding the force of air and a game of table tennis could initiate a discussion of controlling movement. One of the great advantages of primary schooling is that connections can be made across the curriculum and at opportune times to reinforce understanding.

Stage 1 – Explore as a class/group:

- Choice of resources to raise questions. Use a selection of balls to include e.g. air ball, large sponge ball, golf ball, rugby ball, ping pong ball, tennis ball, football, marble, bouncy ball, using ramps, thinking about how each ball behaves in water and air, on different surfaces, slopes and being dropped, rolled or kicked. Play with the balls in several scenarios and observe differences.

- **Talk about** questions raised e.g. 'Which ball makes the biggest splash?' 'Does the depth of the water make a difference to the splash?' 'Does the height of the drop make a difference to the splash?' 'Why do big balls not roll so fast?' 'Why doesn't the football roll so well on wet grass?'

- **Negotiate** identification of a question to investigate e.g. 'Do bigger balls always make a bigger splash?' Different groups might choose different questions using the same resource, e.g. 'Does the surface of the slope make the balls travel faster?' 'Does the angle of the slope make the balls travel faster?'

Stage 2 – Discuss and decide in small groups:

- setting up the test, choice of equipment;

- making predictions, individual or group if a consensus is reached;

- making an hypothesis, individual as well as group i.e. giving reasons for predictions;

- deciding on variables to control, change and measure, joint decision;

- carrying out the investigation, the process can be adapted as problems identified with previous stages such as making a prediction are considered;

- collecting data, how will this be done and by whom;

- recording results, choosing a way which can be discussed and clearly explained, selecting from e.g. data logging, ICT, art, drama, audio/video, pictorial representation.

Stage 3 – Share and debate:

As a class/group, this element of the process will need well-focused teacher direction to use pupils' findings to facilitate learning. Teacher input will be relevant to choices made and questions, making learning personal.

- Analysis of data
- Interpretation of results
- Validity of findings
- What was discovered, confirmed or not verified.

Stage 4 – Compare as a whole class, teacher directed:

- findings, looking for patterns and similarities;
- surprises;
- questions raised;
- problems encountered;
- adaptations needed;
- decisions made.

Stage 5 – Identification through teacher-led dialogue:

- future questions to investigate.

This structure resembles many such examples provided to support children through the process of inquiry. What is different is the degree of choice and negotiation expected. Pupils and teachers can adapt ideas and procedures at any stage of the investigation. Stage 4 is often neglected but it is an important part of the development of an attitude to science that values debate and disagreement. It is important to remember that ethos as well as process needs to be taught and accepted as good practice. Choice at all stages of the process is an option, and planning to give choice provides an opening for creative thinking.

Planning for choice

Choice does not mean that planning is disorganised or haphazard but rather that contingencies are in place. All good plans allow for adjustments but creative planning goes a step further. We can see how this works by looking at the National Curriculum Science 1, 'Scientific Enquiry', in addition to the previous examples:

A question and answer format set out in two stages investigating natural dyes from plants indicates how plans might be completed to be creative in design within a clear framework. Answer 2 is not separate from Answer 1 but follows on, adding a creative element not obvious in Answer 1.

Stages of planning creatively

Q. Why am I teaching this?
A.1. It is part of the school's medium-term plan and addresses 'Scientific Enquiry', part of the National Curriculum.
A.2. Pupils raised questions after a blackberry-picking excursion ended with stained fingers. I thought they would be interested in making and investigating natural dyes from a variety of plants, giving them a wide variety of plants, fruits and berries to compare.

Q. What am I planning to teach?
A.1. How to extract natural dye and test its permanence in comparison with other samples in a controlled experiment, accuracy in measurement, precision in conclusions drawn, perseverance to overcome obstacles and re-articulation of aims through careful analysis of information to answer the question, 'Which plant makes the strongest dye?'
A.2. How to evaluate differences in the properties and behaviour of pigments extracted from a variety of plants by comparing methods of extraction, differences in strength, permanence, application on natural and synthetic fabrics, reaction to heat, light and ways of fixing, ordering shades of colour and variation.

Q. How will I organise the children's learning through this process?
A.1. By setting up groups and providing a question to investigate, selecting a range of resources, asking certain questions and guiding them through the process of controlling variables.
A.2. Encouraging pupils to make their own choices, predictions and comparisons, allowing group or individual enterprise to plan tasks and evaluate findings, consent to pupils setting their own success criteria and pursue negotiated lines of enquiry. Giving a broad remit such as 'What can you find out about the dye we get from these plants?'

Q. What methods will I use to achieve what I want children to learn?
A.1. Small group work with a class introduction and plenary.
A.2. Initiating dialogue, using pupil observations, making suggestions and raising questions to encourage decision making and independent tasks, using children's suggestions for experiments.

Q. When will I do this?
A.1. During timetabled science lessons.
A.2. Also at opportune moments, during class discussion, at a formal presentation of findings.

Q. How will I assess children's learning?
A.1 Formatively through dialogue and summatively through questioning and evidence in written work.
A.2. Application of findings through visual presentations e.g. a selection of tie-dyed materials placed in a sequence to denote strength, a quiz chart to match dye to the plant from which it was extracted, an account of the different way materials absorbed each dye, a flow chart of the process, a collage of berry-dyed fabric and a collage of leaf-dyed fabric, painting with yellow dye and blue dye to control mixtures.

Imagination and originality

The above example, although structured, bombards children with ideas and resources from which they can make choices. In this way they are using their imagination to search for new relationships and connections. It is they themselves who are being creative, by applying what they know in different situations and ways. Observant teachers recognise capabilities dormant in the child's imagination and use them to develop understanding. Scientific comprehension is broadened by helping them in linking facts and ideas and searching for new relationships. There is evidence of this way of thinking in the work of many scientists, including Edison's inventions and Einstein's theories. In these examples the use of imagination is not spontaneous but as a result of looking differently at known facts and ideas.

Although creative thinking is sometimes spontaneous, presenting ideas out of the blue, the imagination rarely manifests itself in this way unless the thinker is already immersed in the subject (Barnes 1989). Immersion in the process is key to developing creative ideas. To support originality and imagination the teacher needs to provide the resources to encourage divergent thinking. Moving away from expected responses and encouraging children to elaborate and redefine ideas is a powerful tool in the creative process. On a practical level this would involve keeping a notebook to jot down ideas, half-formed flashes of knowledge and questions to explore. One problem teachers will encounter is that activities of this original nature cannot be measured in terms of achievement against set criteria. The criteria are often adjusted as ideas develop. For example, *pushing against a wall* may come about in response to pupils' questions about balanced forces. The teacher can encourage this action from a pair of children to include several others and continue to test different ways of pushing. This way of working will not necessarily fit into the desired outcome of the lesson but as an educational experience will increase understanding of the force exerted by inert objects.

There is a danger in an assessment-driven curriculum that planning is controlled to measure achievement through specific outcomes. Creative planning is not concerned with merely judging achievement through convergent thinking or the 'right answer syndrome' but values imaginative and original ideas.

Planning for divergent thinking

Planning for divergent thinking depends on providing opportunities to link ideas to make unusual connections and sense what is probable. *The Earth and Beyond* (NC Sc4, 3) is an ideal theme. It is an aspect of science easily recognised as ripe for exploration, with new theories and discoveries frequently reported. Discussion founded on speculation is easily recognised as valid. Imagination and reality are valued in the pursuit of truth. The history of theories about the Earth and beyond offer a wide range of ideas based on understandings of the time. Children would find it useful to consider why people held such ideas. Knowing that people believed (and some still do) that the Earth is flat or that the Sun moves round the Earth is widely taught but the reasons for such beliefs need to be explored to give them credibility. To appreciate that the ideas we hold today are also based on limited knowledge and understanding and will be changed in the future is liberating. Considering possibilities through well-selected questions to encourage divergent thinking can be planned. For example: the question 'What is beyond our solar system?' provides answers such as, 'Space is silver starry soot' (Ian age 10), 'Black holes, black no sound, no nothing' (Lewis age 10), and 'Aliens but we can't see them but they can see us' (Jasmine age 9). Planning activities to develop ideas through debate and drama, producing books of facts to complement books of ideas, biographies/interviews with recognised scientists from the past and people e.g. sailors who navigated by the stars engages pupils in speculation and ordering and sequencing ideas. Application of ideas such as designing a spaceship, space suit, envisaging zero gravity by explaining how to carry out everyday tasks, inventing a planet to include alien life forms and asking questions, 'What would living things be like?', 'What would they need to survive?' and 'Would they survive on our planet?' encourages divergent thinking. Linking reality and fantasy mirrors the way in which children try to make sense of the world. The examples given use the NC as a starting point and broaden the experience of learning by planning for imaginative thinking as a launch pad for developing scientific understanding.

Imaginative planning using the NC

The National Curriculum offers a great deal of scope for teachers to be creative and relate their teaching to the needs of their particular class or group of children with whom they are working. There is a freedom of choice to plan, but this demands confidence. By comparison, the restrictive nature of any prescribed scheme with suggested activities makes a creative approach to teaching difficult. In the following examples, frequently taught QCA units of work will be compared with alternative ideas and suggestions which aim to offer a more creative way of working. The content of the National Curriculum remains in each case the focus for planning. The structure of the QCA is recognised as a means of covering the curriculum but the activities recommended go beyond the commonplace. They are demanding of the learner, with an expectation of participation not evident in some suggested schemes of work.

Creative lessons

The life cycle of a butterfly Year 1 Sc2 1a, 1b

Lesson 1

Louisa began the session with the children seated on the carpet listening to the well-known and well-used story of the hungry caterpillar by Eric Carle (Carle 1969). She showed pictures and wrote key words such as egg, caterpillar, chrysalis, butterfly on the board at appropriate times during the story. The egg was represented by an old ball which had the top cut off and a felt toy caterpillar placed inside. The top of the ball had been replaced so that the caterpillar could not be seen until it emerged at the appropriate time in the story (to gasps of delight from some of the children). The cocoon was represented by an old sock which was wrapped around the caterpillar and eventually out came a beautiful, felt butterfly. Comments from the children included, 'How did you do that?', 'It's magic!', 'I really enjoyed that', 'Do caterpillars really do that?', 'Does every caterpillar turn into a butterfly?' and 'Does it hurt when they burst their skin?' The children were amazed and involved. Curiosity and wonder were palpable. To help consolidate understanding the children were then shown a short video explaining the life cycle of the butterfly. Once again, words on the whiteboard were pointed to and simple explanations were given to support understanding. Questions followed. The children were animated and keen to put forward views. 'I like caterpillars', 'I saw a caterpillar on a cabbage in my granddad's garden' and 'Are caterpillars all the same?' Some queries had more potential than others for the teacher to develop scientific understanding. These were identified and supported by resources such as coloured photographs of three different caterpillars and the butterflies they turned into and a broccoli plant stripped by hungry caterpillars. The follow-on part of the lesson encouraged pupils to work independently. The class was organised into work stations with resources set out prior to the lesson. The activities were explained and the children were given a choice as to the order and number of tasks undertaken.

The activities included:

- Four ink stamps of the various stages of the life cycle which the children had to order and write one of the words egg, caterpillar, cocoon or butterfly under each printed picture.

- Pieces of paper which became progressively larger were on a table with a selection of green, yellow and black crayons, the expectation being that children would choose a piece of paper and draw a caterpillar to fill the paper.

- Counters to represent leaves and a chart of the week were placed on the table. The children were asked, 'If the new caterpillar ate one leaf the first day and twice as many on the next day, how many would it eat in two days? If it carried on eating twice as much every day for a week, how many leaves would it eat in a week?' The teacher worked with this group.

- The children used head phones to listen to a tape describing the life cycle of a butterfly.

- Painting half a butterfly with two wings already outlined on a larger sheet of white paper which is then folded in half symmetrically to represent a butterfly.

The lesson concluded with a discussion of surprises noted by the pupils, including the fact that each caterpillar would have eaten 128 leaves in a week, the state of the broccoli stalk and the need for caterpillars to protect themselves; camouflage of the cocoon like a dead leaf progressed to a statement from a 5-year-old girl that 'the eggs are green and small and under the leaf so they are camouflaged too'.

Finally, in drama the children acted out being an egg, a newly hatched caterpillar, eating all day long, getting bigger and fatter, bursting out of its skin and turning into a chrysalis and eventually a butterfly which had to sit in the sun and wait for its wings to unfold and dry out before it could fly away.

After the lesson a display was mounted of the progressively larger caterpillars and leaves, some with eggs on and some eaten (the children looked carefully at cabbage and broccoli leaves in an art lesson and produced wax rubbings). The display included charts showing how many leaves were eaten in a week. There were also modelled butterflies and cocoons suspended throughout the class collage.

Lesson 2

The children watched a video of the life cycle of a butterfly. The teacher asked questions to ascertain understanding; she differentiated questions to the needs of the children. She continued to ask questions until the main facts had been repeated and she felt confident that the responses were accurate. She then drew a flow diagram on the board in the shape of a circle to show the four main stages in the life cycle of a butterfly. Following this, the children watched a video of the life cycle of the cabbage white butterfly. Key points were reinforced by the teacher. The children were then set a cloze procedure task of filling in the missing words, egg, caterpillar, cocoon and butterfly, in a simple text. Five of the children with poor reading skills were given four pictures showing caterpillar eggs, a caterpillar, a chrysalis and a butterfly under which they had to match up the correct word. The work was collected in and the lesson finished with the teacher reading the story of *The Very Hungry Caterpillar.*

Lessons 1 and 2 were both carefully planned by the teachers, with Lesson 1 having more opportunity for developing a creative approach.

Lesson 3

In Lesson 3 there is the added element of negotiation. The plan (Figure 3.3) shows the teacher's plan in bold black and added pupil suggestions in green. Look at the checklist of what creative teachers plan for and compare the difference.

Many resources used in the examples were identical. So what was different? Certainly expectations of involvement and choices offered varied considerably. Decisions made by the children were negotiated at different levels, as were opportunities to try things out. Ask yourself about the considerations and decisions you make in planning science lessons. The following questions could act as a creative planning checklist.

This topic was planned by Helen Miles and the children of Ash class
(reception year) at Wicklewood Primary School.
My ideas are in black type and the children's ideas in green.

Read 'The Very Hungry Catepillar'
By Eric Carle
    - Looking a life-cycles
    - Find out what a cocoon is made of

Caring for mini-beasts
Find out where they live

Keeping other sorts of
mini-beasts in classroom

Read 'The Bad Tempered Ladybird'
by Eric Carle

Use non-fiction texts to find information

Looking a live mini-beasts in
the classroom (found and brought in
by the children)

Mini-beast hunt in school
grounds

Making a film about mini-beasts, all
dress up and film it...
- Plan the film with a story-board and
write a script
- Use costumes

Making Lego mini-beasts

Mini-beast movements

Look at spots on mini-beasts use
for counting and doubling

MINI-BEASTS

(TOPIC FOR YR)

Making a Wormery
- layers of coloured sand
- Finding the worms
- Finding out what worms eat
- Thinking about how they move

Creating symmetrical pictures of
mini-beasts:
- ladybirds
- Spiders
- Butterflies

Find out what lady-birds are made from

Making mini-beasts out of boxes (junk
modelling) paint them and hang them from
the ceiling so they can fly. Put crawling
bugs on floor

Making clay mini-beasts
- planning
- evaluating

Using red and black clothes with spots

Make flowers and leaves
and soil for role-play area

Classifying mini-beasts
What is a mini-beast?

Creating a role-play area- chosen by children

Pretending to be mini-beasts

Making costumes
to dress up as bugs

Creating a 'bug room'

Bringing in costumes from home

Use instruments to create sounds
for different mini-beasts, then
match the sound with the
mini-beasts

11/6/2004- School 1, Final Teaching Practice

Figure 3.3   Mini-beasts

Questions to ask in planning creatively

- Are resources stimulating, varied and thought provoking?
- Are openings made to raise questions?
- Will pupils feel a sense of autonomy?
- Will pupils start with a position of strength?
- How will boundaries be set?
- Will negotiation be encouraged?
- What evidence will demonstrate engagement?
- Why and how will learning be assessed?

The above questions are helpful in considering a creative approach to planning but do not fit so readily with the notion of teaching to specified objectives. Learning begins with helping children make sense of experience and starting with strengths is an important part of that. In deciding how to do things to engage the learner the teacher makes choices which relate to beliefs about learning. Designing challenges to meet NC requirements with creative beliefs in mind is a priority for many teachers. The following example takes a commonly taught area of science with prescribed learning objectives and illustrates how an original approach can increase motivation and develop subject knowledge. In each case the plan is a starting point but children's suggestions and questions have been used to prompt other explorations and negotiate a flexible approach.

Thermal insulation materials and their properties (QCA Unit 4C 'Keeping Warm' (QCA 1998))

Lesson plan
PGCE trainees (Charlotte, Eileen and Rebecca) were given the challenge of using the QCA learning objectives creatively to devise practical activities to teach Year 4 children about thermal insulation. They worked with 60 Year 4 children from a local middle school at the university.

The children were given questions before and after the teaching session to ascertain their understanding of concepts relating to the thermal insulation and properties of materials e.g. If you put a coat on a snowman will it take longer for the snowman to melt? (Brenda Keogh and Stuart Naylor, 1997). If you wrap an ice pop in newspaper will it stay cold longer? Interestingly but not surprisingly, most children agreed that the coat would make the snowman melt faster but the newspaper would keep the ice pop frozen for longer. This simple comparison clearly shows that experience has taught the children that newspaper acts as a thermal insulator. The concept of thermal insulation has not as yet been assimilated as an abstract idea to be applied in a different context. After completing three practical activities all the children were able to answer questions which had previously confused them. The lessons demanded very little writing from the pupils. The focus of instruction was through dialogue and questioning, focusing on observations. High value was placed on oral communication, quality of debate and consideration of ideas. Formulating explanations was seen as intrinsically important to the creative style of teaching adopted.

Children were encouraged to share their thinking and listen to other viewpoints. Progress was monitored through discussion, making connections between observations, and scientific understanding was established in a non-threatening way. Explanations were given in context, which meant that activities within the children's experience could easily be related to theory. Pupils were helped to recognise that objects cool or warm to the temperature of their surroundings and that some materials slow down this process because of their insulating properties.

The following three lessons formed a block of work to progressively build understanding of thermal insulation. Lesson 1 links closely with the suggested activity in the QCA scheme. The practical activities in Lesson 2 and Lesson 3 are more creative, both in use of resources and expectation of pupil participation. The pupils moved from predicting to observing to controlling variables. Through interaction and dialogue decisions were made and testing was refined, factors were controlled and measurements taken, and many aspects of Sc1 were covered independently. Challenging misconceptions and building more accepted scientific views through structured practical activity which is fun can be highly motivating. To be successful this must be approached in a way which recognises levels of understanding and uses resources within the child's experience. This was achieved in Lessons 2 and 3.

Lesson 1: Following the QCA

'Which is the best material to keep an ice pop cold?'

It was relatively easy for children to recognise that ice pops stay cold longer if wrapped in newspaper, bubble wrap or tin foil (QCA) *e.g. using an ice cube as a cold object and trying out different wrappings, bubble wrap, sponge sheeting, aluminium foil, polythene.* They learnt that the thickness of materials is a factor and that the air temperature makes a difference to the rate of change from a solid to a liquid. This is all well and good and fits in with the requirements of the National Curriculum but many opportunities to encourage higher-order thinking, help pupils make connections and consider wider possibilities are lost. Carrying out an experiment to control the rate of heat loss from an ice cube or water in a container helps them recognise that some materials are better thermal insulators than others. It was accepted by the 60 children questioned that if you wrap a choc ice in newspaper it will stay cold longer.

Consequently, in Lesson 1 understanding is confirmed rather than challenged. In this case Lesson 1 becomes a procedure to verify established ideas and build on them, with little demanded from the learner other than following a process. Process skills of science such as predicting, controlling variables, measuring using a thermometer and recording data are all used in a practical context but developing understanding of thermal insulation is not challenged.

Some might argue that young children will be unable to make connections or apply knowledge in other contexts and the expectation is too demanding. This will probably be true if the context is unfamiliar and there is no practical application. The following two lessons show how a creative stance can help children develop their understanding through challenging accepted ideas. Instead of taking the suggestion of wrapping ice cubes in various materials or trying to insulate a cup of warm water, a more creative and imaginative set of resources are used. Intended outcomes are unknown by the children and surprise is a planned prerequisite to learning.

Lesson 2: Challenging children's ideas

'Will wearing clothes stop the ice man from melting?'

To a child it seems obvious that a coat will keep them warm and logically a coat will make the snowman melt. Children are used to being told 'Put your warm coat on' or 'You need to wear warm clothes, it is cold outside'. Experience and intuition inform them that clothes are warm and consequently they will warm the ice figure and make it melt. Without exception all the children predicted this would happen. The intention to challenge thinking was achieved. As time passed and the volume of water increased more rapidly in the beaker containing the figure without clothes and the one with layers of woollen clothes stayed frozen, puzzlement and surprise were obvious. Children were asked to explain what they observed; responses to justify their claims included: 'The clothes stop the water coming out: the ice man with clothes is colder' and 'The one without clothes is melting faster but then it will slow down'. As time passed explanations were replaced by statements and finally questions: 'I thought the clothes would warm it up but they didn't' and 'Why does it melt faster without clothes?' None of the children found it easy to understand what had happened but the desire to know the reason was unanimous. When using clothing as a thermal insulator the explanation that materials can keep cold things cold was not easily assimilated. What had to be explained at this point was that clothes keep us warm because they help us retain our body heat and not because they are warm. Children were given several small practical tasks to help them understand this, including wearing a coat with just one sleeve on, lying in a sleeping bag.

Figure 3.4   Ice people

Lesson 3: Incorporating children's ideas

'Does how we cook baked Alaska make a difference?'

The creative ideas and original use of resources and activities sparked questions which otherwise would not be appropriate or even thought of. The children said, 'We could use a blow torch to see if we could melt the meringue', 'Can we put the baked Alaska in a microwave?' and 'I think we could put it in tin foil and it would cook.' Unfortunately, lesson plans cannot indicate this element of involvement and questioning derived from dialogue but being responsive to children's ideas and developing plans accordingly is fundamental to a creative approach to teaching and learning.

For example, the suggestion incorporated into Lesson 3 to compare the baked Alaska cooked in a conventional oven with one cooked in a microwave came from the children. Taking the initiative, the teacher helped children follow a line of inquiry not previously thought of. Because the plan came from the pupils there was a sense of ownership. If the teacher had suggested this, there would probably be interest as the prediction held by many was that it would be messy, blow up, explode and the meringue would be fragmented. This is logical because food in a microwave can explode. The consequences of the experiment were known by the trainee teachers but they recognised the value of giving pupils the opportunity to find out for themselves.

Imagine the surprise when there was no mess and the baked Alaska was retrieved from the microwave in apparently the same state as when it went in. The surprise increased when it was discovered that on slicing through the uncooked meringue the ice cream was soft; the complete reversal of the baked Alaska cooked in the oven. This raised many questions and conflicting explanations which challenged well-held ideas. It is possible to see how this physical example can be used to teach children high-level science about heating by convection and induction, thermal conductivity and electrical energy as well as the insulating properties of air and water.

Some would argue that the level of knowledge is too high for primary children to grasp. But within this unusual context, understanding of the insulating properties of materials was increased, with all children scoring well on a summative assessment task satisfying planned learning outcomes and more. What is more important to recognise is that the implications for learning spread far wider to include aspects of subject knowledge, including for example how a microwave works, what is a colloid, how air acts as an insulator and why some things explode in a microwave. Questions as to why plastic and paper do not burn in a microwave oven were followed up by using science sites on the internet using Google as a search engine and although the level of explanation was too advanced on many sites, http://www.howstuffworks.com was useful in initiating discussion. As with any aspect of science the primary teacher has to decide how to explain concepts and answer questions at a level to enhance understanding and not confuse the learner with language that is too technical. In this instance the children were assured by the explanation that one special thing about microwaves is that they only act on some things to make them hot. An experiment was planned to follow this idea with water and sand separately measured and put in a microwave oven to compare the temperature difference after a few minutes. The children could see very quickly that the water heated rapidly in the microwave and the sand did not. The children then wanted to know why metal makes sparks and you must not put it in the microwave. It was explained that microwaves acted differently on metal and that this would damage the oven. However, some packaging of ready meals has a small film of metal in the packaging to speed up the heating process and act as a mini frying pan.

Giving children space to follow their own ideas or questions is not easy in a busy science lesson, nor is spontaneity always possible, but selectively using pupils' ideas can enhance and support learning opportunities. Reflecting on what the learner thinks, statements they make and questions they ask gives indications of levels of understanding. Using this information in planning can act as a catalyst for creative lessons. With the examples of Lessons 2 and 3 this is certainly true.

Lesson 2

NC Objectives: Sc1 1b, 2d, 2f 2j, 2k, 2l; Sc3 1b, 2a, 2b

QCA: Unit 4C Through this unit children build on their ideas about temperature as a measure of how hot or cold objects are and learn about thermal insulators as materials which can help to keep things warm or cool.

Learning objectives: Certain materials act as insulators; A fair test is essential to justify the results of an experiment; Make predictions and compare with results.

Vocabulary: Insulate, melt, warm, cold, temperature, prediction

Introduction: Recap of last sessions, keeping things warm and keeping things cool. Which materials were the best insulators? Remind children about fair testing and ask for examples based on previous experiments. Introduce activity by showing children three identical ice blocks that have just been taken out of the freezer. Ask what will happen if clothes are put on the ice figures. Discuss the snowman Concept Cartoon (Brenda Keogh and Stuart Naylor 1997)

Main activity: Three identical ice figures are placed in measuring containers such as calibrated jugs. These figures have been made by filling plastic bottles with 1 litre of water and placing them in a freezer overnight. The bottles are discarded and each ice figure is placed in an identical measuring container. One is not dressed, one is dressed in light cotton summer clothes and one is dressed in several layers of woollen winter-type garments. Dolls' clothes are used and many layers are placed on the third figure. The rate at which the ice melts is monitored at regular intervals and the volume of water collected in each container is measured to see which figure melts the fastest. Pupils are asked to predict what they think will happen. Do they think the clothes will speed up the melting process? Ask them to explain their predictions. The Concept Cartoon of Snowmen can be used to compare and elicit ideas. As time passes and evidence is collected and data analysed children are asked if they have changed their ideas. Explanations are given for original predictions and changed views discussed as a result of evidence.

Extension activities:

1. Place the figures in warmer and cooler locations using the same three levels of insulation. Do the children think that the temperature of the location will cause the ice figures to melt more or less? Are the results the same as the original room temperature experiment?

2. Set a challenge for group collaboration. *Insulate your ice figure so that it takes the longest time to melt*.

Lesson 3

Explaining why ice cream inside a layer of meringue will stay solid in a hot oven is a much more challenging task and will require pupils to explain their reasoning.

QCA: Unit 4C Through this unit children build on their ideas about temperature as a measure of how hot or cold objects are and learn about thermal insulators as materials which can help to keep things warm or cool.

Learning objectives: Certain materials act as insulators; A fair test is essential to justify the results of an experiment; Make predictions and compare with results.

NC objectives: Sc1 1b, 2d, 2f 2j, 2k, 2l; Sc3 1b, 2a, 2b

Vocabulary: Insulate, melt, warm, cold, temperature, prediction

Introduction: Recap of last sessions, keeping things warm and keeping things cool. Which materials were the best insulators? Did the same materials that kept hot things hot keep cool things cool? Remind children about fair testing and ask for examples based on previous experiments. Introduce activity by showing children a block of ice cream that has just been taken out of the freezer. Ask for suggestions on how to keep it cool.

Main activity: Baked Alaska. Tell the children that we are going to put this ice cream into a hot oven. What do they think will happen? Can they think of a way to stop it melting? Make up the meringue with children's help, and ask the children what they can see happening to the egg whites and sugar (the mixture now contains air). Ask them to predict what will happen if the ice cream is covered with meringue before going into the oven. Explain that we will try a variety of layers of meringue, keeping the temperature of the oven and the amount of ice cream the same; one dessert will have a thick layer of meringue, one a thin layer, and one a thick layer with a hole in the top. Ask children to make a prediction of what will happen in each circumstance. Put the baked Alaska into the oven, mention safety points. After ten minutes remove baked Alaska and use data logger to measure the temperature of the ice cream before cutting into it. Show the children that the ice cream has melted the least in the baked Alaska with the most meringue covering it. Why? Did this match their predictions?

Extension activities:

1. Using the same three levels of insulation with meringue, use a blowtorch to brown the meringue. Do the children think that this will cause the ice cream to melt more or less? Are the results the same as the baked Alaska that went in the oven?

2. Use a microwave to make baked Alaska, made with a thick layer of meringue. Are their predictions the same? Show children what happens and explain about microwaves heating from the inside.

Danielle, a trainee teacher (2005/6), decided to carry out the same investigation looking at thermal insulation using 'ice people' as described above. After the experiment one of the children remarked, 'Do you think the same thing would happen with Coke?' Danielle took up the challenge. The children, now familiar with the routine of measuring water in large plastic bottles and freezing it before adding layers of insulation (dolls' clothes), set up a similar 'fair test' using Coca Cola instead of water. As before, one ice person was dressed in winter clothes. This time the hat was made of tin foil. Whilst observing and comparing what happened, the children realised that the 'syrup' behaved differently from the water and the brown ice people lost colour. At the same time gas bubbles 'escaped' as the solid changed to a liquid. As time passed the evaporating gas built up under the hat and blew it off. A Year 1 child was passing by just as this happened and was amazed. The event was talked about across the school. This was certainly not a planned outcome. The discussion generated by the surprise of the hat being blown off surpassed any expected result. So what has this little anecdote got to do with creativity? To me it demonstrates both the creative thinking of children and the creative approach of the trainee teacher. The children raised questions, considered possible alternatives and found the ordinary fascinating. The teacher encouraged autonomy, maximised an opportune moment and helped turn predictable outcomes into something better. The fact that the teacher was also surprised delighted the children. Their next question was, 'Would the hat blow off an ice person if it was wearing just a hat and no other clothes?'

Scientists make changes, refine ideas and use their judgement, so why shouldn't children? It is a sad indictment of science teaching if children's questions are not given consideration or lines of inquiry pursued as a result. Far from being uncompli-cated, the venture of doing science is one of trial and error which is constantly scruti-nised for its effect and impact. Scientists play with ideas, make judgements and attach importance to what they understand. Children need the opportunity to do the same if their questions are to be valued.

Conclusion

Much of what has been discussed in this chapter is concerned with short-term plan-ning, adapting schemes of work and responding to pupils' ideas. These aspects of planning are strongly influenced by the daily remit and concern of how children learn. The driving force is the child rather than the teacher, but learning is supported with sound scientific knowledge. Questions and discussion push forwards the learn-ing needed to understand the scientific principles and content. Teachers will be able to identify with the buzz felt when a plan initiates inquiry and expands as pupils take charge of their learning. They will also be able to identify with the feeling that con-trolling the learning environment will demand skill to prevent chaos. The reward for doing this is to teach in a way that makes even lessons taught before seem new and vibrant. The teacher is rewarded by being involved in a lively new debate resulting from purposeful inquiry.

Summary of main points

- Planning creatively is possible within the constraints of the NC.
- Creative planning needs construction within a flexible framework.
- Adaptation of resources and ideas are part of a creative approach.

- Creative planning involves making interesting connections.
- Planning to use and develop children's ideas creatively widens understanding.
- Unknown outcomes are inevitable if flexibility is valued.
- In creative planning negotiation is crucial to decision making.
- Creative planning does not limit science to a specified time slot.

Issues for reflection

- What do you feel about prescribed schemes of work as the basis for planning? Do you feel confident and secure in the knowledge that well-used schemes of work have been well thought through?

- Have you ever adapted published science schemes of work to make them more creative, practical or useful for your pupils? Why did you think this was necessary?

- Do you think about how to incorporate children's ideas and use their questions to create a sense of ownership or do you feel this is too time consuming and not practical?

- Do you look forward to planning meetings? If you do, why is this? If not, what could you do to improve them?

- Given free choice, how would you go about planning science teaching?

Discussion points

- It is now very easy to lift plans from the World Wide Web. How does this fit with a creative approach to planning and learning?

- Does the prescriptive nature of an outcome-driven NC science curriculum stifle creativity?

- Planning creatively would benefit from a collaborative team effort in which ideas are discussed and a whole-school approach is adopted.

- What makes planning a creative experience?

References

Barnes, R. (1989) *Art, Design and Topic Work.* London: Unwin Hyman

Carle, E. (1969) *The Very Hungry Caterpillar.* London: Hamish Hamilton

Keogh, B. and Naylor, S. (1997) *Concept Cartoons.* Hatfield: ASE

QCA, Q. a. C. A. (1998) *Science Teacher's Guide, A Scheme of Work for Key Stages 1 and 2.* London: Department for Education and Employment (DfEE)

CHAPTER 4

Inspiring inquiry

Pupils should be taught that science is about **thinking creatively** to try to explain how living things and non living things work, and to establish links between causes and effects.

(National Science Curriculum for Key Stage 2 1999)

Weisberg (1986) states that creative scientists differ from non-creative scientists in distinct ways. Broadly speaking, creative scientists need to be free of rules to allow for flexible thinking. This flexibility enables them to know when to abandon non-productive efforts and change approaches. They waste little time on simple solutions and recognise the potential for significant breakthroughs. They may also be aware of a problem or solution that others miss. They are open to experiences, will be alert during investigations and observe things others may fail to notice. Playing with ideas is a key feature of their work. To inspire creativity in carrying out Science Sc1 (Scientific Enquiry) of the National Curriculum teachers also need to encourage flexible thinking. Is this easier said than done? Of course, but without the effort teachers and children can miss so much they would otherwise gain.

If we want to inspire inquiry we need to understand that this may result in a jumble of scientifically wrong ideas which need to be questioned. Here lies a paradox. If we want scientific inquiry and teaching science to be 'right' we need to encourage it to be 'wrong'. What is right in science is often determined by knowing what is wrong along the way. This does little for a teacher's confidence unless it is seen as a route to success and that ultimate golden nugget of deeper understanding. There is nothing new about mistakes and failure on the route to success. It is just a little difficult to live with when the safe and expected scientific outcome can *apparently* be demonstrated more easily. Confidence in failure is hard to come by. It is human nature to want things to be 'right' and forget the old adage that 'The person who never made a mistake never made anything'. Confidence in tolerating ambiguous and sometimes wrong scientific answers comes from success after taking the first risk. Not all teachers are initially prepared to do this:

> They are only 5. They cannot do an investigation.
>
> They are playing and they will find things out but that is not investigating.
>
> There is not time to let them investigate. If we want them to learn certain things then we have to set the agenda.
>
> (Teachers 2005)

Some reassurance that curriculum requirements are being met is understandable. After all, teachers are accountable and there is no point teaching children science that is plainly misleading. Fortunately, inspiring children with a desire to know about their world can still be achieved by risking the appearance of those scientific misconceptions that ultimately need a good clean-up. Inspiring inquiry is achieved through rigorous verification of outcomes, not just letting children live with their misconceptions.

In the 1960s 'Discovery Learning' gained a foothold in primary education and was often misconceived as a teaching method where the teacher played the role of a helpful ignoramus. Children actually discovered a great deal and were often fired up by having control over their learning. The teacher was a facilitator and guide enthusing over what was found out. A missing element in teaching and learning was that very little verification of outcomes seemed to take place. The more astute teachers taught skilfully and were aware that they were much more than facilitators. Often the daily agenda for 'Discovery Learning' was decided by the child and freedom of expression was a common feature. All this has changed and developed with the introduction of the National Curriculum and Ofsted inspections. Inspired investigation still puts the child at the centre of learning but there is a difference. Children's discoveries are honed, verified and corrected through the teacher's grasp of essential scientific knowledge. Professionalism comes through verifying in such a way that children's scientific errors are the building bricks of accuracy and accepted thinking.

Risking unexpected outcomes

As part of an investigation into how materials freeze, a child raised the question 'What happens if we freeze cotton-wool?' This investigation is discussed in more detail later in this chapter (Example 2), but here is one investigative response.

> We put cotton wool in the freezer. We thought it would go icy around the side. It was the same when we took it out, and the only change was it was softer. It felt softer. It surprised me because I thought it would get harder. We tried it for a longer time 'cause sometimes you can't find out, can't be exact, can't find out the answers in the time. So I

put some in my freezer at home but it was still soft. We put lots in but it was still soft. So we tried a bit of water just round the edges then it did go hard and crunchy when we took it out but it was still soft in the middle bit, that didn't go hard only where we put water. I watched a programme at home about chemicals like what happens when you freeze things.

(Becky age 8)

Children want to be intrigued and fascinated. Without the desire to find out, learning science would be a sterile occupation. Not knowing is the condition that makes people continue searching.

Some writers (Driver 1985; Elstgeest 1985; Elstgeest and Harlen 1990) argue that a child is a scientist before it can read or write, or even before it can use language at a simple level. Babies and young children instinctively explore the world in which they live. They are drawn to reflections, they compare and consider them, they watch how porridge falls off a spoon, they make banging noises with saucepan lids, and they repeat these experiences; working at controlling them is a mission. They are experimenting. Curiosity is instinctive. Children want to find answers and make sense of the world. What they do not have is the ability or schema to order their thinking to follow productive lines of inquiry.

This does not stop at school, but it can become camouflaged when constraints of time and curriculum coverage dominate. On the one hand, the benefit of an inquiry-based approach to learning is certainly recognised by many teachers, philosophers and educators (Gardner 2004; Harlen 2004; Hunkin 2004). On the other hand, there never seems enough time to let children play with ideas and make their own mistakes. Yet some teachers manage to inspire inquiry because they know that children do not learn in a vacuum. Most learning is achieved through experience.

Inquiry is not predictable. It relies on interaction, dialogue, trial and error and manipulation of ideas. When this becomes inspirational it has several features.

- Children have differing views about the same observed event and wonder why.
- Teachers see 'wrong answers' as a successful outcome because misconceptions can be unravelled.
- Children experience success through finding answers to scientific puzzles and predicting outcomes.
- Children learn it is positive to be wrong and find out why.
- Children develop better understanding through verifying what they have found out.
- Children are likely to continue questioning their world.

This is rule-breaking that Weisberg (1986) would probably approve of. It comes nearer to the practice of scientists who think creatively and is far removed from instruction, supported by a demonstration. The teacher who works creatively does not set out merely to prove a scientific point or reproduce predictable results. When we think of what children remember and understand of our lessons from day to day it is probably not much. Unless, that is, their experience becomes much more meaningful through investigating, much in the way rule-breaking scientists do.

A further reason for working creatively is that puzzling about the world can resonate in children's minds the following morning. Inspired inquirers are those who turn over ideas to find plausible answers to intriguing scientific problems. Rather like hearing a tune the following morning, scientific investigation can resonate with involvement, just as a superb concert, book, play or film does. Not everyone may be curious about the world to the same extent, but could that be because no teacher ever challenged their assumptions as a child? We cannot know, but how energising it is for teachers to find their pupils coming up with questions of mind-blowing infinity.

They asked me if rubber would freeze and 'Does milk freeze quicker than water?' That set me wondering myself, so we needed to try it out . . . but how would we know? How long should we take? I remembered that if you try to make ice-cream you have to stir it. So what happens if we stir partly frozen water and partly frozen milk? And when can we say it is completely frozen? Is it skimmed milk or full milk? It isn't straightforward, is it?

(Teacher 2005)

Example 1. Playing with ideas; an imaginative task

In this example imagination is seen as a vital ingredient in the process of inquiry. Accumulated experience and reason help the learner to make sense of data but it is the imagination that triggers new ideas and opens up possibilities. There is no expectation of a specific conclusion and in fact the conclusion is adapted through discussion and consideration of factors involved. Playing with ideas and where they can lead is a powerful feature of inspiring inquiry. Without the constraint of being concerned about accuracy of scientific detail, pupils can let their imaginations lead thinking.

The children were asked to think about inventing an imaginary planet. Choices made would need to be considered scientifically viable, although imaginary aspects would be expected. Linking fantasy to fact was not seen as a problem. Children could present their work how they wished. Through encouraging speculation and consideration of possibilities the teacher hoped that several aspects of the curriculum would be covered in a motivating way. Everyone was asked to include six facts for discussion and be ready to answer questions about their planet.

Before the children began working, a class discussion covered information about the Earth, including the

- atmosphere;
- conditions for life;
- composition of materials;
- dimensions;
- living organisms;
- place in the Solar System;
- place in space.

Each of these would need to be thought about when designing an imaginary planet. Without a catalyst or frame to aid planning, inquiry would be random. A structure or guide helps children to be systematic. This supporting structure can sometimes be disregarded so as not to give the impression that creativity is being marginalised. What needs to be understood is that creativity is about organising, pattern forming and questioning with originality. Encouraging creativity requires tolerance of ambiguity, accepting conflicting information and valuing individual endeavour.

To be creative in methods of inquiry children need to have different models so as not to be mere technicians but find ways to formulate ideas and make simple connections and choices. Demonstrating several ways of opening up inquiry is essential to avoid rigidity of thinking. With this knowledge children will have a choice of routes to follow. One child might begin by drawing land animals, considering where they live. He will need to think about the gases used by the animals and realise that once one imaginary decision has been made then there will be a cause and effect relationship to explore. Another child might begin by drawing the whole planet as seen from space and talk about meteorites circling it. Decisions might be taken about where to place water on the planet. Talking about the Earth could promote imaginative ideas which would focus thinking. To imagine an unknown planet can link imagination and fantasy with scientific fact. Inventing many examples of planets is a benefit and not a limitation. Through comparison and examination of peculiarities critical evaluation can be developed in a non-threatening way. Anything is possible but scientific considerations are put in context. Inquiry becomes open to all.

Gup

The creutwer spits the blood out so it digests is own silver

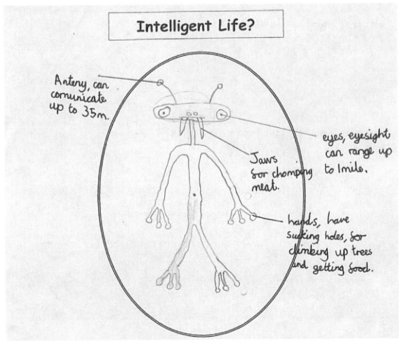

Intelligent Life?

Anteny, can comunicate up to 35m.

eyes, eyesight can range up to 1mile.

Jaws for chomping meat.

hands, have sucking holes, for climbing up trees and getting food.

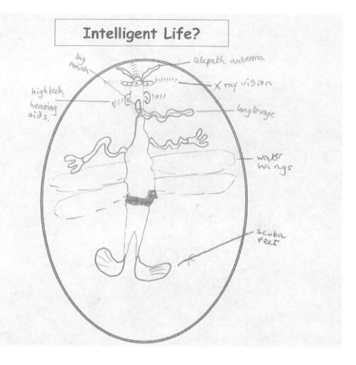

Intelligent Life?

big mouth
telepath antenna
X ray vision
high tech hearing aids
long tongue
water wings
scuba feet

Figure 4.1a, b, c   Intelligent alien life

Creatures on my planet don't need to eat because they digest their own spit. The creature spits the blood out so it digests its own saliva.

(Glyn)

Spiked feet were needed on each leg to climb on the ice. They didn't have toes just spikes 10 on each foot.

(Parvati)

They had 4 eyes with night vision 'cause the planet had been hit by a meteorite and they lived underground. They came out at night because they couldn't see in the day.

(Paul)

Plants rule my planet, they eat anything that moves but now there are hardly any animals left they grow them in farms; worms and slugs are best, they are easy to catch.

(Asaf)

Nothing lives on my planet, they have all gone to another planet because it is warmer.

(Daisy)

Plants on my planet grow in the air so they don't need soil but they do need clouds for rain.

(Matthew)

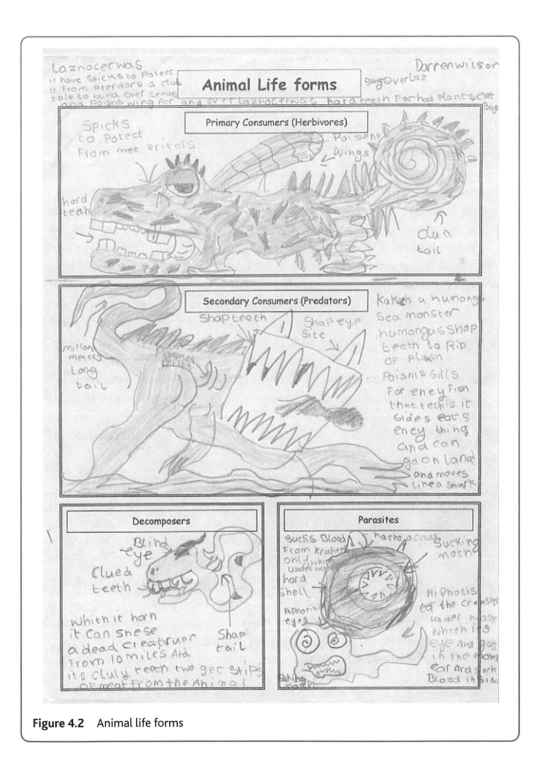

Figure 4.2 Animal life forms

What an opportunity this is to verify the logic of how things grow and what the make-up of planets is. Two obvious verification questions address what processes are possible:

> How is your planet NOT like Earth?
>
> How is Earth NOT like other planets?

Verifying understanding can concern scientific processes such as what happens to mountain climbers at high altitude if they are starved of oxygen. Is this the same as a deep sea diver? And are there other sources of oxygen apart from air? Why do we need oxygen anyway? It is also worth evaluating ideas, for example in terms of establishing a food chain and looking at ours. Verification is not just a random business. There needs to be some emphasis on what the teacher wants to achieve and make use of. This gives learning a focus because scientific vocabulary and discussion of life processes can be set against the needs of the National Curriculum. The follow-on work looked at National Curriculum SC2 Life Processes, particularly *to make links between life processes in familiar animals and plants and the environments in which they are found.* Development of understanding was apparent as pupils made links between their imaginary beings and those within their experience. It was as if their thinking was focused on the big ideas of adaptation, ecosystems and climatic implications to life processes. They were able to make links between cause and effect,

> When the planet got hot it was because there were no clouds and there was nowhere to hide. All the creatures lived in the ground, they built tunnels and came out at night. It was so swampy and gooey that the best surviving animals liked water and had big feet. They squashed the little ones with their feet and sucked them up a tube. When their children were hungry they sucked the tube for bits that were left.
>
> (Asaf)

The children gained a great deal from this way of working. The teacher was able to help pupils make links between many aspects of National Curriculum science, including characteristics of living things, environments, habitats, interdependence and food chains.

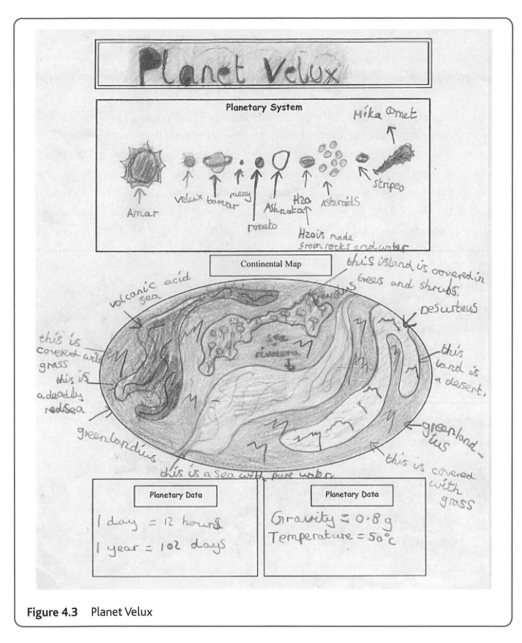

Figure 4.3 Planet Velux

Example 2. Raising questions; pursuing ideas

Jo felt that the children were bored by the way she taught science and so was she. She decided to try a different way of teaching her class of 8-year-olds. The children were learning about materials and their properties, physical change, mixing and mixtures. Instead of focusing on specific learning objectives Jo decided to give children the freedom to test things and find out what happens by pursuing their own ideas. The children were given a range of familiar materials found either at school or at home, including some liquids. They were asked two questions,

> What do you think will happen if you mix some of these materials together?
>
> Is there anything else you want to find out about these materials?

Jo was curious to see how the class would react to this freedom and she had some concerns about the value of such an activity. It was obvious from the start that the children enjoyed mixing things to see what would happen. Initially this was an arbitrary process, exploring possibilities without a system or notion of control. Very soon several pupils progressed to asking questions about freezing some of their mixtures. This was not the teacher's idea but nevertheless she encouraged the children where possible to follow their ideas. She asked them to come up with some questions to which they would like to find the answer.

Questions raised by the children

- What happens if you freeze cotton wool?
- If we put oil and water in the freezer together will they both freeze?
- How long will it take for a cup of water to freeze?
- Will paint freeze?
- If you mix vinegar, flour and tomato sauce what will it look like frozen?
- What happens when you set light to cotton wool?
- What happens when you put paint in the oven for an hour?
- What will happen if we mix beer and orange juice?
- What happens if you freeze rubber?
- What happens if you put salt, water and ketchup in the freezer?

The following accounts describe the way in which some of the above questions were followed up. The conversations took place six weeks after the experiments were completed. This is significant because the detail and accuracy are remarkable considering the time lapse between 8-year-old children doing the experiments and talking about them. It would be interesting to see if the same children could give an animated, detailed account of a teacher-directed science lesson which had taken place six weeks previously.

We had an empty bottle and put oil and water, the oil on top, then we tipped it and put it in the freezer. The next day oil was on top, the water had frozen but the oil hadn't. Oil wouldn't freeze at the temperature of the freezer. I measured how much water was in the 500ml bottle, I put 250ml in, the next day oil was on top. When I took it out the water had frozen and gone to 400ml. I think that's to do with air.

(Latasha)

We put a plastic cup half full of water in the freezer and looked at the clock every ten minutes. We timed it. It took 4 hours 55 minutes to freeze. I couldn't believe it.

(Latasha)

We predicted that paint would freeze but it went hard inside but watery round the edges, sort of mushy, it was wet around the side. It surprised me, I thought it would either freeze or not.

(Becky)

It's messy; we used an ice cube container. First we put in vinegar, then ketchup, then water. Then we put it in the freezer. The water froze mushy even after two days. Because vinegar and ketchup are just like water I thought they would freeze. I wondered if hot water would be different to cold water. I put in sugar and salt, we noticed it dissolved, you couldn't see it, after one hour it started to freeze only a thin layer. I opened the fridge the next day and it was brown, you couldn't see the vinegar, you still couldn't see the sugar and salt. Even though the hot started hotter but in the freezer all ended up the same.

(Latasha)

It's easy to see that children would be motivated by playing around mixing their own concoctions and that science would be seen as fun. But what is really noticeable here is what the children are learning, including:

- **Developing testing skills**: 'We looked at the clock every ten minutes, we timed it.'
- **Challenging understanding**: 'I wondered if hot water would be different to cold water. It took 4 hours 55 minutes to freeze. I couldn't believe it.'
- **Making a simple hypothesis**: 'Because vinegar and ketchup are just like water I thought they would freeze.'
- **Increasing their subject knowledge**: 'That didn't go hard only where we put water . . . oil wouldn't freeze at the temperature of the freezer.'

The lines of inquiry and the direction these took were not predetermined in any way. The learning resulted from pupils taking responsibility in pursuing questions independently using resources supplied by the teacher. Although the teacher decided which resources were to be used, it is unlikely that she pre-empted the exact detail of questions raised or explorations which followed. By focusing on pupils' questions, surprises and evident misconceptions, the teacher opened up dialogue to increase subject knowledge. As they were working the children decided what they would like to find out. If the teacher had given pupils an ice cube and instructions to time how long it would take to change to a liquid, it is unlikely that their attention and motivation would be sustained. Because they wanted to find this out, motivation was high. The process skills of setting up an experiment, recording and measuring in a systematic, controlled and accurate way were all evident. This degree of independence was possible because the teacher:

- triggered initial motivation by sharing information and offering resources;
- used information to make predictions and hypotheses about what might happen;
- responded to children's ideas positively;
- valued questions raised;
- helped set up situations and intervened to guide thinking;
- accepted that pupils respond and learn in different ways;
- promoted a willingness and confidence to abandon certain lines of inquiry;
- encouraged creative thinking.

As in the planet examples, inquiry was inspired by an imaginative approach. Elaboration is a key feature of creative thinking. It enables pupils to pay careful attention to detail in explaining their discoveries and planning their own search to answer questions of interest. Without an environment conducive to interpreting carefully collected data, much creative endeavour would be lost. However, if a teacher started a lesson with 'Today we are going to see what happens when we put cotton wool in a freezer', they would be surprised to find pupils motivated or inspired to investigate. The lesson would probably be over before it began. Because the teacher encouraged exploration, ideas emerged at random. The pupils set the agenda and provided explanations, making learning a flexible process with no expectation of a correct answer.

How teachers work

Not all teachers adopt such a creative stance. Decisions made put a very different expectation on the learner. If teachers want children to accept the explanations or answers given to them without question then their way of teaching will mirror this. If they are concerned with initiating inquiry, raising questions and encouraging speculation, their approach will demand interaction, decision making and speculation.

Anna began the lesson with questions. 'Do you think you could squash an egg? If you hold an egg between your finger and thumb and press as hard as you can, do you think it will break?' She demonstrated placing her thumb under the egg and her index finger on top, so that the vertical plane was longer. 'Does anyone want to have a go?' Several children put their hands up and made an attempt. The effort was visible on their faces but all were unsuccessful in applying a force strong enough to break the shell. Not only were they surprised but also intrigued. Anna started talking about strong shapes, the shell shapes of the bones in babies' heads which need to withstand pressure at birth, and drawings of bridges designed to carry heavy loads.

A rather dull alternative would have been to explain that 'Forces are pushes and pulls and they can be measured using a force meter.' By placing a mass on the hook of a force meter the weight could be measured and recorded. The trouble with this is it is almost invisible as a means of understanding how forces work. It is not enough to give information and demonstrate a skill without engaging involvement in thinking about cause and effect if we want to inspire inquiry.

Placing value on discovery

There are many skills and processes involved in developing scientific rigour and understanding. If children are to be inspired they need to be intrigued to continue rather than be satisfied with one answer. Responding to instruction to carry out a process of inquiry will not necessarily achieve this. Science presented as a set of skills and concepts as though they are inevitable misses the opportunity to raise questions. Through placing value on discovery, as in Anna's lesson, the stage is set for building vital connections. Actually doing something practical alerts pupils to the need to engage in, not only the activity, but also thinking about it. At primary level discovery is usually engineered by the teacher to achieve desired outcomes. Consequently the ideas that the teacher gives will guide but also restrict thinking. Care in recognising pupils' response and interpretation of data will open up new pathways.

Curriculum requirements

Scientific inquiry in National Curriculum terms is concerned with the process of science; key features include exploring ideas, collecting evidence, evaluating evidence, testing ideas and trying to make sense of findings. Within this broad framework skills are developed, including those of observation, questioning, analysis and fair testing. In Key Stage 1 children are taught to collect evidence, plan by asking questions, recognise when a test is unfair, obtain and present evidence, make simple comparisons, review their work and explain what they did. In Key Stage 2 children are taught to make links between ideas and explain things using simple models and theories. They are expected to think about the positive and negative effects of scientific and technological developments. They are expected to carry out more systematic investigations and take a rigorous approach to obtaining evidence, measuring and recording. Appropriate use of ICT is a requirement and should be used as a resource at all levels.

Guiding inquiry

Young children do not have the experience or ability to transfer abstract thinking in the way that adults do. Their interpretation of words and concepts is often literal and subjective. For example, their experience of seeing pre-packed food will not necessarily help them realise that chips are made from potatoes which grow as tubers in the ground or sprouts grow on a stalk or peas grow in a pod. In the classroom, learning from practical experience alone is not enough to increase understanding. Discussion among peers and with the teacher will help pupils move on and make sense of what they are doing. Structures need to be in place; familiar models and routes to follow to support the process of inquiry need to be taught. This may seem contradictory to the notion of creative autonomy but freedom works best when choices can be made in a secure way. There is no doubt that children enjoy being able to take their time, work with friends and do things by trial and error but the big question as to what they are learning must be what drives teachers' thinking. To encourage inquiry a teacher must organise the lesson to give children a sense of freedom and ownership but also ensure that their understanding of the process of science and subject knowledge has increased as a result of the experience.

For example, if children are presented with a variety of seeds to observe and compare, then it will be relatively easy to instigate a discussion as to their appearance, size and shape. Sorting and classifying exercises are useful in themselves but also set the scene for a more theoretical dialogue. It is unlikely that children will recognise which seeds will grow into which plants unless their experience is of growing flowers and vegetables at home. To organise lessons in which children have a sense of freedom to inquire can come from such a simple beginning. Suppose a child comes up with a query: 'Does the biggest seed make the biggest plant and the smallest seed make the smallest plant?' Then they will have a sense of ownership from the start. But we all know this does not readily happen and definitely not to order. The teacher needs to have questions prepared as starting points or to be pursued fully. Such as:

> Do bigger seeds grow bigger plants?
>
> Does a small seed grow into a small plant?

To respond to these questions with any accuracy it is necessary to understand which conditions plants need to germinate and grow in a healthy way. This subject knowledge is not implicit and will need to be taught. It is also necessary to record and monitor growth in a systematic way. Methods of recording and accuracy of data collected will need to be checked. So where does this allow for freedom and ownership? Freedom comes from making choices as to what to investigate, how to investigate, how to adapt investigations and whether another question is more interesting. In this case:

- **What to investigate:** choice of seeds, selecting large and small e.g. avocado, poppy, carrot, marrow, hollyhock, leek.

- **How to investigate:** choice of place to plant, ways of ensuring healthy growth, what to observe, how to record and measure data.

- **Adapting investigations:** changing conditions to suit the plant.

- **Pursuing a more interesting line of inquiry:** following a question generated from the initial inquiry, for example 'Why do some beans grow curly and some grow straight?'

It is with this last statement that freedom to follow an idea has a real sense of purpose. Teachers do not know in advance what observations will be made but if they can allow them to be followed a sense of ownership is established.

Ways to inspire inquiry

Asking questions; fair testing

Questions to which no member of the class knows the answer, as the answer will be subjective to the inquiry, is a good starting point. This way of beginning an investigation puts everyone on an equal footing. To start an investigation with the question, 'Which biscuit is the best dunker?' gains attention. Tea and biscuits are enjoyed by most people. Dunking biscuits holds a fascination and can be amusing. The question is deceptively simple and might appear trite, but the scientific possibilities are there: *dissolving, physical change, suitability of purpose, chemical construction, food facts, dietary information, effect of heat, manipulation and control of variables, setting up a fair test.*

By providing a variety of cups and mugs, a selection of biscuits carefully chosen for different properties and lukewarm tea (for safety reasons), children are able to feel confident that there is no right answer, no correct way of dunking and they can explore the possibilities freely. What they soon realise (and this is the teacher's intention) is that some control is needed if results are to be compared and have meaning. Questions are quickly raised indicating awareness of fair testing. Once they begin to compare results, children recognise that the test is not fair: cups are different sizes, they are made from different material, they have different surface areas; the tea varies in quantity and temperature; the biscuits are different shapes and people have different methods of dunking. Conversations are about trying to control variables. The teacher can use this opportunity to identify factors in setting up a fair test. A list of *what will make a difference to the test* can be started and added to as the children come up with more suggestions. They will be developing an understanding of variables and the effect they have on data without using complicated terms.

Although the language used is child friendly, concepts are soundly embedded in good scientific practice. Before the experiment can progress, children need to clarify terms by deciding what they mean by dunking. This will be an individual construct and a consensus on how to dunk the biscuits will be needed. Imaginative and varied responses may include dipping the biscuit halfway into the tea and counting to 5, quickly dipping the biscuit in and out three times, submerging most of the biscuit for 10 seconds and dipping for 2 seconds five times which are all possible suggestions. If the list of *what will make a difference to our test* is used appropriately to identify what will be kept the same, what will be changed and what will be measured then pupils will set up a test that is controlled. The cup and the liquid will remain constant and the control variable, the biscuit, will change.

Encouraging independent decision making

There is a real buzz in the classroom when pupils collaborate to set up a test themselves. A good teacher will manoeuvre an activity with science skills firmly embedded in the task, allowing children to develop and build on these skills in a non-threatening context. Pupils decide what they are going to change, measure and record. Enjoyment of the activity should not detract from the fact that they are learning to identify, control and manipulate variables. Although the subject knowledge covered can be minimal in this type of investigation, pupils learn to follow a process of inquiry with a degree of independence. Fair testing and consideration of factors can be explored. Dunking biscuits is fun.

By comparison, a lesson in which children tested the effect of insulating cups of tea using different fabrics to find the best insulator would be less purposeful. Wrapping cotton wool, quilted cotton or wool material round a cup of warm tea has little relationship to experience; except perhaps wearing gloves when holding a cup of tea. If heat transfer is considered it is more relevant to think about how the cup is able to be held rather than how the temperature of the tea is affected. At worst, the pupils would follow instructions and copy the conclusion from the board along with a chart showing cooling curves of each sample of tea.

If independent decision making is encouraged more often this results in children taking ownership of the activity. This is an unpredictable route, as these responses show.

I decided to make the ramp higher so that the car would go further, but it didn't so then I put it just a bit higher and then put candle wax on the tyres. It didn't work so we got a smooth piece of plastic stuff instead of wood to make the ramp. Then it worked.

(Dani age 9)

The woodlice like it dark so we put some black paper over the dish, then we tried different things like putting mud and leaves or stones or sand, it was still dark but we wanted to see where they went in the dark. It was my idea to put sand.

(Abi age 10)

What is important is that decisions to see what happens are made by the children themselves and questions to investigate result from explorations and speculation. 'How can we make the car travel further?' 'In the dark, what conditions do woodlice prefer?'

Opening up lines of inquiry from children's ideas

There are ways of opening up lines of inquiry to support children in following their ideas. To achieve this the teacher will need to monitor conversations, respond to suggestions and interpret body language. Identifying questions which children may want to ask cannot be done in isolation (see Chapter 3). Young children will not necessarily have the language or way of thinking to formulate specific questions. They will, however, be intrigued or puzzled by things they have noticed or experiences encountered. Observation of children's play and exploration is a good way of gaining evidence of their ideas and thinking. It is only by watching closely how pupils interact and respond to situations that decisions can be made which inform teaching. In a lesson based on negotiated learning teachers and children become involved together. This participation can be exciting and stimulating. There is a shared sense of purpose. The process is developmental and open to change. The following examples are a direct result from teachers' observation and participation, with an initial exploration of certain phenomena and experiences.

- **Setting a challenge**: Can you slow down the speed at which the car travels down the ramp?
- **Generating ideas through debate**: I think the glue made with just flour and water is stronger than the glue made with flour, water and egg white.
- **Turning pupils' observations into questions**: 'It's difficult to cut this furry material' becomes 'Which material is the easiest to cut?'
- **Using pupils' questions to open up lines of inquiry**: 'Why don't parachutes with a hole in the top crash?' becomes 'How does the size of a hole in a parachute affect the fall?'
- **Encouraging collaborative exploration and discovery**: Do more people make tug-of-war easier or harder?
- **Looking at cause and effect**: How can we move the paper clips without touching them?
- **Taking risks about uncertain outcomes**: Which is the best way to keep our picnic fresh?
- **Making connections**: In which part of the school grounds is there most pollution?

Objectives related to Science Sc1 such as *developing an understanding of how to control factors to ensure a fair test*, as in the dunking biscuit example, can be effective starting points. The emphasis placed on preparation will be concerned with thinking of ways to encourage observation, identify patterns, look for discrepancies, raise questions and use resources appropriately. Encouraging speculation and debate takes a great deal of planning. It does not happen or become productive by chance. The creative teacher will use observations and comments to help children develop a line of inquiry and pursue an outcome. Sometimes this will result from

- a conversation outside a science session;
- a question raised;
- an observation made as a result of doing science;
- an idea children want to pursue.

It is rare, however, for children to independently come up with questions to investigate without the facilitation of the teacher. Turning pupils' observations into questions and using pupils' questions to open up lines of inquiry is a skill which teachers use to encourage ownership and open up possibilities. In supporting children to follow ideas, teachers lead children through a series of steps. In Sc1 this is focused on developing the process skills concerned with inquiry, looking at cause and effect, making predictions, forming simple explanations and giving reasons for theories and carrying out a fair test in a controlled setting (Goldsworthy and Feasey 1994). This is best achieved through a systematic line of inquiry to develop scientific rigour and meaning. The following example offers a model for stages to follow in carrying out an investigation. Children may come up with their own formats such as a runner bean plant, each leaf representing the next stage of a plant investigation, or a train, each carriage depicting the next step in an investigation of forces. The creative teacher will alter and adapt ways of presenting data to make the experience relevant, accessible, attractive and fun.

Most aspects of Sc1 need to be taught. Children need to be taught how to plan an investigation. Children need a model, a clear structure to follow. A focus from a learning point of view is important if Sc1 is to be addressed effectively. Offer a model, a way of working, then have the confidence to step back and allow children to take control. The Planning House is just one example of a model which can be offered to very young children or those with little prior knowledge or training in Sc1.

The house is made of durable material such as plastic-covered card. Each layer is independently movable. Begin at the base with, 'What do we need to find out?' The teacher can be the scribe for those children with inadequate writing skills. Children with writing skills can write their answers on a piece of paper and Blu-tack their suggestions in the box. Answers can be compared at this stage, before taking the next step in the process: 'How will we do it?'

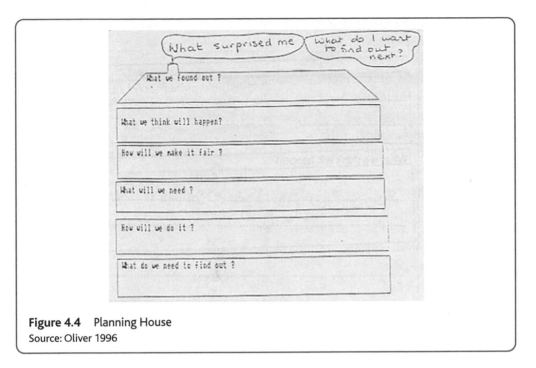

Figure 4.4 Planning House
Source: Oliver 1996

The house is built layer on layer until the roof is added at the end of the investigation, culminating in 'What we found out.' A record of the stages of the investigation is now available for the children to interpret; they have a clear model to follow. Children's answers can be photocopied as a permanent record. Answers are then removed and the house is ready for use again. Once the children have become confident using this model they can take responsibility for organising and carrying out their own investigations.

What cannot be investigated can often be modelled

Parents can face questions of mind-numbing complexity from their toddlers. Why is the sky blue? Why is the sun red before it disappears? These are two phenomena that we probably take for granted because they are just part of everyday experience in good weather. Explanations were found over a hundred years ago, but have not found their way into classroom investigations. One reason may be because they involve an understanding that there are such things as molecules. Another is that invisible gases are involved and children are more able to tackle things they can see. John Tyndall (1820–1893) gave us an explanation, but this would not have been possible if he had not himself investigated gases in the Earth's atmosphere (Greenfield, Singh and Tallack 2001). He was one of the first scientists to recognise that climate change was possible if gases in the atmosphere changed.

A simple explanation given is that the sky appears blue on Earth because large molecules in the atmosphere scatter blue light from the Sun more than any other colours. This explanation needs back-up if it is to have meaning. Since sunlight appears white but the sky is blue, it must be that the scattered light excites our blue sensing cones more and our red sensing cones less than the original sunlight. The colour vision receptors in our eyes, the cones, are of three types: blue receptors that respond to light over a broad range of frequencies, green receptors that respond to medium frequencies and red receptors that respond to low frequencies. The distribution of frequencies in scattered light must be biased towards high frequencies. A similar reason explains why, when the Sun is visible near the horizon, the large molecules in the atmosphere turn it red as light has to travel further to the viewer. The blue light and other colours are scattered, leaving only the red light. This is now known as the 'Tyndall effect'. A simple model can be found to demonstrate this effect at http://chemlearn.chem.indiana.edu/demos/Tyndall.htm (Indiana University 2005).

Two simple questions could not be practically investigated, but they could be modelled, using milk and a light source.

Sky in a jar

What you need:

- A clear straight-sided glass beaker
- Water, milk, light source (torch, light bulb)
- A dark room or blackout tent.

What to do:

- Fill the glass about $3/4$ full of water (300–400ml).
- Add 1 teaspoon of milk and stir.

In a dark space:

- Hold the light source above the surface of the water and look at the water from the side. It should appear blue or at least have a bluish tint.
- Hold the light to the side of the glass and look through the water directly at the light. A reddish tint is observed.
- Put the light under the glass and look down on top of the water. The reddish tint will be deeper.

In using this model it is important to explain not only what happened but how this relates to observations of the colours we see in the sky. The small particles of milk suspended in the water scattered the light from the torch, just as dust particles and air molecules scatter light from the sun. When the light shines in the top of the glass, the water looks blue because we see blue light scattered to the side. When we look directly at the light we see red because some of the blue has been scattered. By using models to offer verification, investigations will take a more informed route to inquiry.

Thinking about why the sky is blue, ask the question, 'Is the sky blue on Mars?' This will bring speculation into the investigative process. Obvious answers include, 'I think it's black because every picture I have seen from space is black' or 'It's blue like it is on Earth.' The colour pictures from Mars Pathfinder are a spectacular reminder that the sky is not blue on Mars. The sky is orange, pink, grey and tan, as was discovered in the 1970s by Viking landers. This is because the atmosphere on Mars is very thin and dusty and light scattering is dominated not by molecules of gas (mostly carbon dioxide) but by suspended dust particles reddened by iron oxide-like Martian soil.

Summary of main points

- Inspiring investigation means encouraging wrong answers.
- Risks are worth taking because of the understanding generated.
- Answers lead to more questions, which lead to understanding.
- Inquiry can have a resonant effect the next day.
- What cannot be investigated can often be modelled.
- Investigation is limited by restraints.
- Verification is necessary for accuracy.

Issues for reflection

- To encourage independent inquiry means not being sure of the outcome. How confident do you feel in encouraging such an approach? What advantages are there in being unsure of the outcome?

- The model or models given to children to develop their understanding of systematic inquiry need to be child friendly, relevant to the context and varied. This is not common practice. What do you think the reasons are for this? Have you considered different inquiry-based models as part of your teaching?

- If creative thinking is to be encouraged, time and space are important when carrying out investigations. Do you feel that there is justification in adopting these requirements? How could they fit within the learning structure?

- Do you feel that there is value in learning the process skills of science without too much concern for the context? Is it enough that children are pursuing ways of doing science or is verification of subject knowledge important to you?

- Think about how you view inquiry. What are the necessary conditions to inspire involvement? How do you provide pupils with these conditions? Does fantasy form part of the agenda?

Discussion points

● What methods and resources do creative teachers use to inspire inquiry?

● Surely it is more important to teach subject knowledge rather than engage children in following unknown outcomes?

● Einstein said that imagination is more important than knowledge. A more commonly held view is that imagination and knowledge are important. Where do you stand?

Recommended reading

Ferri, G. (2000) (ed.) *Everything Has a Shadow Except Ants* (2nd edn). Reggio Emilia: Comune di Reggio Emilia

Goldsworthy, A. and Feasey, R. (1994) *Making Sense of Primary Science Investigations.* Hatfield: ASE

Greenfield, S., Singh, S. and Tallack, P. (2001) *The Science Book.* London: Weidenfeld & Nicolson

Hunkin, T. (2004) *Hunkinsexperiments.* Brighton: Pelham Projects

Kaku, M. (1998) *Visions.* Oxford: University Press

Vernon, P.E. (1970) *Creativity.* Bungay: Chaucer Press

References

Driver, R. (1985) *The Pupil as Scientist.* Buckingham: Open University Press

Elstgeest, J. (1985) 'Encounter, interaction and dialogue', in W. Harlen (ed.), *Primary Science: Taking the Plunge.* London: Heinemann

Elstgeest, J. and Harlen, W. (1990) *Environmental Science in the Primary Curriculum.* London: Paul Chapman

Gardner, H. (2004) *Changing Minds: The Art and Science of Changing Our Own and Other People's Minds.* Boston: Harvard Business School Press

Goldsworthy, A. and Feasey, R. (1994) *Making Sense of Primary Science Investigations.* Hatfield: ASE

Greenfield, S., Singh, S. and Tallack, P. (2001) *The Science Book.* London: Weidenfeld & Nicolson

Harlen, W. (2004) *The Teaching of Science in Primary Schools* (4th edn). London: David Fulton

Indiana University (2005) *The Tyndall Effect.* Available: http://chemlearn.chem.indiana.edu/demos/Tyndall.htm [2005, 11/04/2005]

Hunkin, T. (2004) *Hunkinsexperiments.* Brighton: Pelham Projects

National Science Curriculum for Key Stage 2 (1999) London: Department for Education and Employment and Qualifications and Curriculum Authority

Oliver, A. (1996) *Science Planning Framework.* Unpublished

Weisberg, R.W. (1986) *Creativity: Genius and Other Myths.* New York: Freeman

CHAPTER 5

Inspiring involvement

I showed my masterpiece to the grown-ups and asked them if my drawing frightened them. They answered: 'Why should anyone be frightened by a hat?' My drawing did not represent a hat. It was supposed to be a boa constrictor digesting an elephant. So I made another drawing of the inside of the boa constrictor to enable grown-ups to understand. Grown-ups never understand anything by themselves and it is rather tedious for children to have to explain things to them time and again.

(Saint–Exupery 1995)

Understanding the child's perspective is often the key to involving children in grasping scientific ideas and developing concepts. The questions children ask, and the speculations they make, demonstrate their actual level of involvement. They also show more about understanding than a regurgitated answer ever could. Providing a safe, secure and positive environment in which children can debate their views with an open mind is crucial to the success of this. Meaningful participation does not happen in a vacuum or with mechanistic expectations. It sometimes happens by accident, without design, but it always requires acceptance of the child's view, however bizarre it might seem at first. A child may look at the moon and wonder why the 'face' formed by shadows from the craters looks different in the morning than it did the night before. If this idea is not explored through discussion then the child may still continue to wonder. The focus of scientific learning is much more effective if we can involve the child in a dialogue based on their individual ideas.

Example 1

Several years ago I was teaching children about 'Earth and Beyond' as required in the National Curriculum. Towards the end of the block of work children began to ask 'big' questions. 'How did the universe begin?' 'What was there before?' 'Where did it come from?' This is a naturally curious response when trying to make sense of the unknown. By developing dialogue in response to children's comments new ideas were stimulated. Several ideas about the beginning of the universe were aired, including simple reiterations of various theories, interestingly including, 'God made the world in seven days.' After a while one quiet boy put his hand up and said, 'What if space has no beginning and no end?' (Andrew age 11). This short question stopped everyone in their tracks. Not just because of the question but because Andrew rarely spoke. The look on several faces showed that a question had been asked which demanded thinking about. It was a question that nobody could answer and was difficult to comprehend but it was interesting. What it showed was a serious and unique consideration of trying to make sense of the problem. The physical evidence of Andrew being involved in the debate had not been apparent until he asked the question. Once the question had been asked, not only did it show Andrew's involvement in speculating what *might be* but it also involved other children. The debate that followed was at a higher level than I had previously experienced. As one trainee teacher commented, 'Creativity is, to me, inspiration. It can come from anywhere and anything. My main source for this is often from the children themselves and to ignore this is missing out on a massive potential' (Phil 2005).

There is no doubt that valuing what children have to say encourages speculation, and in the right climate children will share their views about science. Listening to other points of view encourages creative thinking but to be creative children need the opportunity to think for themselves. They need to form independent judgements and be proud of their understanding. To feel involved children need to have a voice. Children gossip and talk, question and argue most of the time. The child's opinion can be more easily heard if science is represented as a set of shifting ideas explained through stories. Making decisions about the way to proceed will, for example, be part of talk. This type of dialogue is especially useful when deciding to reject some ideas and follow others. For example, in constructing a cantilever bridge a group of boys decided to adapt their plan after discussing possible ways of adding components. This was not just a case of trial and error. Decisions about how to strengthen struts, balance forces and reject redundant parts were all talked about before action was taken. The level of involvement was quite sophisticated and required not only well-developed collaborative skills but also appropriate science knowledge. There were 'doers' and 'watchers' as in any group. Often very little notice is taken of the 'watchers' and assumptions are easily made about their lack of involvement. However, Andrew's comments about the universe show that 'watchers' can also participate at a deep level. This is something that teachers need to be aware of in order to nurture opportunities to give each child ways of expressing their thinking.

Promoting discussion

By contrast, in following instructions in a model of teaching where the child is a recipient of knowledge, few creative skills are required. If this is followed by narrow assessment strategies to provide a certain outcome, the learning agenda is soon recognised by the child as requiring specific responses. This mode of working concentrates on facts and functions. It is not about involving the learner to imagine, speculate or discuss possibilities or wonder at diversity. For example, the teacher might explain the function of muscles and describe the way they work. The child might be set the task to make a simple model to show how muscles work in a pulling action to demonstrate the cause and effect of contraction. This method of teaching has some practical application. However, it does little to create a climate where awe and wonder are present or surprise triggers thinking. Another point worth considering is how many children actually recognise the significance of the model. It is often made with elastic bands and lolly sticks. Are they able to relate this model to what is happening when movement occurs? If they do make the leap of understanding required, does this help them marvel at the complexity and variety of muscles used by humans or other species?

Teachers could use practical 'hands on' experience in identifying certain muscles. For example, identifying triceps and biceps in the arm would be an obvious choice to help children make connections of understanding. The gluteus muscle in the hind limb or 'bottom' in the case of humans is as easy to identify but not so commonly mentioned. Discussing ideas about movement and muscles involved in going to the toilet, swallowing, vomiting and breathing would involve children in thinking about voluntary and involuntary muscle action. Knowing that there is more muscle tissue than any other tissue found in the human body might surprise them. Recognising that muscles can be increased to three times their size through exercise will help understand a cause and effect process. Understanding that retaining a certain posture, balance or stillness is as a result of the use of particular muscles can help dispel the myth that muscles are only used for movement.

Example 2

James (a newly qualified teacher 2005) performed a dissection demonstration of an uncooked chicken leg to show his class how the muscles are attached to the bone by tendons and how the bones are joined by ligaments. He used an Intel microscope and a data projector to show this on a screen. The muscles were clearly evident. He made one of the muscles contract as the children watched. This demonstration understandably received a mixed response, 'Yuk, that's gross', 'It's amazing', 'I don't want to eat any more chicken', 'It's fascinating how all those bits know what to do' and 'Have we got so many things in our legs?' Involvement was obvious. Throughout the day pupils talked about what they had seen, including dinner time when turkey was on the school menu. There is no doubt that by watching a demonstration pupils had learnt about muscles, but more importantly, their interest was sustained. This example demonstrates the way whole-class teaching can initiate discussion and involve the learner. Involvement is not just about individual enterprise. A measure of involvement is the discussion it creates.

The following examples could all be used to promote discussion. Thinking about muscle action which appears to make the impossible possible, there are boa constrictors, weight lifters, pearl divers and garden worms. All these examples stretch the imagination. There are also simple exercises to do in the classroom, such as pushing against scales with legs at right angles to the wall, carrying a bucket of water with just a finger and thumb, or touching your nose with your tongue.

Creative involvement demands application of knowledge to include imaginative possibilities but this is not achievable without a degree of subject knowledge. An holistic approach in which several ideas and examples are considered to show muscle function will increase understanding of diverse functions. Observation of animal movement will create the opportunity to compare not only movement but adaptation too. In dance and PE, as in all sports, muscle action is controlled to achieve certain outcomes but these outcomes would not be possible without the action of voluntary and involuntary muscle action. The way small muscles have a tremendous influence in keeping absolutely still will raise important questions about muscle function. A creative outcome might be to invent a puppet character or robot or an alien and draw, list and describe muscles needed by each to operate successfully.

Minimal resources

Helping children become involved in learning science is not always about providing 'wow' resources, going on science trips or having experts come into the classroom. In creative teaching this is something of an illusion and not necessary. It is true that children can be stimulated by a wide range of resources, but some of the most creative outcomes involve few materials. Lack of resources or minimal resources can prompt creative thinking because resourcefulness and ingenuity are required to make the best use of them.

In one of my recent science workshops, trainee teachers explored the notion of creativity and the use of materials. After an initial brainstorm of criteria for creativity and references to well-used quotes, including those presented on the QCA website: www.ncaction.org.uk (QCA 2005), a group of four trainees set the remainder a challenge. The trainees were divided into three groups. Each group had a different selection of resources with the same instruction, 'to make something for a Year 1 class for Christmas'. After about an hour each group presented their finished work to be assessed. Two groups produced Advent calendars and the other group made a Christmas tree adorned with snowflakes, decorations and cards. This was not a 'fair test' as resources were not shared equally.

Group 1
Resources included a piece of A3 white paper and pencil.

> With only a sheet of paper we had to think about joining, without glue, 3D shapes; origami came to mind. It took a long time to get an idea and we talked about possibilities. Then we set to work as a team, tearing snowflakes, building a tree, adding small hanging decorations and cards to go round the tree. We were pleased with the result and felt we had been creative because we made something interesting with just a sheet of paper. The expression 'less is more' popped into my head several times, as I had only recently taught a Year 6 science lesson, in which I planned for simple resources. The

children used creative ideas to construct different shapes from single sheets of A4 paper to see how each one was affected by air resistance. I think if I had provided too many resources, the lesson would not have been so effective.

(Sandra)

Group 2

Resources included a sheet of A3 white paper, a range of coloured felt pens and two illustrated Christmas story books.

With a sheet of paper, coloured pens and two picture books, starting points were different. Two people looked at the books for inspiration whilst two others rejected this idea as they felt the images would hinder rather than stimulate creative thinking. Once again discussion to focus on a particular idea took time but once an Advent calendar had been agreed, particular tearing, folding and drawing jobs were shared. It was decided to make four star-shaped windows, one for each week of Advent. Rather than just produce a stereotypical calendar, a 'science of Christmas theme' was adopted. Each window depicted an aspect of the Christmas story, baby in a manger, stars and moon over the crib, sheep on straw and the three kings carrying gold, frankincense and myrrh. These were used to initiate discussion. Areas of science included: thermal insulation, properties of materials, suitability of purpose, classification of materials and needs of a newborn baby. Although members of the group were proud of their achievement, they felt less confident.

I feel creativity can be squashed when you know you have to present something back to the group. I end up scrapping my own ideas and produce something I know will be accepted by others.

(Jodie)

Initially I did look to the books for inspiration. I think I was scared of doing the wrong thing, especially knowing we had to present to the group. I therefore wanted to look at the books to get ideas. However, with hindsight I would have probably copied one of the pictures and can see how such resources can hinder and stifle creativity.

(Louisa)

Group 3

Resources included a wide variety of coloured paper, pens, glue, sticky shapes and scissors.

With a wide range of coloured paper the group thought 'ah, green, a Christmas tree' and made a pretty, well-presented resource for children to use. Precision of cutting and careful presentation were evident and each day of December had a separate window, with a drawing behind and crackers below. With the tools available the speed of production was faster than the other groups and less discussion preceded the activity.

> The thing that struck me was that group 3 clearly produced the most aesthetically pleasing piece, yet it became apparent that they were the least satisfied with their achievements. This suggests that the self-imposed success criteria by which the groups judged their pieces was the creative thinking process, not the creative outcome of the exercise.
>
> (Emma)
>
> I felt that we had to produce something quite impressive because we had the most resources. I thought that the other groups had been a lot more creative and this was to do with the limited amount of resources they had. Our group didn't really think very much about what we were going to make, there was not much discussion.
>
> (Sally)

As groups 1 and 2 realised, creative thinking requires persistence and the desire to produce a unique product.

> I felt we had been creative because the finished article was completely different from the other groups' work. We really had to think 'outside the box' on how to construct a 3D object from flimsy paper that could stand unassisted. It was amazing to take part in a simple task that generated so much positive energy amongst the group. Real creativity is when magic happens, where people are involved and find tasks involving.
>
> (Paul)

Time to consider ideas and discuss alternatives before embarking on the project were cited as important to the creative process. Perseverance and motivation over a substantial period of time with the opportunity to revisit ideas were also considered necessary.

Conditions

Psychologist Carl Rogers (1969; Rogers 1995) argues that human beings require two conditions if they are to function creatively. These are psychological safety and psychological freedom (Popper 1968). Psychological safety and psychological freedom are difficult to achieve in isolation and do not fit easily with the ethos of a busy classroom or teacher-directed learning. But if a child is to be involved creatively in the process of doing science, as well as learning about science, a degree of autonomy is needed. Security to try out creative thinking in a primary classroom is more easily achieved through group work where generating ideas and not rushing towards judgements are accepted as good practice. Through collaboration, co-operation, and sharing fresh and different ways of looking, children will become familiar with considering new ideas. Such principles help children think about alternatives and expand their own ideas within an environment conducive to debate. With freedom to explore thinking, pupils' autonomy and security will be increased. Creative science teaching which is good inspires and enthuses children to compare findings, raise questions, interrogate data and raise more questions to answer (Oliver 2001). There are many examples of teachers and educationalists who firmly believe that involving the learner in a collaborative process is crucial to success. As the National Commission on Education Report, *Learning to Succeed* shows, 'Concentrating on a fixed-pace, whole class teaching can leave the learning requirements of many pupils unsatisfied' (NCE 1995). Relying on self-paced work can result in low productivity. Learning in groups can be more effective than either of these if members of the group have the right mix of ideas and approaches (NCE 1995).

Group work

In a collaborative venture children require both social and creative skills. The range of abilities in any primary class is wide and this is equally true in science. Being able to differentiate for the needs of individual children is a fundamental teaching skill. This is especially true in teaching practical science. To encourage pupil involvement in doing science a teacher needs to consider:

- the scientific ability of each child and not rely on their literacy or maths achievement to determine their ability to do science;
- the place of Sc1 at all levels of participation;
- the needs of the individual and groups in developing process skills and solving problems;
- developing a collaborative approach to doing science.

The four considerations provide a structure for teachers on which to organise and manage their teaching groups. It is not much use having an inspiring idea if this cannot be used to match the needs of a class or is delivered in a way inappropriate to those needs. The questions, 'How will children respond to this?' and most importantly 'What will they learn as a result?' must be asked when planning lessons. 'How can involvement be instigated and sustained?' is an equally important consideration but is often not given the status it deserves. The organisation of groups needs careful consideration and will vary according to the task. All teachers know that just because children are taught something it does not mean they have learnt it and that they might be even more confused after having been taught a particular concept (Lightman and Sadler 1993; Sadler 1994). Pupils can be present in a lesson, passively follow the prescribed route to learning and be perfectly behaved. They can contribute relatively little to the process intellectually. The expectation that they are required to contribute needs to be made explicit.

Intervention

Thinking about science can happen by chance but this is random and not likely to inform the learner without adult intervention. Importantly, such opportunities need to be planned but also responded to as a result of children's responses, requests and problems. Intervention to support creativity is a delicate balance between encouraging speculation, promoting divergent thinking and keeping a focus on the chosen activity. Creative teaching operates on many levels to include a sense of purpose, community and challenge, as the following example shows.

Example 3

Paul was working with a Year 6 class. They had just completed the statutory science tests. Prior to testing, science lessons had followed the policy of revision exercises. Paul was very aware of the need to differentiate tasks to accommodate the abilities of individual children. He wanted the children to make decisions so that his role became one of facilitation. Intervention strategies would prompt involvement in the task and focus learning. His concern was that pupils should take a more active part in their learning. He was not interested in working to prescribed outcomes which did not encourage creativity or demand higher-order thinking. Although the class had performed well in statutory tests, he felt that there had been little scope to encourage involvement or decision making. He felt that the more able children were going through the motions of reiteration and that they had not been challenged creatively. With the support of a local project called 'Creative Partnerships' (2004), he embarked on a small piece of action research to address this concern (Haydn, Oliver and Barton 2004). The following lesson was planned as part of the research.

'Cheesy Co.'

The four most able pupils were set the challenge of producing a documentary using a video recorder, with sound and editing facilities. The documentary had a scientific theme. Paul invented a company called 'Cheesy Co.' 'Cheesy Co.' set the task of asking four eminent scientists (the four most able pupils) to decide the best way to keep a cheese sandwich fresh. The remainder of the class were divided into small groups. The scientists worked for 'Cheesy Co.' but were in competition with each other to come up with the best solution. The scientists decided to carry out fair tests, observe the effects of micro-organisms and find out ways of preventing the action of decay. Some groups did research on decay in different temperatures, some looked at trying to slow down the action of decay and others used the same cheese sandwich but placed it in various locations. Once they had completed their tests and observed changes over a period of a week, each group was interviewed by the 'Cheesy Co.' management team. Interestingly, what came out of this was the lack of structure of questions used by the interviewers. They were able to manage and organise their teams to follow procedures of testing, adapting tests and presenting findings through interrogation of data. When it came to recording this information and outcomes for the filmed documentary, questions were haphazard and random. This finished documentary did not reflect the buzz of excitement or collaboration evident in the classroom.

Although involvement was sustained, scientific rigour was lacking in presenting findings. This is not surprising as research clearly shows that 'interpretation of data' is the aspect of fair testing which is given minimal time in science teaching. Paul's expectations of the more able children had been challenged, not in setting up the tests but in the analysis of data. The information he gleaned from this exercise gave him the impetus and knowledge to focus his teaching on helping children explain ideas and findings. He recognised that children can be helped to progress beyond their first ideas to consider alternatives before making a decision.

Initial ideas

Many children fall short of their creative potential because they stick to their initial thoughts or explanations that come into their head. The level of involvement in such cases is weak and demands very little attention or speculation. To think creatively means investigating further and looking again at what they normally take for granted. Techniques to promote involvement in science also promote creative thinking. Fisher (1990) identifies techniques to support creative thinking to include: divergent thinking, deferring judgement, extending effort, allowing time and encouraging play. As Fisher states, 'Certain techniques can be applied to improve the range and quality of ideas gathered' (p. 41). In teaching science the teacher can use such techniques to encourage psychological safety and psychological freedom.

- Divergent thinking – the kind of thinking which generates many different answers, not being concerned with right and wrong, works well with the principle that science is a 'journey' and not a 'destination'. Examples include: making a shadow picture using various light sources, composing a piece of music to demonstrate how sounds can be made by blowing air, creating a list of possible outcomes of global warming/freezing, the best way to keep a cheese sandwich fresh.

- Deferring judgement – think now, judge later, removes anxiety and prevents imagination being hampered by judgement and is especially useful when brainstorming ideas. Examples include: What would happen if worms grew bigger? Can we make different kaleidoscopes? Sorting photographs of people by perceived age and race.

- Extending effort – attitudes displaying interest; questioning and stimulus of adults, not just accepting a first answer or moving on too quickly; encouraging lots of ideas from which to select. Examples include: selecting a healthy diet, why do only some tomatoes float? Compare ways of making colours using natural dye.

- Allowing time – set aside time for the incubation of ideas, the do-nothing stage is vital, several projects at once, learn techniques, problem solve, use skills later or find out a new skill. Examples include: Collect leaves each week and compare them at the end of the term, design a habitat for a red-eyed alien, make 3D sunglasses, find the most polluted place in the school grounds.

- Encouraging play – involvement in play and the creative impulse go hand in hand. Examples: Watch marbles travel through different liquids. How big can you make a bubble? Make a demolition ball to knock down a wall. How many ways could you use a coat hanger? Pick up things without touching them.

Learning science using these techniques fits well in a climate where the 'journey' is considered more useful than a 'finished product', and also fits well with creative methods of teaching. If such techniques are used to build on children's ideas and questions then involvement will be stronger because the individual desire to know or 'find out' will be followed through.

Encouraging responses

Responding to pupils' comments and questions constructively (Bruner 1983) is not only good teaching but a sure way to sustain involvement. There are endless examples of children's creative questions which can easily be followed practically, such as, 'Will the splash be bigger if we drop the ball from a greater height?', 'Will a string telephone work round corners?', 'Can static electricity move hot water?' In asking questions of this nature the child is puzzled, unsure or curious and wants to find out. To deny this desire to know would be counter-productive in helping children be involved in appreciating the value of exploration. Obviously some questions that children ask are not so easily followed and have a more esoteric nature, such as 'If icebergs melt will penguins die?' In such cases an encouraging response requires discussion or explanation. Genuine interest can only be fostered if comments and questions are taken seriously.

An encouraging response to a child's practical question might be, 'Do you want to try to find out?' or 'Have a go and see what happens.' For example, in predicting which fruit will float, discussions move on to reasoning why some things float and others don't. It is a fun thing to do. To try to make sense of what is happening requires an explanation. Many children think small things float and are surprised when grapes sink. Statements such as, 'If we squash them they will float 'cause they spread out,' 'If we cut weeny bits off then the little weeny bits will float' and 'They will float if they are small grapes' can easily be followed up in the lesson to try out ideas. It could be argued that this does not help understanding of why some things float but what it does do is recognise the value of linking learning to questions raised, thus involving the learner in trying to answer questions which are not imposed but are asked in response to observations made. In this context, one creative way to dispel the misconception that 'small' things float is to compare what happens when a grape and a coconut are placed in a tank of water. Children will see that the large coconut floats and the small grape sinks. This will not help them understand why things float but it will challenge the idea that small things float.

Example 4

Dawn and Sandra (trainee teachers 2005/6) used involvement techniques to encourage psychological safety and psychological freedom. They also structured the lesson to ensure that pupils were practically engaged and that expectations of achievement were not paramount to success. Encouraging responses as to why things happened was built into their plan. The session began with a story and a challenge.

'Secret agent 003.5 happens to be a small toy bear. His mission is to land and deliver a highly important message. To do this he needs to make a parachute to drop him slowly to earth at a secret destination.' Teachers will recognise this type of introduction to a lesson. What the teacher is doing is setting a challenge within a story to encourage involvement and give purpose to the task. This is a common ploy for developing and explaining subject knowledge in context. However involved in making parachutes pupils become, the underlying learning purpose is to consider air resistance as a force which acts on materials and the effect it has on different shapes.

The lesson began with a simple demonstration; two sheets of A4 paper were dropped simultaneously. One was carefully balanced horizontally to the floor and the other was screwed into a ball. This is nothing new and many teachers use this demonstration. What was unique was that the entire lesson was spent observing what happened to sheets of A4 paper. At first the groups of children copied the demonstration, made paper aeroplanes, folded the paper in half and tried simple concertina folding. As the session progressed they became more creative. One group decided to puncture holes in their paper; this idea was copied and other groups added more and more holes to a single sheet. For a while the challenge shifted to see 'how many holes could be accommodated without altering the rate of fall'. Another group decided to make a ring of paper and adapted this to a saucer-shaped ring with a hole in it. To their amazement they could slow down the fall depending on the lip of the saucer. A third group observed a flip motion of a concertina shape and a spiralling motion of a cone twisted shape. They began to discuss why these things happened and talked about air pushing 'up' and altering the balance so 'it flipped' over. After 30 minutes the teachers suggested that it was time to move on and build the parachutes for 'Secret Agent 003.5'. This was met by cries of 'Can we do just one more?', 'We haven't finished yet', 'We want to see if we can make it flip', 'We haven't tried one with thirty holes yet.'

The trainee teachers were amazed at the effort and concentration evident and how simple instructions and simple resources encouraged creative thinking and involvement. What had happened was that as each example was demonstrated, encouraging and constructive criticism had been given. This prompted adaptations. New ideas developed were copied and refined. The feedback concentrated on the science involved, for example 'air pushing up over a larger area, balance of push and how different shapes move through the air'. The level of science knowledge shared was appropriate to encourage thinking.

Blind alleys, consideration of alternatives and speculation cannot be based on an inflexible outcome. The excitement of science as in the paper-dropping exercise must be concerned with thinking about connections, discovering something new and asking questions which may be puzzling, and ultimately using that knowledge with purpose. Trying things out to see what happens and considering the evidence through debate and dispute reflects the fact that science is often not simple, stable or easily understood.

Hindering involvement

There are several reasons why in the primary classroom a trend to conform, contextualise and present science in a factual way is usual practice. It is rare to see lessons based solely on pupils raising questions or observing something in detail or being encouraged to raise their own challenge. Staying with the topic of forces, how much more magical is it to 'move objects without touching them' than to identify what force is involved in the movement or draw diagrams of force represented by arrows for direction and size? Moving objects without touching them requires creative thinking of how to use resources provided. If a teacher shows imagination in choosing resources and encourages a policy of ownership in which pupils have some autonomy in selecting additional resources, pupils will quickly realise that individual endeavour is valued, which is what happened in the above example. The children were inspired to continue the exploration because they were given time and space to form their own views. The sense of fulfilment in finding out superseded the need to know. There was no need to fear analysis or scrutiny because the focus of teaching was on not only the outcome but the reasons for the outcome, as the example of 'holes in the paper' shows.

Children are a good barometer for indicating how involved they feel. Although they have a limited understanding of complicated concepts and little science knowledge, they do have strong views on how they would like science lessons to be. 'I like it when I can choose and don't have to hurry. I like drawing better than writing' (Parveen age 7). 'My best time was when we went outside and I rode my bike in paint and it made marks, but not so good on the grass and it stuck to the sand. And then we painted sand pictures and the paint stuck to the sand' (Eliza age 6). 'I like making models where you have to measure exactly. We made one of the phases of the moon in a sweet tin and you could look through the holes. The best bit was telling my dad how to do it and he made one. When Granny came to tea we showed her and everyone had a go' (Evan age 11). Perhaps children's views need to be assimilated more readily and used in planning science sessions or even the whole curriculum. As the statement by

Jonathan (aged 17) suggests, 'My ideal school would be holistic; education can often be divisive, splitting subject from application and mind from soul. The education would be best where art, music, maths and English blend and integrate and where one is not expected to forsake being a human being to teach or be taught' (Burke and Grosvenor 2003). Interestingly, science is not mentioned in the list of subjects but the premise is sound. Children do not learn in compartments and the benefit of cross-curricular learning is well documented. This does not mean that subjects are devalued but rather the experience of learning science is put in context.

Linking subjects

Science and art

In the grounds of Waddesdon Manor there is a bronze sculpture by the artist Fairhurst (2002) of a gorilla carrying a fish, entitled 'A couple of differences between thinking and feeling'. In the dining room, hanging over a round table, there is a large, white lamp commissioned by Lord Rothschild. The lamp is constructed from broken pieces of white china, including plates, coffee pot, saucers, suspended on metal wire, including a silver spoon. On entering the room the viewer could be forgiven for thinking that the lamp is delicate, perhaps constructed from feathers. The sculpture of the gorilla, by contrast, is robust, sturdy and in no way delicate. Both works, however, invite comment. For example, with the gorilla, 'Why is a herbivore carrying a large fish?' In each piece a different way of looking is described. Materials are used creatively. There are many parallels to be drawn with science. In physically producing the sculptures, 'suitability of purpose' is understood within 'limitations' of the materials used. Imaginative alternatives create a unique piece of work. Different ways of looking question the norm. Using materials in diverse ways will help children recognise properties and limitations of materials. Science and art link well. The materials used provide opportunities to be creative by looking differently, considering alternatives and accepting new ideas. The example of the lamp constructed with broken china lends itself to discussion not only of the aesthetic qualities but also brittleness, shadows formed, reflections, joining materials, strength and durability.

Example 5

Jenny took her class of children to an art exhibition to see the work of Cornellia Parker. The work of this innovative artist acted as an inspiration for a science session where children looked at ways of deforming commonly used implements. Her work, 'Thirty pieces of Silver (exhaled) cake stand', is constructed with crushed metal. Thirty silver-plated items, crushed by a 250-ton industrial press and suspended by metal wire, are formed into a circle. After seeing this work at Norwich castle, children used Coke cans and plastic drinking cups to explore how crushing and deforming materials is affected by the properties of particular materials. Having fun stamping on Coke cans whilst wearing heavy walking boots and squashing plastic drinking cups in a variety of ways ensured participation. They were playing, having fun and enjoying the experience. The teacher intervened to highlight comparisons. Stiffness and flexibility, stress fractures, compressibility, tension, bending, tearing, elasticity and plastic properties were all observed. Children talked about Coke cans being squashed because the volume, or amount of can, did not change. A 'wow moment' occurred when one child placed a plastic drinking cup on the palm of her upturned hand and covered it with her other hand before squashing it flat between her hands. The 'wow moment' was when she removed the force applied by her top hand. The flattened cup very slowly sprang back into shape, one part at a time, until it resembled a crumpled version of the original cup. The children watched with big eyes and soon tried this out for themselves, delighting at their new-found 'magic'. This simple exercise did not work so well with all the various plastic cups available. The children began to sort them into those with greater or less elasticity without any prompting from the teacher and at this stage not understanding about elastic properties. The opportunity to talk about the difference between elasticity and plasticity, compressibility and squashing presented itself in context. The follow-on lesson involved the children making suspended sculptures using squashed cans and deformed plastic cups. They were then encouraged to think about how they might light their work to make a shadow picture on a large white board, bringing another area of the science curriculum into an art project with purpose. It is this type of link that encourages involvement. It is not forced but requires a creative attitude.

Science and poetry

> Trees Eat Sunshine
> It's a fact
> Their broad leaves lap it up like milk
> And turn it into twigs.
>
> (John Updike 1964)

This simple, imaginative poem paints a picture to support the child's imagination in understanding the process of photosynthesis. All the words used are familiar and explain photosynthesis in a non-scientific manner. This is important. Young children need complicated ideas explained in a way that 'paints pictures' in their mind. It helps them make connections between accepted science theory and day-to-day experience. Images within the child's experience can be translated to explain functions and phenomena which would certainly confuse them if presented scientifically. Poems, drawings, scenarios, stories, descriptions and diagrams can all be used to inspire involvement in thinking about difficult concepts. To be effective they must enable the child to see differently, make connections and select relevant information. Anne Osbourn's (2005) 'SAW' project, www.sawtrust.org, linking science, art and writing, does this very well.

Example 6

Anne began the project with the premise that science, art and writing could be explored creatively and influence the creativity of those involved. Photographs of scientific images were used as a starting point to explore ideas, raise questions and stimulate interest and discussion. The photographs were of high quality and covered a wide range of scientific phenomena, for example magnified images of the e-coli virus, sheet lightning, thermal imaging, a cheek cell, pollen grains and a distant planet. Jill Pirrie and Matthew Sweeney, well-known poets, worked with Anne and the class teacher, using the photographs as a resource and stimulus to generate ideas. After a while themes began to emerge. The poets helped children identify appropriate poetic phrases and language to support ideas. After several drafting exercises some truly remarkable poems were created, not just by a few children but by the whole class. These poems have been published, in *SeeSaw* (2005).

STRUGGLE FOR LIFE

Here I see cliffs of sea green,
Craters of brown and blue,
The cells are swimming,
Drowning,
Then many are found
I feel waves,
Lapping against rocks,
Arches of candle wax,
Running through the labyrinth
Of dark holes and unknown curves,

I smell salty sea,
And the honeycomb pieces,
I hear voices of motivation,
And the struggle for life.

(Phoebe Wall Palmer Year 7)

A CHRISTMAS ROSE LEAF

The inside of a leaf looks like the sea
With plants growing and a cave collapsing.
The whale calls for a friend to swim with him.
The waves crash and splash against each other.

(Jacob Beckley Year 4)

Phoebe and Jacob have both written poems as a result of looking at a coloured electron micrograph of a section through the leaf of a Christmas rose. The upper surface is at the top. The long cells just beneath this are the site of photosynthesis. The blue spots are vascular bundles, stomata are seen towards the bottom.

Although the above examples of science link specifically to individual areas of the curriculum, single subject links are not the only way. Having a class allotment, for example, would involve children in studying seed packets, reading gardening books, following instructive texts, planning areas of planting, designing the plot, measuring the ratio of seeds required, considering the use of pesticides and fertilisers, preparing the plot, thinking about crop rotation, compost heaps and conditions for healthy growth, insulation, watering and weeding, following the life cycle of plants and finally harvesting, storing and cooking the produce. This type of venture would not only involve the children learning through practical application but also offer a context for a healthy eating debate. The Royal Institution Christmas Lectures for children 2005 took the theme of food. There is a national concern for the eating habits of our children, famously highlighted by the chef Jamie Oliver in his television programme, 'Jamie's School Dinners' (BBC 2005). Involvement in science is truly useful if it affects decisions made about lifestyle. All children will need to make decisions about what they eat and this is one way to raise awareness and help them realise that not all potatoes come in the shape of a dinosaur.

Games

All aspects of science can be taught through games. To play a game children have to be involved. The scope is endless and can be invented, adapted or presented by either the teacher or the children themselves. For example, considering difficulties in adaptation, avoiding being eaten, how to breed, how to get food would lend itself to the model presented by a game of 'snakes and ladders', with the dangers being represented by snakes and the benefits by ladders. Children could make cards to be used in the game. A game of snap could be used to identify matching properties such as diamond/hard, talc/soft, glass/brittle, bamboo/tough. There are many game-type resources on the market, such as a T-shirt displaying felt replications of internal organs put on with velcro in place or magnetic games which allow the child to draw safely with iron filings. These all have a place in stimulating interest and making learning fun but they lack the opportunity for children or teachers to be creative. In inventing a game which successfully adds to science knowledge and understanding there is the opportunity to be creative. Not only is good science subject knowledge required but also use of the imagination in providing a unique experience. For example, a Year 2 teacher wanted to improve the children's knowledge of musical pitch. She devised a game of musical chairs. When the children moved they had to be mice making a squeaky high-pitched sound or elephants moving in a lumbering way making a low noise, depending on the music played (two tape recorders were required). Afterwards she drew some sound pictures to represent high and low pitch and this time the children moved to the pictures and not the music.

Recognising that involving the learner requires understanding of how children receive information and how they respond to it will certainly inform creative teaching. Considering what hinders involvement needs to be high on the agenda when considering teaching and learning. Feedback from teachers and other pupils and adults can have a positive or negative effect on pupil involvement. It is doubtful that each pupil wants to be a Sherlock Holmes or a Miss Marple but when participation is evident then a teacher knows that attention is focused on doing science. If science is timetabled for the last thing on Friday afternoon and pupils are reluctant to stop working because they just want one more look under the microscope or they need a few more minutes to check the force required to break a plastic bag, then participation is evident. Unless engagement in the subject is achieved then learning will be limited. Involvement and learning go hand in hand; without involvement there will be no learning. All teachers know that there are different levels of engagement and to be fully absorbed in an activity requires sustained motivation. To be involved requires interest, curiosity, inquisitiveness, questioning, concentration, concern, meditation and application.

Summary of main points

What hinders involvement

- Lack of communication
- Lack of motivation
- Intervention of a negative nature
- Perceived lack of purpose
- Interruption
- Lack of self-reliance
- Overambitious expectations
- Lack of equal opportunity

What stimulates involvement

- Sense of purpose
- Sharing ideas
- Having a voice
- Intervention of a positive nature
- Feedback to prompt thinking

- Not being concerned with the correct answer
- Wanting to know or find out
- Enjoyment
- Application

Issues for reflection

- Do you think involvement in doing science can be achieved using minimal resources? Can you think of any successful science lessons in which minimal resources were used creatively?

- How do you encourage children to go beyond their first idea? Do you ask them to share ideas, listen to other ideas and then refine or adapt their own? Do you think children are comfortable with this way of working?

- Is it possible in a primary school to create an environment where children have a sense of psychological freedom and security to learn science? How might you go about this?

- Have you taught science sessions where the children planned the agenda or where you planned the lesson in response to questions children asked? If you have worked in this way, what did you observe about the level of involvement?

- Do you see the value in linking science with other areas of the curriculum? Which subjects do you think fit most creatively with learning science? Have you had the opportunity to link art and science in your teaching?

Discussion points

- How can involvement, participation and engagement in learning science be achieved in a busy primary classroom? What factors hinder involvement?

- It has been suggested that offering children a wide range of ideas, resources and stimuli will encourage thinking about science creatively. Do you see this suggestion as such an opportunity or just as a dead-end exercise?

Recommended reading

Enion, D. (2002) *Creative Child.* London: Hamlyn

Fisher, R. and Williams, M. (2004) *Unlocking Creativity.* London: David Fulton

Johnston, J. and Gray, A. (1999) *Enriching Early Scientific Learning.* Buckingham: Open University Press

Osbourn, A. (2005) *Seesaw.* Norwich: SAW Press

References

Bruner, J.S. (1983) *Child's Talk: Learning to Use Language*. Oxford: Oxford University Press

Burke, C. and Grosvenor, I. (2003) *The School I'd Like*. London: Routledge Falmer

Creative Partnerships (2004) *We Can: The Norfolk Story So Far*. Norwich: Arts Council

Fisher, R. (1990) *Teaching Children to Think*. Oxford: Blackwell

Haydn, T., Oliver, A. and Barton, R. (2004) *Providing Time for the Development of Creative Approaches to Subject Pedagogy: Three Case Studies*. Paper read at BtRA 2004

Lightman, A. and Sadler, P. (1993) 'Teacher predictions versus actual student gains', *Physics Teacher*, 31 (3): 162–7

NCE, N. C. o. E. (1995) *Learning to Succeed: The Way Ahead/A Report from the Paul Hamlyn Foundation*. London: National Commission on Education

Oliver, A. (2001) 'Teaching science', in A. Cockburn (ed.) *Teaching Children 3–11: A Student's Guide*. London: Paul Chapman

Osbourn, A. (2005) *Seesaw*. Norwich: SAW Press

Popper, K. (1968) *The Logic of Scientific Discovery*. London: Routledge

QCA, Q. a. C. A. (2005) *National Curriculum in Action*. Available: http://www.ncaction.org.uk[03/08/2005]

Rogers, C. (1969) *Freedom to Learn: A View of What Education Might Become*. Columbus: C.E. Merrill

Rogers, C. (1995) *Freedom to Learn* (3rd edn). New York: Merrill

Sadler, P. (1994) *Simple Minds*. QED: BBC2

Saint-Exupery, A.D. (1995) *The Little Prince*. Ware: Wordsworth Editions Ltd

Updike, J. (1964) *Telephone Poles and Other Poems*. London: Deutsch

Creativity in the Foundation Stage

Alan Howe

Thank goodness I was never sent to school; it would have rubbed off some of the originality.

(Beatrix Potter)

Introduction

You might know Beatrix Potter as an author and artist. She was also a talented scientist with particular interests in the natural world. She had a rare ability to make connections between her art and her science through her stories and illustrations. She was a very creative individual who did not see the world in terms of separate subjects – perhaps precisely because she didn't study them formally in school. You might also know that before children arrive in school they do not see learning in terms of discrete subjects. They are, however, curious, imaginative and playful learners and do not see things the same way as most adults do.

Science is a core subject that children will study throughout compulsory schooling but the Foundation Stage curriculum for England and Wales is rightly structured around areas of learning. So how can science be relevant to the early years? The place for science in the early years curriculum, it is often said, is in 'Knowledge and Understanding of the World'. The *Curriculum Guidance for the Foundation Stage* does state that 'Knowledge and Understanding of the World forms the foundation for later work in science, design & technology, history, geography, and ICT' (DfEE/QCA 2000: 82). However, in our view there is not a straightforward correlation between 'subjects' and 'areas of learning'. We must not have too narrow a definition of science if we are to recognise it in the activities that happen in Foundation Stage classrooms. If we see science as *active enquiry* – something children do in order to find out about the world – then we can identify many opportunities for science and argue that science-based activities and experiences can contribute greatly to children's learning across the learning goals of the Foundation Stage.

We show throughout this book how science is a subject that develops and requires creativity, although the Curriculum Guidance emphasises that the area of 'Creative Development' relates to 'art, music, dance, role-play and imaginative play' (DfEE/QCA

2000: 116). Each of the 'arts' can be combined with science in ways that lead to creative development. We show below how art materials can be a source of inspiration not only for creative expression but also for creative play that leads to new knowledge and understanding. Furthermore, through the very act of exploring art materials, making sounds with instruments or trying new ways of moving their bodies, children perform 'experiments' with both *artistic* and *scientific* intentions. There is currently a great deal of interest in the adult world of art about rediscovering links between art and science (see the work of the National Endowment for Science Technology and Art (NESTA) and the Wellcome Trust) – young children have not yet lost this knowledge.

Craft (2002) takes issue with those that suggest science is fundamentally uncreative. Some research has found that children who are 'convergent' thinkers do well in science and maths at school because they are required to provide the one right answer (Hudson 1973). School science may perpetuate the view that science is mostly about recalling facts, and older children do tend to experience this misconception at first hand, yet this is to grossly misrepresent the real nature of science.

> If, from our own educational experience, we see science as a factual body of knowledge about the world, concerned with laws and formulae and 'discovered' through complex experiments, we will find it difficult to recognise the scientific significance of four-year-olds pushing each other around on wheeled toys. If, on the other hand, we regard scientific knowledge as shifting and tentative – inherently rooted in the 'here and now' of everyday things and events – early years science will appear as a natural component of young children's learning and development.
>
> (Davies in Davies and Howe 2003: 3)

Fortunately, most practitioners in England tend to take the latter view (Johnston and Hayed 1995) and subscribe to a 'process based' model of science. Scientific processes (exploration, observation, asking questions, trying things out) are certainly very important aspects of early years science. Indeed, we would argue that the younger the child, the greater the emphasis that should be placed on the procedural ('doing') aspect, in comparison with the conceptual ('understanding') components of science.

Scientists communicate their ideas by telling us stories. Their stories are about how the world began, how the mountains and seas, animals and plants came to be. They tell us how they carried out their work and what they found as they delved, dissected and deliberated over the universe. Many of their stories are 'true' – the authors are usually convinced about this – the readers or listeners need to make up their own minds about that. Some scientist tales may turn out to be false, or better stories take their place. Communication, particularly *narrative*, is essential to human experience and therefore to science (Black and Hughes, in Davies and Howe 2003). As children develop their ability to communicate, they too will tell stories about their explorations and their discoveries. They will 'use language to imagine and recreate roles and experiences' and 'use talk to organise, sequence and clarify thinking, ideas, feelings and events' (DfEE/QCA 2000: 58).

Our scientific stories should always be thought of as a rough draft, not a final edition. Every day scientists solve problems, generate new ideas and imagine how things might be. Their creativity leads to new knowledge, new understanding, and new ways of doing things. Making connections between previously unconnected ideas is a central part of creativity. In science we try to make connections between what we already know and new experiences in order to develop better understandings of the physical world. Really good scientific theories unify different bits and pieces of knowledge. For example, Darwin's Theory of Evolution connected a range of ideas and observations about geology, island populations and fossils. This connection making is similar in some ways to how young children think and learn. Although Piaget probably wasn't the first person to notice that children think differently to adults, he was certainly the first to take children's thinking seriously enough to base his career on exploring them (Papert 1999). After hearing of 'childish' ideas – that 'the Sun and moon follow us as we walk' or 'trees waving their branches make the wind', Piaget wanted to find out if all young children had similar beliefs. He found that many did. He went on to explore children's thought processes and concluded that they have their own distinct order and special logic. They were like little scientists, carrying out their own investigations and constructing their own theories of the world. My daughter, when 3 years old, thought the way to tell if stones were alive was if they had a face (i.e. marks that looked like eyes and a mouth). This seemed consistent with her observations that (a) all living things she had encountered had a face (mum, dad, brother, dogs, cats) and that (b) some stones seemed to have faces. It is these 'theories', also called 'alternative frameworks', that many science educators believe should be the starting points for teaching in science.

If we accept that children are creative thinkers actively trying to make sense of the world then we need to take account of the investigations they have already performed and the conclusions they have already reached if we want to help them progress in their learning. Furthermore, it has been noted that adults often underestimate young children's mathematical and scientific abilities and knowledge (British Educational Research Association Early Years Special Interest Group 2003). Fortunately, there is a range of research into children's common ideas in many areas of science and these can be useful to teachers wanting to 'tune in' to children's creative thinking (see Recommended Reading below).

Time, space and resources

Time

Our discussion so far has identified that a curriculum organised around subjects is inappropriate for the Foundation Stage and is also contrary to DfEE/QCA guidance.

We have also begun to explore the connections between 'knowledge and understanding of the world', 'creative development and communication', 'language and literacy'. If areas of learning can be integrated in the ways described, perhaps children's 'connective' thinking and learning will remain intact. Another artificial divide known to inhibit creativity is the timetable (Shallcross 1981).

De Boo (1999: 2–3) identifies the tension between the nature of early learning and the requirement to use time in a structured way:

> As the infant grows there is more to learn and less time in which to learn it, less time for the countless repetitions of infancy . . . In nurseries or early years classrooms, time has to be structured so as to give children the maximum experience of familiar and unfamiliar phenomena in as short a time as possible, whilst still allowing enough repetitive play to convince them and enable them to make reasonable generalisations . . . if we are successful in helping children to be confident explorers, aware of their own scientific skills, how to apply them more consistently and economically (time-wise) . . . we will have equipped them for life-long learning.

It is thought that a key characteristic of creativity is total engagement in an activity – known also as 'being in the flow' (Csikszentmihalyi 2002). This concept is echoed in the findings of the Effective Early Learning Project (EEL) (Pascal and Bertram 1997). Amongst its many findings, the project has identified as very useful a number of signals that indicate a child's level of involvement and therefore the extent to which the child is gaining a deep, motivated, intense and long-term learning experience. Pascal and Bertram have used Laevers' (1994) 'child involvement scale' to identify effective early learning. The scale includes the signal of 'Complexity and Creativity' that is shown when a child 'freely mobilises his cognitive skills and other capabilities in more than routine behaviour'. The child involved cannot show more competence – he/she is at his/her very 'best'. The child exhibits an 'individual touch' and what she/he does furthers his/her own creative development. The child is said to be at the very edge of his/her capabilities. The Laevers (1994) 'child involvement scale' used by Pascal and Bertram discussed above is available on http://www.eddept.wa.edu.au/lc/pdfs/involvementworkshop.pdf

Research into creativity offers powerful support to the notion that there should be opportunities for children to remain uninterrupted during those times when their involvement is at its most intense. Easier said than done, of course, but a day with the minimum number of compulsory breaks and switches of activity would appear conducive to creativity. Restructuring the school day to suit children and learning rather than adults represents a fundamental challenge to educators in the UK. It is too big an issue to resolve here. Many UK settings are looking to the approach taken by the Reggio Emilia schools for inspiration and guidance and further reading on this is given at the end of the chapter.

Space and resources

One aspect of provision less daunting than restructuring timetables for practitioners to consider is the creative use of spaces to support learning in science. An essential part of teaching for creativity in science is the development of a 'creative ecosystem' (Harrington 1990; Davies *et al.* 2004; see Chapter 9) in which physical and human resources are brought together to support and nurture the learner's creative development. The 'ecosystem' should have a number of components, including a choice of resources that can be selected by the child. This approach to resource-provision is usually found in good early years settings but it might be worth auditing the resources available to check if they provide for scientific play and activity. Resources such as magnifying aids, binoculars, torches, mirrors, weather boxes (see Table 6.1), non-fiction books on scientific topics, collecting boxes and measuring equipment can all encourage science-orientated activity.

One way of ensuring children are provided with the right sort of resources is to offer them on the basis of children's schematic development. Davies and Ward (in Davies and Howe 2003) propose possible connections between a child's early schema – an individual's habitual way of acting and understanding – and scientific concepts. For example, a child with a 'transporting' schema who enjoys exploring moving objects or materials from place to place in different ways should be provided with a range of containers, vessels, toy vehicles etc. plus a range of materials – bricks, sand, water, soil, gravel – with the aim of supporting and extending the child's exploratory play.

This approach to individualised provision, while ideal, presents the practitioner with a challenge – to identify each child's schema and to offer appropriate resources. This clearly demands a systematic programme of child observation by the teacher or learning assistant with time for reflection on the child's needs. For a teacher to work in this way she needs to be accepting of what the child wants to do with resources even if it isn't what they were intended for. As a child wraps masking tape round and round the legs of a chair it is tempting to think of it as a waste, more difficult to think 'I never thought of doing that.' The teacher will need to make a judgement about what is acceptable – she will be able to accept that sand mixed into the play dough is 'creative play' only so many times.

One additional suggestion for a resource for creativity is what one teacher calls her 'magicians' box' – which contains anything that can be imagined – like enough cold ice lollies for the whole class or a puppy trying to get out. This kind of prop for the imagination can be used for the development of creativity and scientific language (What does it feel like? What does it sound like?) and thinking ('How shall we find out?' 'What would happen if . . .?'). The practitioner will need to model imaginative language first and the children will quickly catch on to the game.

The *Curriculum Guidance for the Foundation Stage* (DfEE/QCA 2000) is clear that practitioners should make full use of spaces for learning indoors and out. Table 6.1 offers some suggestions on the uses of spaces for science, apart from the classroom itself, and indicates the kinds of resources that could be provided to guide play and discovery in scientific directions.

Play

It is likely in early years settings that the elements of provision described above will be often combined through a play-based pedagogy. Play is of course a fundamental part of early years provision.

Table 6.1   Spaces and resources for creative science

Spaces	Resources
The outside area/patio	Play with large toys can encourage thinking about forces (pushes, pulls, twists). The weather can be a resource too – rain, sun, wind or ice can all be explored scientifically. Weather boxes filled with sunglasses, gloves, windmills, kites and the like will encourage exploration. Large-scale water play with drainpipes, guttering, watering cans, funnels and hosepipes can lead to co-operative and creative problem solving. Large-scale sand play can lead to similar outcomes.
Dark corners and cupboards	A dark, dark cave with torches, luminous (glow in the dark) toys, mirrors, coloured filters and lights will promote explorations into light, colour and reflections.
Kitchen or cooking area	A cooking lesson (making a cake, making toast) can provide a good context for discussions about materials and their properties, changes of state, temperatures, the senses.
School hall	Large-scale apparatus for climbing, balancing, jumping, swinging; balls, cylinders and hoops for rolling, stopping and catching – all these can provide experiences that will help with the understanding of (a) forces and (b) our bodies.
School grounds or gardens	Gardening equipment, magnifying aids, 'bug' collection equipment, a log pile, bird table or pond will enhance greatly the range of creatures to be found.
Local shops and businesses	An organised trip to the local shops offers stimulation and provocation for learning in a number of areas of science; food shops or restaurants can provide a focus on food and the changes that food goes through when it is prepared or cooked. The garden centre offers potential for learning about seasonal changes, growth and life cycles, and hardware/DIY stores can encourage children to think about materials and their properties.

What we know about play is:

1 Young children learn through play (Sylva *et al.* 2003).

2 Scientific learning will occur during some types of play (Howe and Davies, in Moyles 2005).

3 Play can be creative (Craft 2002).

Hutt's (1979) taxonomy of play differentiates between three play types: *Epistemic* (with materials and objects), *Ludic* (socio-dramatic, language and roles) and *Games-play* (rule making and following). Within each category there is wide scope for creativity and science, although play is not *necessarily* creative.

The British Educational Research Association Early Years Special Interest Group (2003) report on critical evidence regarding adult interaction and the quality of play provided by Hutt *et al.* (1989). Their study noted that in the pre-school settings observed, children often engaged in stereotypical, repetitive behaviours (which is difficult to relate to creativity), particularly in sand and water play, and there was little evidence of cognitive challenge. Adult interventions were predominantly monitorial and did not involve sustained conversations. The activities where an adult was present (commonly collage and junk modelling) produced more sustained engagement and lively discussions. A consistent theme running through these studies is that educators need to be active and *create* the conditions for learning through play. This contrasts with the notions of 'discovery play' that prevailed in play-based pedagogy of the 1960s and 70s. Gura's (1992) study concluded that a number of learning-relevant conditions were necessary to support high quality play. These factors are closely linked to ideas about creativity already discussed and include:

- enabling children to take risks, be creative and playful in their ideas;
- organising the physical setting to maximise learning opportunities;
- adult involvement;
- allowing children to share the initiative about what is to be learnt;
- developing effective systems for observation and record keeping, and using these to inform curriculum planning.

These factors are illustrated within the discussion on play types below.

Play with materials and objects

Craft (2000, 2002) has proposed the concept of 'possibility thinking' to be at the core of creativity and a foundation for knowledge. She sees possibility thinking as posing questions and 'a continuum of thinking strategies' from 'What does this do?' to 'What can I do with this?' (Craft 2002: 113). These questions are *generative* and therefore at the heart of creativity, in the sense that they lead to new actions and the creation of new knowledge for the learner. Generative questions are the kind that children will 'ask' as they play with materials. I recall my children playing with 'ice balloons' for the first time in their paddling pool on a warm summer day. Although they didn't speak out their questions and predictions, it was apparent they were asking through their actions: 'What does this do – does it float? Can you sit on it? Can it break? Can it spin round and round? Can I hold such a cold and slippery object? Can I break the ice? I think it will break if I hit it. Can I suck the ice? I think I know what will happen when I put it down my brother's back.' Their play moved from one type of question to the other and as they went their knowledge of the properties of ice, water, and concepts of mass, temperature, melting and friction developed.

We know that young children do need opportunities to repeat actions and experiences in order to consolidate their understanding and we should not be in too much of a hurry to 'move them on'. On the other hand, it is possible that after a while experiences can become stale and lead to repetitious behaviour. Take water play, for example. After a term of pouring, sieving and splashing in the water tray, any benefits of repeating actions and explorations may be minimal (Hutt *et al.* 1989). Children can be prompted into making new connections by presenting them with materials in new ways. Tonie Scott and Sandie Shepherd, from the Bishop Henderson School Early Years Department, encourage this connection making by changing the contents of the water tray to promote new thinking. Their 'sparkly water tray' contains a range of objects small and large, some of which float, some sink, some reflect and some refract the light, creating changing colours. What any child will make of the experience is difficult to predict but it is guaranteed to encourage new interest and prompt new experimentation: 'What do these things do when they get wet?' 'This wet mirror is a bit like the one in our bathroom that gets "steamy".' 'Is this the same tinsel that was on the Christmas tree?' 'Can I stick the wet sequins to my arm?' 'Why do some sequins float and some sink?'

Perhaps the best materials for encouraging possibility thinking are those gathered from nature. For as Howe (2004: 1) points out, 'natural materials do not come with an instruction manual. Their uses and applications are only as limited as our imaginations.' As children play with 'natural materials' – leaves, pebbles, soil and clay, fruits, shells etc. – possibilities emerge:

> How can I classify these leaves (e.g. the ones I like, the ones I want to use)?
>
> How can I these order these stone (e.g from big to little)?
>
> What can I make with this mud (e.g. a castle)?
>
> How shall I test this fruit (e.g. by digging my finger into it)?

Natural materials are of infinite variety and therefore more capable of provoking original responses compared to manufactured, uniform resources. What can be done with a pile of autumn leaves? They may provide a 'habitat' for the toy dinosaurs, they can be scrunched to make a satisfying noise, torn to create confetti, sorted into pretty ones and not so pretty ones . . . my limited imagination is not providing any more ideas but I am quite sure a group of children in a reception class would find many more ways of playing with them.

When children are apparently doing 'art' activities, or playing with art materials, they may also be carrying out a scientific enquiry. Consider a child mixing wet paints together on a sheet of paper, swirling them with a brush and watching them merge, change colour and drip down the easel. Another child has a lump of clay and adds more and more water to make it 'muddy' – slipping and sliding between her fingers – and then proceeds to make a hand print with the 'mud' rather than make a model like the rest of the table are doing. The first thing to be said is that the children are learning science through play – for example, about the properties of materials. We may think that such activities are creative play, but just because art materials are involved it doesn't necessarily mean that any activity counts as 'creative'. Notice in both the above scenarios there is no mention of the child necessarily working towards an end point – a painting or model. An important feature of creative play is that it is centred on what the child wants to do at that moment, not on what an adult might want as a product. To check further our 'hunch' that this example of play is creative we can test how it relates to the National Advisory Council for Creative and Cultural Education (1999) definition for creativity – *Imaginative* activity fashioned so as to produce *outcomes* that are both *original* and of *value*. If you are happy to think you know creativity when you see it, you may want to skip the next paragraph.

There is much academic debate about the meaning of each of the italicised words above, and therefore of 'creativity' itself. The outcome of mixing paint (the new colour) could be original (to the child) and of value (to the child or her teacher). The meaning of 'outcome' *could* be interpreted as the *knowledge* that has been generated about paint and colour. Perhaps what is most difficult to establish with certainty is the level of imagination the child has shown in mixing the paints. Craft (2000), among others, proposes that imagination is in evidence when one is aware of a convention (e.g. that paint is mixed in a palette) and chooses to move beyond it (e.g. by mixing paint 'in the eye' as Suerat did with his paintings using dots or points of colour). Does the child know artists usually mix paints before they apply them – perhaps not? The child with the clay may know one usually makes 3-D models with clay in school – by doing something *post-conventional*, is this a child who is more imaginative? By the time the intentions of the artists have been analysed in our scenario, they have probably taken off their art aprons and moved to the role-play area! Perhaps we should accept at this stage that *some* elements of creative play have been exhibited here and move on to see what they do next.

Role-play

Being imaginative, playing make believe, pretending, imaging (seeing reality in the mind's eye) – all these are features of children's *ludic* play. A key feature of such play and one reason why it is so valuable to the development of children is that it is a low-risk way of 'rehearsing' for the real world. In setting up a role-play area practitioners hope to provide children with opportunities to develop their imagination and be creative – although in reality that is not always the case. Broadhead and English (in Moyles 2005) have found that *pre-themed* role-play areas can actually be *less* good at stimulating co-operative play and higher-order learning than practitioners assumed. Their research has focused on the setting up in reception classes of open-ended role-play areas or 'whatever you want it to be places'. Two key features of these places are:

- play-resources that can be used for a variety of purposes;
- extended play periods with regular access so children can become 'expert players'.

These observations present a challenge to practitioners who wish to utilise a themed play area to promote play in a certain 'scientific' direction – typical themes might be 'the hospital' or 'the garden centre'. Children cannot create play in contexts they haven't experienced. They will need to be provided with knowledge on which to base their creativity. A key ingredient of the research of Broadhead and English is the provocation of a theatre performance where the actors 'suggest' ways in which the play-props might be used. Children will mimic adult behaviour whether it is in the contexts of a play or 'real life'. Visitors to the classroom or visits to workplaces can be used to provide new knowledge and ideas about how adults interact and behave. These experiences can in turn stimulate play.

Reception teacher Alison organised a trip to the local garden centre for her reception class. In the classroom she began to set up a 'garden centre' area where children could play the adult roles they witnessed during the trip. Involving children in setting up the area became a genuine context for creative thinking. Alison planned further opportunities in school for the children to plant seeds and potatoes, care for and watch plants grow. In this way the children's scientific knowledge was developed which informed further role-play.

Playing games

Playing games with rules might not seem to offer much scope for creativity. Rules that are open to interpretation or allow for creative responses, however, offer a clear structure within which creative thinking can be developed. Davies (in Davies and Howe 2003) writes about 'playing the scientist game' with young children and offers a set of 'rules' or steps to be followed. The rules are expressed in terms of questions that guide the process of scientific enquiry:

- What have we noticed? (observation)
- What are we going to find out? (question)
- What do we think will happen? (prediction)
- What we will do/what we did (test)
- What we found out (interpretation, communication)

Armed with magnifying aids and note pads, children can be encouraged to be scientists as they make observations, perform 'investigations' and report back their findings. They might be guided to make 'discoveries' by practitioners modelling scientific behaviour themselves. Expert practitioners are able see the everyday through a child's eyes – the shape of a snail trail, the flow of sand, the smell of an apple – and these 'commonplace' observations can promote questions – 'Where is the snail now?' 'Does the sand feel wet?' 'Does an apple core smell different to a whole apple?' By modelling questions, practitioners can show children how to put their natural curiosity into words.

Games with a basis in logic can also promote connection making and creative thinking. A collection of objects from the kitchen or garden can be sorted and linked – how are these items different? How are they the same? These games are further described in Chapter 8 on materials and their properties.

Teaching creatively in the Foundation Stage

Turning predictable outcomes into something better

While this is essential to motivate older children who may be less engaged with science, it is difficult to imagine that most 4–5-year-olds find many scientific phenomena 'predictable'. In one sense young children will need to realise that they *can* predict what might happen based on their prior, albeit limited, experiences of the world. It may be, however, that they might find the contexts in which phenomena are presented to them are predictable – water always in the water tray, food always as a part of 'cooking'. Practitioners may find that during the reception year they can revisit phenomena such as food changing, ice melting, clothes drying or objects floating and sinking by presenting them in a variety of contexts to allow for the consolidation concepts that the children are beginning to develop.

Making the ordinary fascinating

As outlined above, the role of the adult, particularly the extent to which an adult is engaged or interested in what the children are doing, is a key element of early years practice. Perhaps it is the adult who needs to see the ordinary as fascinating as young children are finding it. In a sense, the adult and child need to swap roles. The adult must become the novice and listen to the expert child. In this way children can be encouraged to articulate their fascination with, and knowledge of, the world.

Sharing a sense of wonder

Although possibly difficult when presented by a child with a live spider or a squashed frog, practitioners who model curiosity and a questioning attitude are powerful promoters of positive attitudes towards science. One outcome of early science education should be to develop children's sense of awe and wonder about the natural world. It was Rachel Carson (1907–64), one of the 'founders' of the environmental movement, who said that 'The more clearly we can focus our attention on the wonders and realities of the universe about us, the less taste we shall have for destruction' (1998). She went on to say:

> If I had influence over the good fairy . . . I should ask that her gift to each child in the world would be a sense of wonder so indestructible it would last through life . . .
>
> If a child is to keep alive his inborn sense of wonder, he needs companionship of at least one adult who can share it . . .
>
> (p. 54)

Many of us have our innate sense of wonder quashed by adulthood and may need to re-learn how to make the ordinary extraordinary.

We have established in this chapter that the early years practitioner should have a secure understanding of how children learn science and adopt an enlightened view about the nature of science. A good understanding of some basic scientific knowledge is a third requisite yet this does not mean she needs to know all the answers to questions posed by children, or if she does she doesn't need to attempt explanations on every occasion. Nolan (2005) discusses the role that wonder and mystery play in keeping our imagination and interest alive in science. He suggests it is sometimes better not to attempt to explain scientific phenomena; rather teachers should welcome creative thinking:

> Knowing how something works can lessen our interest in it, but good scientists . . . take pleasure in both knowing and in not knowing . . . we are coming to realise that great scientists become interested in science not because of the things we know but the things we don't know.

Seeing differently

We say the most creative scientists and artists can see objects 'in a new light', or 'from a new angle'. We can take these phrases literally as a starting point for classroom work. In one reception class children were given coloured light filters or made their own 'colour telescopes'. By providing torches or illuminating items from below on a 'light table' children can be encouraged to see the familiar differently.

Maximising opportune moments

Nicholls (1999) argues that young pupils' scientific work should not be constrained by a rigid curriculum framework, but should be prompted from natural curiosity. It is difficult to predict the focus of children's curiosity; if we are to be able to respond to it then a flexible 'framework' is required.

   In their analysis of the Curriculum Guidance, Siraj-Blatchford and Siraj-Blatchford (2001) find that it does indeed support the idea that practitioners should make effective use of unexpected and unforeseen opportunities for children's learning and that there is a general acceptance in the document of the appropriateness of 'emergent' learning. The Curriculum Guidance does not state which specific scientific or technological knowledge is to be gained during the Foundation Stage. Practitioners should see this as a freedom to explore 'opportune moments' on a daily basis. The key is to recognise the potential in the moments when they arise.

Summary of main points

- Whilst science is not a subject to be taught in the Foundation Stage, scientific contexts can make an essential contribution to all areas of early learning.

- In the past, 'school science' may have promulgated perceptions that science is not creative. A more enlightened view of the nature of science is to recognise it as an active endeavour that requires inquiring and creative thinking.

- Provision for creativity in science depends on skilful use of time, spaces and resources.

- Creativity and science can be unified through a play-based pedagogy.

- Creative teaching of science demands the practitioner adopts an inquiring, open-minded and flexible approach rather than a concern to teach specified scientific concepts.

Issues for reflection

● Does your own experience of learning science in school influence the way in which you approach science in your teaching?

● Can you recall seeing teachers using 'opportune moments' creatively to provide a springboard for learning in science?

Discussion points

● What are the connections between Gura's (1992) 'factors for high quality play' (above, p. 110) and Harrington's 'creative ecosystem' in Chapter 9 on physical processes?

● In what ways could the 'sand tray' be presented to children to encourage wider exploration and creativity?

Recommended reading

Davies, D. and Howe, A. (2003) *Teaching Science and Design and Technology in the Early Years.* London: David Fulton

Howe, A. (2005) *Play with Natural Materials.* London; David Fulton

Thornton, L. and Brunton, P. (2005) *Understanding the Reggio Approach.* London: David Fulton

References

British Educational Research Association Early Years Special Interest Group (2003) *Early Years Research: Pedagogy, Curriculum and Adult Roles, Training and Professionalism.* London: BERA

Carson, R. (1998) *The Sense of Wonder (Introduction by Linda Lear, Photographs by Nick Kelsh).* London: HarperCollins

Craft, A. (2000) *Creativity across the Primary Curriculum: Framing and Developing Practice.* London: Routledge

Craft A. (2002) *Creativity and Early Years Education.* London: Continuum

Csikszentmihalyi, M. (2002) *Flow.* London: Rider

Davies, D. and Howe, A. (2003) *Teaching Science and Design and Technology in the Early Years.* London: David Fulton

Davies, D., Howe, A., Fasciato, M. and Rogers, M. (2004) 'How do trainee primary teachers understand creativity?,' in E. Norman, D. Spendlove, P. Grover and A. Mitchell (eds) *Creativity and Innovation – DATA International Research Conference 2004.* Wellesbourne: Design and Technology Association

De Boo (1999) *Science 3–6: Laying the Foundations in the Early Years.* Hatfield: Association for Science Education (ASE)

Department for Education and Employment/Qualifications and Curriculum Authority (DfEE/QCA) (2000) *Curriculum Guidance for the Foundation Stage.* London: QCA Publications

Gura, P. (ed.) (1992) *Exploring Learning: Young Children and Block Play.* London: Paul Chapman

Harrington, D.M. (1990) 'The ecology of human creativity: a psychological perspective', in M.A. Runco and R.S. Albert (eds) *Theories of Creativity.* London: Sage Publications

Howe, A. (2004) *Play with Natural Materials.* London: David Fulton

Hudson, L. (1973) *Originality.* London: Oxford University Press

Hutt, C. (1979) 'Play in the under-fives: form, development and function', in J.G. Howells (ed.) *Modern Perspectives in the Psychiatry of Infancy*, 94–144. New York: Brunner/Marcel

Hutt, S.J., Tyler, S., Hutt, C. and Christopherson, H. (1989) *Play, Exploration and Learning: A Natural History of the Preschool.* London: Routledge

Johnston, J. and Hayed, M. (1995) 'Teachers' perceptions of science and science teaching' European Conference on Research in Science Education, Proceedings, Leeds 1995. Leeds: University of Leeds

Laevers, F. (1994) *The Leuven Involvement Scale for Young Children LIS-YC.* Manual and Video Tape, Experiential Education, Series No 1. Leuven: Centre for Experiential Education

Moyles, J. (ed.) (2005) *The Excellence of Play* (2nd edn). Maidenhead: OUP

National Advisory Council on Creative and Cultural Education (NACCCE) (1999) *All Our Futures: Creativity, Culture and Education.* London: DfES

Nicholls (1999) 'Young children investigating: adopting a constructivist framework', in T. David (ed.) *Teaching Young Children*, 111–24. London: Paul Chapman

Nolan, S. (2005) *The Joy of Not Knowing.* http://www.nesta.org/inspireme/think_nolan.html

Papert, S. (1999) 'The century's greatest minds', *Time* magazine special issue, p. 105, 29 March

Pascal, C. and Bertram, A.D. (1997) 'The effective early learning project: achievements and reflections', *Early Education*, no. 22. 4 pp. insert

Shallcross, D.J. (1981) *Teaching Creative Behaviour: How to Teach Creativity to Children of All Ages.* New Jersey: Prentice-Hall

Siraj-Blatchford, I. and Siraj-Blatchford, J. (2001) 'A content analysis of pedagogy in the DfEE/QCA 2000 guidance', *Early Education*, 35, 7–8

Sylva, K., Melhuish, E., Sammons, P., Siraj-Blatchford, I., Taggart, B. and Elliot, K. (2003) *The Effective Provision of Preschool Education (EPPE) Project: Findings from the Preschool Period.* London: Institute of Education

CHAPTER 7

Creative teaching and learning in 'Life Processes and Living Things'

Kendra McMahon

A flower is relatively small.

Everyone has many associations with a flower – the idea of flowers. You put out your hand to touch the flower – lean forward to smell it – maybe touch it with your lips almost without thinking – or give it to someone to please them. Still – in a way – nobody sees a flower – really – it is so small – we haven't time – and to see takes time like to have a friend takes time. If I could paint a flower exactly as I see it no-one would see what I see because I would paint it small like the flower is small.

So I said to myself – I'll paint what I see – what the flower is to me, but I'll paint it big and they will be surprised into taking time to look at it–

(Georgia O'Keefe 1939)

Introduction

As a teacher I shared some of Georgia O'Keefe's paintings of flowers with a class of children. They described looking at them as like imagining that you are a bee and 'zooming in'. This idea of 'zooming in', and also of 'zooming out' – of looking at things on different scales – is important to biology as well as to art. We zoom in by using hand lenses and microscopes to look at the detail of living things – a common wood-louse is pretty impressive when magnified! Zooming out – we think about living things in relation to other living things, and the environment, moving to global ideas about sustaining life on our planet. If creativity can be stimulated by looking at familiar things in different ways then this topic lends itself well to thinking about things on different scales.

The quote at the start of the chapter indicates a personal, emotional connection with what the artist is looking at. Perhaps we traditionally view science as cold and objective, but how does that fit with the other image we may have of the scientist as passionately interested in their topic of study, utterly immersed and engaged with it? It seems unlikely that creative thought emerges from boredom and dissociation. Of course, in science, ideas need to be put to the test of logic and evidence, but perhaps this isn't so different from creative processes. Dust (1999) suggests that at least four phases of creativity are commonly identified:

1. preparation – investigating the problem and gathering data;
2. incubation – usually an unconscious/subconscious phase;
3. illumination/revelation – the insight, the moment of creation;
4. verification/reframing – the 'testing', and through communicating the outcome to others for their approval or otherwise.

These have parallels with the processes of science; first of all, the scientists would need to be interested in a problem or phenomenon and go through a phase of initial exploration and gathering together of ideas. This might be followed by a period of 'mulling over', perhaps talking with others, during which the mind is making links and generating ideas, leading to the suggestion of new explanations or applying ideas in a new context. In the fourth phase, 'verification and reframing' takes place when these ideas may be focused as a hypothesis to be tested out and subjected to criticism by other scientists. The ideas are likely to be further changed and developed through this process. Thinking about science in this way emphasises processes that are imaginative and creative; usually it is the last phase in which ideas are formalised and tested that is labelled as investigative science. By valuing the initial processes more, we might shift what we do in the classroom that we label as 'scientific enquiry' and spend more time gathering together resources and ideas from a range of sources and exploring them physically and verbally.

The study of living things is full of opportunities for awe and wondering, and children find animals in particular to be fascinating. Teachers can make the most of this natural curiosity and help children both to formulate questions and try to find answers. Through supporting children in scientific processes, in raising questions, suggesting explanations and testing out ideas, teachers are supporting children in being creative.

What though, if through carrying out enquiries children come up with 'the wrong answer'? One of the conflicts that teachers experience when thinking about how they can both teach creatively and help children to be creative in the context of science is that there will be particular scientific knowledge, 'content', that teachers want children to learn. This dilemma is exacerbated by an over-packed curriculum and high-stakes testing (Harlen and Qualter 2004). However, there is also a tension embedded within science as a subject. In Chapter 6 of this book Alan Howe explains that, in science, theories are always 'a draft', they are the best explanations that we have at the moment, but are only tentative and open to be changed. Bearing this in mind, how are we to help children understand the 'big ideas of science', as they are currently understood, because these ideas are useful in helping us to make sense of the world, but not to see them as finished, fixed things? It is challenging and uncomfortable for children and some teachers to learn to live with the uncertainty of scientific knowledge. But learning to accept this is essential if teachers are going to support children in understanding science as a creative process. We want children to be able to question scientific ideas, not just accept them. One way we might do this is by thinking about the ways we talk with children during science lessons, and this is explored later in this chapter.

Time, space and resources

Learning about living things also offers opportunities to get outside of the classroom and explore bigger spaces. Although there are many organisations and places to visit, exploring living things in different spaces needn't require expensive trips – it could be to a parent's allotment, to a park, or a garden centre. Also, it is worth considering how the space within the school grounds can be used on different scales – you could plant a tub to attract butterflies, build a pond or create a shady area.

Another possibility is working on time scales that may be different from a standard medium-term planning block of a few weeks, particularly when looking at plants and the environment. Children could do a year-long study of a tree – do they observe any changes to the bark, underneath, the leaves, buds or fruit? In the first week of the year the class could dig a patch of newly bare earth and over the year – what grows first, next; what animals do they find there? Enquiring into animal growth and change may also involve longer-term planning; many schools incubate and hatch chick eggs, some observe silk moths emerging from their cocoons. What happens in 'A day in the life of a dandelion flower'?

Cross-curricular links

This area of science provides many opportunities for cross-curricular links and thematic topics. Koestler's (1964) definition of creativity as 'the ability to make connections between previously unconnected ideas' is useful in helping explain how powerful it is for teachers to think about cross-curricular links when they are planning topics. The process of looking for links and connections can generate all sorts of new approaches and ways of thinking about familiar topics. The ideas suggested below are intended to illustrate this and provide some hooks and suggestions to further stimulate ideas and not to replace this process.

There are many possible links with the work of artists such as Georgia O'Keefe, Rennie Mackintosh and Van Gogh who have taken nature as a focus for their painting and drawing. Children could look at their work and use it to inform their own drawings and paintings of flowers, leaves, or the bark of trees. Still-life paintings such as those by Cézanne might inspire observations of fruits. Beatrix Potter illustrated her own stories using her observations of wildlife (she was an expert in fungi) to inform her work. Children might look at her books, perhaps comparing them with less realistic illustrations of plants and animals. Andy Goldworthy's sculptures using natural materials could be used as a stimulus to help children engage with the environment in different ways.

Stories that feature animals can be used to contextualise work in science and develop ideas further. Children could be encouraged to write their own stories taking animals as lead characters, having researched some details of how the animal lives first. The traditional story of the elephant and the ant arguing over which one was the strongest provides a simple plot (after the elephant demonstrating his superior lifting power with tree trunks, the ant gives his brother a lift home on his back, and the elephant concedes that he couldn't do that) and children could be challenged to develop the plot into an engaging story, including details about the life of an elephant or an ant, such as what they eat and the environments they might share. It also could be used as a starting point for discussions: 'How do you compare "strength"?' or 'What if an ant was as big as an elephant?' It might lead into talking about how different animals are suited to their particular habitats.

Alternatively, different kinds of texts can be used to gather information about topics in science. The book *Dear Greenpeace* (Simon James 1998) is a wonderfully engaging story about a girl who thinks she has a whale in her pond, and she exchanges letters with Greenpeace who provide lots of information about whales in an attempt to convince her that it couldn't possibly be a whale. After enjoying the story, children could work on a collaborative group activity to extract the information and present it in a different form. Perhaps the class could watch the movie *Bugs Life* and collate information about 'mini-beasts' they have learnt from it. Older children could be encouraged to check this using another source.

Poetry can provide a starting point for discussion of scientific ideas, e.g. Brian Patten's poem 'Poisoning down', about pollution, can be found in his book *Gargling with Jelly* (Patten 1986). Poetry can also be an alternative way of communicating ideas that children have developed. The publication *STAR (Science Technology and Reading) – A Resource for Teachers* (ASE 2000) is a useful source of ideas for using poetry to support learning in science. An advantage of linking science with fiction and poetry is it supports the emotional aspect of science – the feelings of curiosity, excitement and awe that are associated with finding out about the world around us, and the world inside us (McMahon and Davies 2001).

Linking maths with the topic of living things suggests opportunities for counting and measuring: How many seeds in a pod? Do all our pods have the same number of seeds? Are dandelion leaves smaller if they grow near the road? How far can I jump? How many times do I breathe in half a minute? Can the biggest hands grab the most sweets? Children are often asked to measure the growth of seeds they have planted in terms of height, but what else could be measured? Perhaps they could record the number of leaves, or compare growth above ground with growth underground. Shape and pattern are other fruitful areas for enquiry; looking for symmetry and patterns in natural structures.

Work on habitats can be supported by geography topics that focus on what particular areas are like physically and in climate and can help to raise questions: Why do different things live in the woods, in the park, in the desert, in the Arctic? Why do we import bananas? Do we need to import apples? This helps to develop ideas about living things being adapted to suit their environment and provides a context to consider concerns many children have about the future of the planet. Oxfam (www.oxfam.org.uk) produce a range of educational materials that can be used to explore how foods are grown around the world, considering the social conditions as well as the physical ones. For example, the big book *One child, One seed* (Cave *et al.* 2003) is the story of a child in South Africa growing a pumpkin seed, illustrated with photographs and aimed at younger primary children. Perhaps children could try to grow pumpkin seeds instead of the typical cress or broad beans. Again, this links science back to people and how they live, and helps to show that science has a meaningful contribution to make to understanding the world.

When children are learning about themselves, about the human body and health, although there is a scientific dimension to this there is also an emotional and social dimension. The kinds of choices children make, and the range of choices they have, for example about what they will eat, or whether or not they will decide to smoke, will depend on their social situation, their relationships with their peers and their personal and emotional attributes, not just their understanding of the science involved (see Chapter 8 in Howe *et al.* 2005).

There are all sorts of other possibilities. Perhaps in a winter project for Design Technology children could evaluate commercial bird feeders and make their own, finding out what species feed on different foods and how their beaks help them to get the food out. Thematic planning with a topic such as 'Our park', 'The seaside' or 'People' all suggest opportunities for work in science. Again, my intention here is to provoke ideas and show how looking for cross-curricular links can suggest new angles on a scientific topic. Children could be involved in the planning process before a new topic begins and their ideas may suggest all sorts of new possibilities and different directions.

Links with ICT

Developments in ICT can also stimulate creative approaches to both teaching and learning. Howe *et al.* (2005), Chapter 9, provide examples of how using digital cameras can enhance children's observation of structures in plants, and in looking for variation (in roots, stems, leaves, flowers, parts of flowers) between plants. Working on different time scales can be facilitated by ICT – making or using time lapse photos of growth of animals or plants, or producing a long-term time line perhaps of the same space at different times of the year. Bird boxes with built-in cameras are now available at prices within reach of school budgets and following the progress of a family of blue tits could engage the whole school community. Digital microscopes and some internet sites are useful to explore looking at things on different scales (e.g. www.visions-of-science.co.uk).

Perhaps children could create a website about their local area, providing details and photographs of the habitats and the living things they have found there. There is also the opportunity to make a real contribution to national databases which depend on the observations of amateurs such as the BBC's 'Springwatch'. Phenology – investigating the time in the year when different plants and animals go through different parts of their cycles (the first cuckoo of spring, or the first flowering of blackthorn, or the first sighting of a bumble bee) – has become increasingly recognised in recent years as a means of exploring the impact of climate change (www.phenology.org.uk).

The popular TV programme *Walking with Dinosaurs* prompted one teacher to invite children to bring fossil dinosaur bones to life. Pictures of skulls were put into a computer drawing program and children drew on top of the bones, building up muscle and skin, choosing colours and textures in much the same way as the scientists had used their imagination to interpret the fossil evidence. Children could be asked to think about how we might use what we know about animals now to fill in the missing gaps in our knowledge. Is an ammonite like a snail? Would it stick its head out? Are there any animals that are more similar? How would an ammonite move?

Assessing children's creativity in Life Processes and Living Things

In Chapter 9, Dan Davies explores in more depth what assessing children's creativity in science might mean, considering how problematic it is, and he suggests how we might view progression in creativity. Whilst acknowledging the complexity of

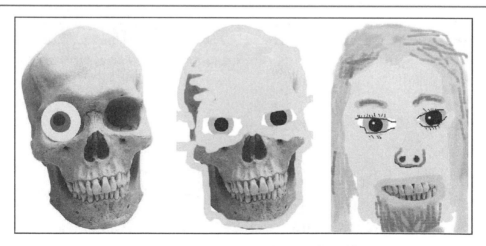

Figure 7.1 Reconstructing a human face! Hattie and Harriet (age 10)

this discussion, here I will take the list of behaviours that QCA (2003) consider provide a means of judging pupils' creativity (subheadings below) and suggest examples of how they might be manifested in the context of Life Processes and Living Things.

Questioning and challenging

We can look for evidence of children asking questions; e.g. 'Why do giraffes have such long necks?', 'What happens to bumble bees in the winter?', 'Where do butterflies sleep?', 'Why do sweets taste so nice if they are bad for you?', 'Do you think the plants near the road are getting polluted?'

In a sorting activity we could look out for children who are disagreeing with how another child has grouped some animals or plants and giving a reason for their view.

Making connections and seeing relationships

Evidence of making connections and seeing relationships might involve making links and drawing comparisons between living things or pointing out similarities and differences between different animals or plants. Another example might be children making suggestions about the relationship between the physical features of a habitat and the kinds of plants and animals that live there; 'I think that butterflies are different colours so they can hide in the flowers.'

Envisaging what might be

Speculating about the relationship between structure and function – 'Maybe that bit is like . . . so it can . . .' e.g. 'I think fish have scales so they can bend and swim' – provides evidence that children are using general biological principles in a creative way. (Look at the case study 'What are flowers for?' for more examples of this kind of speculation.)

Responding to 'What if . . .?' questions (Feasey 2005), e.g. 'What if teachers really did have eyes in the back of their heads?', 'What if plants could move about?', might be another way of assessing children's creative visualisation, and thinking of some 'What if . . .?' questions of their own would take this even further.

Exploring ideas; keeping options open

Are children making really careful observations – noticing more than the immediately obvious features of animals and plants? Are they finding their own ways of recording their ideas, observations and results? If children are demonstrating that they are exploring possibilities in a topic, this may be evidence of how they are thinking about their own experiences in relation to the topic, and as they get older, asking other children for their ideas and opinions too.

Reflecting critically on ideas, actions and outcomes

Being prepared to change their ideas in the light of new evidence, e.g. to be surprised by the results of a test, to be able to say that it wasn't what they expected, perhaps that plants grew really tall in the dark, and then to consider alternative explanations, is an example of critical reflection. So is listening to the ideas of other children and comparing them with their own: 'You know Alisha said that chocolate is bad for you, well I think it's OK if you don't have too much.' If children are arguing by presenting reasons for their ideas then they are taking this to a higher level.

Debating the personal and social implications of knowledge in science, 'I think people shouldn't keep tropical fish as pets because their natural habitat is a huge ocean', would be evidence of a greater depth of critical thought.

One of the challenges for teachers in making judgements about children's creativity is how they are going to access the children's ideas. Questions and hypotheses may be unspoken. Being explicit with children about how creative responses are valued may be part of the solution, as Marshall *et al.* (2003) describe the importance of communicating clear success criteria to children. For example, the learning objectives for observational work in a habitat might be: 'I am looking for children who notice something about the hedge that they haven't noticed before', or 'I am looking for groups who think of lots of different ways of grouping their collection of leaves.' Perhaps a poster in the classroom could invite children to tell their teacher something they have noticed that surprised them that week. Or there could be a space devoted to recording 'questions we can't answer . . . yet!'

However, there may be some conflicts experienced by teachers in valuing children's ideas, particularly if they are not in line with the scientific view. Creating a classroom environment in which thoughts can be freely expressed, but also challenged, requires children to learn to work collaboratively to explore ideas (Mercer 2000). It also requires teachers to reflect on the hidden messages they are expressing in their own talk, as children are adept at working out what teachers really value (Lemke 1990). A first step for teachers might be to review the opportunities that currently exist in their classroom for making judgements about children's creativity and how these could be increased.

Planning for creativity in Life Processes and Living Things

Although it is useful to have a framework for medium-term planning that helps to build in progression, and identifies some key aspects of learning, very detailed plans leave little room for responding to children's interests and ideas, and for developing aspects of a topic that seem to take on a life of their own. Where teachers have a good understanding of the key aspects of scientific knowledge that are important, they often feel more comfortable about taking different pathways through and towards the same content knowledge. The challenge for writing this chapter was how to support teachers in deciding what the most important parts of the topic would be, and initiating a planning process that is both creative for teachers and provides opportunities for children to be creative too. One approach might be to think about each topic in four different ways:

- What are the 'big ideas' of the science content?
- What contexts might be used to explore these ideas? Are there any cross-curricular links to be made?
- How can we find different starting points for enquiry?
- How can the topic be made rich in human experience and emotions?

The intention of this section is to use these four questions to provide examples of how planning might be approached.

So a first step is to identify the 'big ideas', or key concepts, within the subject area of living things. Of course, teachers are obliged to meet the statutory requirements of the curriculum, and the English National Curriculum (DfEE 1999) has been used as the starting point in Table 7.1. Thinking about each area of the science curriculum and the contribution it makes to our understanding of living things may open up opportunities for a diversity of approaches and flexibility in planning.

Contexts sometimes seem to be firmly embedded in schools' planning by the use of topic titles, and available resources. Drawing on the interests and expertise of children, teachers, parents and members of the local community can suggest alternatives that are more meaningful for those involved. If children are invited to respond to some initial ideas about the topic through a discussion prior to detailed planning, then all sorts of ideas and opportunities may emerge as they make links between the content and their own experiences. 'Brainstorming'-type sessions or question-raising activities can be useful here. If parents are informed about the topics that are coming up and invited to share expertise, all kinds of hidden skills and interests may be revealed. Parents who are health professionals may be an obvious possible source of ideas, but what about the parent who breeds dogs, or who keeps tropical fish? Looking around for local industries and services may suggest opportunities for visits and visitors. Identifying any cross-curricular links might be useful at this stage to open up ideas.

One way in which biologists try to make sense of what they see is to look at the way that living things are structured, how they have been put together, and they try to work out how that helps them to stay alive or to reproduce – they look for relationships between 'structure and function'. The underlying question 'How does this help it to live?' can be applied to all living things, parts of living things and systems of living things. For example: 'Why do humans have bones and snails have shells?', 'What does a fish scale look like using the digital microscope and why might it be like that?' or 'Why don't lions and tigers live in the same places?'

Another important way in which biologists work is to examine the variety of life and classify it. Fossil collector Mary Anning's patient and delicate work in extracting fossils from rocks in Lyme Regis made a huge contribution to our understanding of extinct animals. Rather rudely referred to as nothing more than 'stamp collecting' by some experimental scientists, the systematic categorising of the diversity of living things has provided insights into evolution and the relationship between living things and their habitats. It is also an area in which there is surprisingly little agreement amongst the scientists – so there is plenty of room for creative contributions to the debates! The underlying questions 'How is this similar to other living things, and how is it different?' and 'Why might that be?' are important here.

The idea of looking at familiar things in new ways was introduced in Chapter 1, and this approach could be adopted by teachers, and also by children, to raise questions and identify areas for scientific enquiry. In the biological sciences, there is less reliance on the 'fair test', and more use of other forms of enquiry such as close observation, pattern seeking and identifying and classifying (Howe *et al.* 2005). By encouraging children to look for opportunities for comparing and contrasting new things, for 'zooming in' and 'zooming out', and asking 'Why is it like that?' (structure–function) type questions, they will be thinking like creative scientists.

The importance of emotional engagement with the topic was stressed earlier in the chapter. Thinking about how children's experiences might be related to each topic also provides a way of thinking about it from different points of view. How can the topic be made meaningful on a deeper level, perhaps by asking philosophical questions? How can experiences be planned to offer rich opportunities for children? Table 7.1 identifies the 'big ideas' of topics in this area and presents a few suggestions for developing both starting points for enquiry and the human, affective dimension.

Example of planning a topic – 'Birds'

Imagine that as a teacher you are supposed to be doing a topic on 'habitats' next term. You have noticed some opportunities for a context; there is a parent in your class who is a keen ornithologist, you have a vague memory of your own school science in which different birds have different kinds of beaks depending on what they eat, the parent teacher association has offered a small amount of funding to help develop part of playground and so you have decided that 'birds' might be an interesting topic. You suggest this to the children in your class who start to talk about feathers they once collected, one child has a bird skull in a box, another talks about their gran's parakeet, and others have enjoyed feeding bread to the ducks in the park. The topic could then be developed by looking for cross-curricular links and areas for enquiry identified by considering the topic on different scales. The children could be included in this process, perhaps suggesting stories that they could share. The web in Figure 7.2 shows how the teacher's initial planning ideas might look.

Table 7.1 Developing planning

Big ideas	Starting points for enquiry	Human experience and emotions
Variation and classification Things can be defined as living/nonliving based on certain characteristics. Plants and animals can be classified and identified based on similarities and differences.	**Comparing and contrasting** Looking for differences and complexities and sub-groups, looking for groups of similarities, and generalising. **Challenging categories** What is a living thing? – a computer? a seed?	**Philosophical questions** What does it mean to be alive? **Awe and wonder** Look at all that amazing diversity of life out there!
Adaptation to habitat Species of animals and plants are 'designed' to live in certain very specific conditions. Changing the environment can mean the living things can't survive.	**Structure & function** 'Zooming in' for a close look at an organism, 'zooming out' to look at its environment, thinking about the links between the two.	**Awe and wonder** How does it feel to be here? 'This wood makes me feel like I'm in a fairy tale.' 'I love it when it's windy on the beach!' **My place in things** How do different things live together? Wondering about the future of the environment.
Nutrition Plants need water and sunlight so they can make their food. Humans need a balanced diet.	**Structure and function** What are different parts of a plant for? Why are there different kinds of teeth? **Comparing and contrasting** How do leaves, roots and stems vary between plants?	**Inside me – outside me** 'Jamie Oliver says we should eat more vegetables but I like chips!' 'How does that fish finger get into my feet?' **Awe and wonder** How did that huge sunflower come from that small seed?'
Reproduction Flowering plants, animals, human life cycle, about animals having offspring	**Structure and function** Looking closely at different kinds of flowers. What are the advantages and disadvantages of live birth, eggs, pouches . . .?	**My place in things** 'Where did I come from?'
Growth Linked with nutrition in plants, linked with human life cycle.	**Comparing and contrasting** How old can living things get? What makes the same things grow differently?	**Things change** 'I felt sad when my Nan died.' 'I can see a tomato growing on my plant!'

(*continued*)

Table 7.1 Continued

Big ideas	Starting points for enquiry	Human experience and emotions
Movement (Animals) includes ideas about bones and muscles.	**Structure and function** How do different parts of the body move? Are they different inside? What are bones like?	**Inside me** Experiences of broken bones. Pleasure in exploring own movement through dance.
Senses A KS1 topic, exploring sight, hearing, tastes, smell, touch and identifying the sensory organs.	**Comparing and contrasting** Exploring different sensations. Investigating similarities and differences between people.	**Inside me – outside me** How do I find out about the world? My likes and dislikes. Do we all feel the same things?
Micro-organisms A KS2 topic, food storage and health, decay and recycling.	**'Zooming in'** How can we find out about things that are really small?	**Awe and wonder** Living things can be so tiny! **Inside me – outside me** What choices are to be made about what goes inside your body?
Health Naming body parts, circulation, exercise, drugs.	**'Zooming in'** How can we find out what is inside us? **'Zooming out'** How can we help everyone to be healthy?	**Awe and wonder** 'Have I really got all that inside me?' **Inside me – outside me** What choices are to be made about what goes inside your body?

There are many aspects of science in the National Curriculum that could be addressed by this topic of 'birds' but the most obvious ones are:

- Plants and animals can be classified and identified based on similarities and differences.
- Species of animals and plants are 'designed' to live in certain very specific conditions.
- Reproduction – about animals having offspring.
- Movement – ideas about bones.

Depending on what the children have learned previously, the teacher might decide to focus on some aspects of the curriculum, perhaps assessing children's understanding

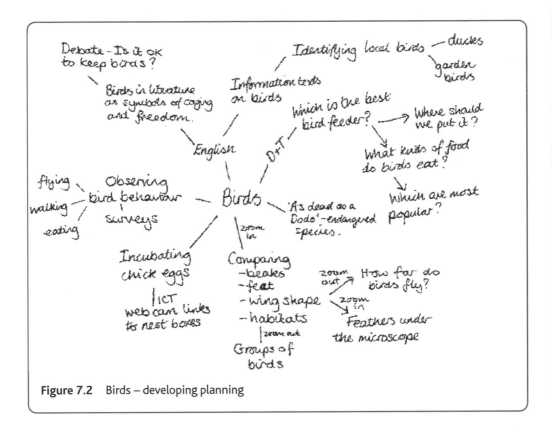

Figure 7.2 Birds – developing planning

of the way animals are adapted to suit their habitats, and seeing the other aspects as enriching children's broad understanding.

Social creativity

Howe (2004) draws on the idea that to support children's creativity, schools and classrooms need to develop a 'creative ecosystem'. This sees creativity as located not only in the head of an individual, but within a culture, as a way of being and interacting with other people. One way of developing a creative ecosystem is to think about the nature of talk, of interactions, within a classroom and whether they are helping or hindering creativity.

Although the relationship between talking and thinking is not straightforward, it seems reasonable to assume that a classroom in which children can express their ideas and have them valued, and also challenged, is more likely to contribute to a creative ecosystem than one in which they are not. Increasing emphasis is being placed on how children and teachers can talk together so that ideas are built on 'cumulatively'. Talk that is cumulative, in which children's ideas are listened to by others and explored together to build meaning, has been referred to as 'dialogic' (Mortimer and Scott 2003; Alexander 2004). Table 7.2 (p. 137) provides a summary of the features of 'dialogic' talk in contrast with 'authoritative' talk. This kind of talk could be important in helping children to understand that science is a social, creative and changing entity, not a rigid body of knowledge to be consumed.

There are particular challenges and opportunities for talk that the topic of living things presents. There are aspects of the curriculum that are not easily accessible to investigative work – what is inside a human, or the role of foods and drugs in relation to health, cannot be explored directly. Instead we rely on using secondary sources of information and providing models – and there is a risk that this approach can make teaching rather didactic, limiting opportunities for talk. However, there are also opportunities. It is a topic in which children will have a wealth of personal experience to draw on. Encourage discussion and speculation, e.g. Is there a better arrangement for parts of the human body? Would eyes in the back of your head be helpful, or not? There are also many opportunities for raising social and ethical issues, in which debating, arguing and expressing opinions become important. For example, a group of children could be given a collection of photographs of different animals (cat, budgie, butterfly, lion cub, snake) and asked to discuss which ones would be OK to have as pets. This could lead into discussions about how different animals feed, their natural habitats, whether or not animals have rights. Duschl and Osborne (2002) suggest that the process of constructing arguments with reference to ideas and evidence is central to learning in science, as it is to the nature of science. Concept cartoons (Naylor and Keogh 2000) provide good starting points for discussions on a range of topics.

Case study – What is a flower for?

The following extract from a class discussion during a topic on plants provides an opportunity to think about how talk can be creative in science, even on a subject that might seem to be rather closed – that the function of a flower is to play an important role in reproduction. The children are in Year 5 (9–10 years old).

Whilst reading the extract it might be informative to identify:

- The different ideas that the children suggest about the purpose of flowers, and how they relate to the scientific view.

- Any evidence that the talk is cumulative, that children and teacher are building on each other's ideas.

- What is the role of the teacher? Is she asking questions? How is she responding to children's comments?

- Ideas that could lead to further enquiries.

The prompt for the following extract from a whole-class discussion was a close-up photograph of a tulip flower. The 'big idea' in the teacher's planning was about linking structure and function – what are flowers like and why might they be like that?

Rosie:	Miss, I never seen it on a close-up picture before but that looks very funny.
T:	It's strange, isn't it?
Rosie:	It's a strange shape.
T:	Mm, I think, was it Lucy who said that different flower centres have all got this sort of thing? They might not look exactly like this, in some they might be smaller, in some they might be different colours.
?:	They might be thinner.
T:	They might be thinner, but all flowers have got something a little bit like this. Matt?
Matt:	Me and my sister was testing if we liked butter and she, she, she put it under my chin and it went up there and lots of little bit of pollen coming off.
T:	So you could see . . . specks . . . what did it look like the pollen that went up there?
Matt:	That much and they looked yellowy and they looked sm—
T:	Ah right, only tiny little bit. Josh?
Josh:	Miss, Luke said to me that . . . A flower that smells like beans!
T:	That sounds like a very unusual flower.
Cameron:	The petals, are they to block the sun from getting around there?
T:	What a good question! . . . Cameron's wondering what the petals are for, what they do and if it's anything to do with the sun. Has anyone else got any suggestions? Alisha, what do you think?
Alisha:	I think the petals are to attract bees.
T:	You think the petals are to attract bees. Ah ha, anyone else want to add anything?
Pete:	We could do an experiment on one flower, pick off all the petals and leave one with all the petals on and see whether the one without the petals still grows.
?:	It wouldn't grow.
T:	Well, it would be worth trying, it would be worth trying. Yeah, I think that sounds like a good idea. That would be a way of testing, wouldn't it, if petals are important or not, if they really matter. Polly?
Polly:	You can make perfume out of petals.
T:	Perfume out of petals. How can you make perfume out of petals?
Lucy:	You put them in water.
T:	It would be nice if people could put their hands up and not talk out loud.

?:	My mum could give you the recipe.
T:	Nadira?
Nadira:	. . . (Inaudible) . . .
T:	Oh, right, so how come you can get perfume from petals? What do you think? Anna?
Anna:	I think the petals are for a runway, 'cos when the bee lands and it wants, it wants some nectar or whatever it is, pollen,
?:	. . . it zooms down and goes bbbbzzzz runway!!!
T:	So a petal is a landing and taking off place. Could be.
Luke:	If it didn't have the petals the water that went up the stem would go out the top.
Rosie:	It holds it in.
T:	Hang on, it's to . . .?
Luke:	The water that goes in the roots and up the stem would go out the top if it never had no petals.
T:	So you think it's a way of keeping the water in. That's interesting. Actually, I think that what happens in plants is that water does go in, some of it gets used up and some of it evaporated out of the top. So there's this constant flow: water going up the roots, some of it being used up, some of it being evaporated out the top, but I like your idea.
Matt:	Some plants, like when insects come to get pollen, some plants eat the insects.
T:	Right, there are . . .
?:	. . . trap them.
T:	. . . a few plants that actually trap the insects, aren't there? They're quite rare and they're quite special, but there are one or two that do that. A few more comments. Jamie?
Tom:	I've got a plant that eats . . . and spiders.
?:	A Venus fly trap.
Tom:	Yeah!
T:	Does it, and have you seen it catch anything?
Tom:	. . . (inaudible) . . .
T:	A moth? Oh I'd like to see that.
?:	. . . put a camera on.
?:	. . . put your hand in . . .

T:	Carla?
Carla:	You know Polly said you can make perfume from petals, I reckon that some petals smell different from others and that's why you get different smells of perfume.
T:	So it's actually the petals that smell different, smell in it as part of it. Darius?
Darius:	You know that somebody said that flowers have pollen . . .
T:	Yes.
Darius:	. . . and you said does anyone else know if they've got something else, well they have nectar.
T:	Nectar, yes, what does the nectar do? Do you know anything about it? I think nectar is . . . does anyone else have anything to say about nectar? Shh. Kate?
Kate:	I think they use it to make bee wax.
T:	To make bee wax, we might need to look into this a bit more closely to see exactly what they do. I think it's something to do with bees. [gap in transcript]
Max:	Without the flower the bees can't get like nectar and they probably will die.
T:	So that helps the bees, how does it help the flower? Aoife, how does it help the plant as a whole?
Aoife:	Oh I wanted to answer the other question!
T:	Oh.
Aoife:	Well, they say, some scientists say that if when you go into space you wear light green then, you can get a better suntan so maybe if you . . . yellow . . . on a plant you may be able to attract more sunlight.
T:	That's a very good thought, isn't it? I don't know the answer.

There are different ideas suggested about the purposes of flowers:

Petals block the sun

Petals attract insects

Petals catch insects!

Petals are for insects to stand on

Petals make nectar

Petals keep the water in

Petals attract sunlight

This hypothesising is a creative response to the question, 'What are flowers for?' and the children are engaging in this speculative process.

The role of the teacher in this discussion is largely as a chairperson. The children have lots to say, they seem interested in the topic and they are making extended comments rather than one-word answers. They are sometimes initiating exchanges and bringing new ideas based on their own experiences into the discussion. They are also using each other's ideas and the teacher's ideas as triggers for new thoughts. The teacher is sometimes asking questions, but not always getting an answer to them! She is trying not to be too overtly judgemental about the children's suggestions, not always successfully, but is aiming to explore the children's ideas and follow them on different pathways. These are characteristics of dialogic talk.

There are links being made to personal experience, hypotheses being developed, and suggestions for possible enquiries are emerging:

- We could compare centres of lots of different kinds of flowers – what are the similarities – and what are the differences?
- We could pull all the petals off a flower and see what happens.
- We could put a camera on a Venus fly trap, or make close observations of a carnivorous plant and compare it with other plants.
- We could try to extract perfume from different kinds of petals.
- We could find out about what happens to different colours in the sun.

There are also questions raised for research in secondary sources – What is bees wax made from? What about honey? Realistically, it is unlikely that all these possibilities can be explored in school, but some could, and others could be displayed, valuing them, and perhaps some enterprising parents would take it further outside of school.

Not all talk in science lessons has to be dialogic. There are times when the teacher might be introducing a scientific idea or providing an explanation in a more authoritative way. But think about how different being provided with an 'answer' feels if you have asked the question, even if this is inside your head. Instead of the teacher being in a position of evaluating the children's ideas, the children are now in a position to evaluate the teacher's – 'Oh, so that's why . . .' or 'Yes, that makes sense.' Perhaps they might challenge the teacher's idea: 'That can't be right because when you . . .', 'But what about if . . .', or extend and apply the explanation 'Does it mean that . . .?' If the general tone of classroom discussion is one that encourages expression of ideas then when the teacher provides information she provides another voice, it will probably be an expert voice, but in a way that encourages children to link the new idea with their own and to go beyond it. So although there may be authoritative episodes interspersed with dialogic ones, the children understand that these are within an overall ethos in which they are to actively engage with ideas and make sense of them for themselves.

Aoife's idea about the colour of petals and whether they attract sunlight got me thinking. I've often thought that there are lots of yellow flowers in early spring, and then more blue ones, and then red ones later – I wonder if this impression would be borne out by a more systematic look at the evidence? Might it be to do with the different height of the sun at different times of the year and might that make a

Table 7.2 Features of authoritative and dialogic talk

Authoritative	Dialogic
General features: Focused mainly on the 'information transmitting' voice. 'Closed' – children's ideas are not accepted unless they are supporting message to be transmitted. The outcome is controlled.	Reciprocal – listen to each other, share ideas, consider alternative viewpoints. 'Open' – new voices contribute to the act of developing meaning. The outcome may not be anticipated.
Nature of teacher talk: Invested with authority which tends to discourage interventions. Intended to convey information. Often based on instructional questions (to which the teacher already has the answer). Often involving factual statements which offer few 'invitations' to dialogue.	Framed in such a way as to be open to challenge and debate. Intended to act as 'thinking devices' or 'generators of meaning'. Often based on open or genuine questions where the answer is not obvious. Directed towards sustaining dialogue. Answers provoke further questions and are seen as the building blocks of dialogue rather than its terminal point.
Nature of pupil talk: Often in response to teacher questions. Often consisting of single, detached words interspersed in teacher delivery. Often direct assertions.	Often spontaneously offered and triggered by comments from other students. Pupils ask questions and provide explanations. Often consisting of ideas expressed in whole phrases and in the context of ongoing dialogue. Cumulative – building on their own and each other's ideas and chaining of ideas into coherent lines of enquiry. Often tentative suggestions open to interpretation and development by others. Supportive – children articulate their ideas freely without fear of embarrassment over 'wrong answers' and they help each other to reach common understandings.

(Adapted from Mortimer and Scott (2003) and Alexander (2004))

difference to the wavelength of light that gets through the atmosphere? I don't know, but I enjoy the feeling of having these ideas and speculating; being curious about the world and trying to explain and make sense of it. That seems to be the part of science that engages people and that makes it a worthwhile human activity.

Classroom approaches to foster creativity in Life Processes and Living Things

Chapter 2 suggests ten approaches to teaching creatively and these have been developed here in the context of Life Processes and Living Things. The points on sharing a sense of wonder and humanising science have been considered in more depth already in the section on planning.

1. Turning predictable outcomes into something better

Probably the most predictable science in primary schools is that children will grow cress or broad beans in containers. How about growing potatoes, or rice, or planting up a bed outside? Try different varieties of tomatoes in a growbag. Which tastes the best? Does growing one species of annual flower attract more insects than another?

2. Making the ordinary fascinating

There is a huge variety in everyday objects that often goes unremarked upon. Challenging children to 'Bring me a leaf' as a homework activity and looking at the range of leaves might provide a starting point for this.

3. Sharing a sense of wonder

There seem to be endless opportunities for promoting awe and wonder at the beauty or strangeness of nature, and the sheer amazingness of life itself! Taking the time to ask children for their emotive responses is important. I once tentatively asked a class if they had a favourite flower, wondering if this was a gender-biased question, and was overwhelmed with the range of responses from all members of the class explaining what they liked about different flowers and the associations they had, often with grandparents or special family events such as weddings. Cross-curricular links have an important role here in providing different ways for children to express themselves, through art, dance or writing.

4. Seeing differently

If children can be helped to find their own ways of seeing differently then the ideas of zooming in and out might be useful approaches to considering living things in new ways. Zooming in: What is it made of, what is inside it – does it have a heart?

Zooming out: How high up can they live – up trees? Up mountains? How far away from here do they live? In the desert? In the Arctic? A habitat can be looked at from different perspectives – we are familiar with the term 'a bird's eye view', but what about 'an ant's eye view'? Using magnifiers and digital cameras are other ways of helping children to find their own angles when observing living things.

5. Maximising opportune moments

The changing weather and seasons provide opportunities to look at habitats in different conditions; a dewy autumn morning might be a good time to go spotting spiders' webs. Children's illnesses and accidents need to be treated with sensitivity, but might provoke discussion: What happens when you fall and cut your knee? What events happen, from the cut to the treatment, and why do they happen?

6. Humanising science

Children can be invited to share their own experiences of different places. This doesn't have to involve long-haul flights but could be about sharing their favourite places in the playground, e.g. sunny spots, places out of the wind, places where you see people, places where you don't. Children could create a picture of an imaginary habitat they would like to live in, and insert a photograph of themselves being there, in role.

7. Valuing questions

Opportunities for children to generate their own questions can come from making collections – ask groups to collect natural 20 items on the theme of:

- spirals
- holes
- shells
- feathers
- a pattern – stripes, spots.

The collections can then be sorted and ordered: 'Can you find some big differences?, 'What about some tiny differences?' If children are unused to raising questions they may need some question stems to get them going such as 'How many . . .?', 'Where did . . .?', 'How did . . .?', 'Which is . . .?' Collections can be provided to stimulate questioning on a particular topic, for example a seed collection could generate questions about growth and conditions and variation and be a preparation for ideas on seed dispersal.

There are topics that raise big existential questions about the origins of life and death. These can be hard to handle, but avoiding them makes science a sterile and inhuman activity. As when teaching RE, sensitive discussion about different viewpoints is important, and evidence for the scientific viewpoint can be considered.

8. Modelling explanations

Pollination can be modelled by drama activities in which children take on the roles of different parts of a flower and insects, or the wind. A similar approach could be taken to seed dispersal, perhaps with appropriate musical accompaniment for wind, water, or being eaten! Food webs can be modelled by giving each child a photograph of an animal or plant to hang around their neck, and then creating a web of links of wool between the eaten and the eater!

Perhaps teachers can model creative thinking by asking questions to which we genuinely don't know the answer, or speculating about the reasons for something when we are not sure. Be honest! 'I think that's because . . . but I'm not really sure.' Teachers have ideas too, but we need to be prepared to justify them – what is our evidence, or trusted source?

9. Encouraging autonomy

Children can be offered a choice of means of recording, of media to draw with, of scale of observations. A structured starting point can then open out with opportunities to diversify and respond to children's ideas. For example, if a child thinks that putting a plastic bag over a plant would stop it growing as it had no air, then encourage them to try this out. Collaborative group work provides children with both support and more freedom to make decisions for themselves.

10. Allowing for flexible beginnings

Finding out what children's ideas are at the start of a topic is widely encouraged – and teachers can plan specific opportunities for this through elicitation activities (Ollerenshaw and Ritchie 1997; Howe *et al.* 2005). However, analysing children's responses is not always easy and can focus on comparing children's ideas with the scientific ones and identifying 'misconceptions'. Although it is important to consider children's ideas in relation to the 'big ideas' of the topic, looking for 'errors' alone is a deficit model. Elicitation provides an opportunity for teachers to gain an insight into children's thought processes, and reasons for their ideas that can be explored and challenged through dialogue. It may be productive also to look for opportunities for exploring unusual ideas and taking the topic in new directions.

Summary of main points

Thinking about life processes and living things on different scales of time and space can lead to new directions for teaching and learning. This chapter also suggested that providing opportunities for children to express emotional connections with topics helps to enrich their experiences. In this way science can be understood as a human activity. The kind of interaction that takes place between teachers and children can support creativity; this chapter explored how 'dialogic talk' may support children in engaging with scientific ideas in creative ways.

Issues for reflection

- How can existing science topics be developed in order to provide more opportunities for children to relate them to their own experiences and the feelings associated with these?
- To what extent does your current teaching support dialogic talk?

Discussion points

- How can teachers both ensure that children understand the 'big ideas' of biological science and take a creative approach to teaching and learning?
- When would dialogic talk be most appropriate? Are there any occasions when talk should be more authoritative?

Recommended reading

DfES (2003) *Speaking, Listening, Learning: Working with Children in Key Stages 1 and 2*. London: DfES Publications. Also available at http://www.standards.dfes.gov.uk/literacy/publications/

Chapters 8 and 9 in Howe *et al.* (2005) *Teaching Science 5–11: A Guide for Teachers*. London: David Fulton

References

Alexander, R.J. (2004) *Towards Dialogic Teaching: Rethinking Classroom Talk*. Cambridge: Dialogos UK

ASE (Association for Science Education) (2000) *STAR* Science, Technology and Reading – A Resource for Teachers*. Hatfield: ASE Publications

Cave, K., Oxfam and Wulfsohn, G. (2003) *One child, One seed*. London: Frances Lincoln Publishers

DfEE (1999) *The National Curriculum. Handbook for Primary Schools*. London: DfEE

Duschl, R.A. and Osborne, J. (2002) 'Supporting and promoting argumentation discourse in science education', *Studies in Science Education*, 38, 39–72

Dust, K. (1999) *Motive, Means and Opportunity: Creativity Research Review*. London: NESTA

Feasey, R. (2005) *Creative Science: Achieving the WOW Factor with 5–11 year olds*. London: David Fulton

Harlen, W. and Qualter A. (2004) *The Teaching of Science in Primary Schools* (4th edn). London: David Fulton

Howe, A. (2004) 'Science is creative' *Primary Science Review* No 81, 14

Howe, A., Davies, D., McMahon, K., Towler, L. and Scott, T. (2005) *Teaching Science 5–11: A Guide for Teachers*. London: David Fulton

James, S. (1998) *Dear Greenpeace*. London: Walker Books

Koestler, A. (1964) *The Act of Creation*. London: Hutchinson

Lemke, J. (1990) *Talking Science: Language, Learning and Values*. New Jersey: Ablex Publishing Corporation

Marshall, B., Harrison, C., Lee, C., Wiliam, D. and Black, P. (2003) *Assessment for Learning: Putting it into Practice*. Milton Keynes: Open University Press

McMahon, K. and Davies, D. (2001) 'Literacy and numeracy in science', in S. Alsop and K. Hicks (eds) *Teaching Science – A Handbook for Primary and Secondary School Teachers*. London: Kogan Page

Mercer, N. (2000) *Words and Minds: How We Use Language to Think Together*. London and New York: Routledge

Mortimer, E. and Scott, P. (2003) *Making Meaning in Secondary Science Lessons*. Maidenhead: Open University Press

Naylor, S. and Keogh, B. (2000) *Concept Cartoons in Science Education*. Sandbach: Millgate House Publishers

O'Keefe, G. (1939) cited in N. Callaway (ed.) (1987) *One Hundred Flowers*. New York/New Jersey: Callaway/Wings Books

Ollerenshaw, C. and Ritchie, R. (1997) *Primary Science: Making It Work* (2nd edn). London: David Fulton

Patten, B. (1986) *Gargling with Jelly*. London: Puffin Books

Qualifications and Curriculum Authority (QCA) (2003) *Creativity: Find it, Promote it*. London: QCA

Creative teaching and learning in 'Materials and their Properties'

Chris Collier

It is a slightly arresting notion that if you were to pick yourself apart with tweezers, one atom at a time, you would produce a mound of fine atomic dust, none of which had ever been alive but all of which had once been you.

(Bill Bryson 2003: 1)

Introduction

From the day a child is born he or she will have a strong desire to find out about the material world: chewing and sucking a toy; splashing in the bath; cuddling up to a soft teddy or a softer mum or dad; dropping toys and listening to the satisfactory noises they make when they hit the hard floor; 'finger painting' with food on their high chair tray. All these experiences provide playful means of finding out about the material world in which we live. When the child leaves the safety of their home another world of materials opens before them:

Each piece of wood, each pebble, and each fruit will have a unique shape, colour and texture to explore . . . the toddler squeezing mud through his fingers in the garden or crunching through leaves in the park is exploring natural materials.

(Howe 2004: 1)

Once children arrive in school they will continue to enjoy activities that allow them to play with, explore and come to understand some of the properties of the materials. Their questions will give rise to investigations that will focus on how the material looks, feels, how it behaves, how it can be changed.

As children enter 'National Curriculum' science, 'Materials and their Properties' *might* sound like an exciting topic for science; on the other hand, the study of inanimate objects *could* lead to a rather dull and unengaging science lesson. How should teachers build on children's natural curiosity and interest in their world through formal learning in science?

One way to think about a creative science lesson is to first think of the opposite – what would a boring lesson be like? The teacher might have identified a learning objective from the National Curriculum – let's say Sc3 1c *'Pupils should recognise and name common types of materials'*. This objective could be met by a well-designed worksheet where children match pictures of material with a word bank of their names – glass, paper, metal etc. After an explanation the children can complete the worksheet. This is a safe and simple way for most children to demonstrate that they have reached the objective. How would a 'creative' teacher approach the same task? How would she plan a lesson to allow for children's own creativity to be developed and applied? It is important to recognise here that teaching for creativity is more difficult and challenging than playing safe. A creative teacher is one that will have to take a few risks. Creative teaching has been described as a high-risk strategy requiring self-confidence and an investment of time and energy (Yeomans 1996). Creative teachers have been described as 'planning geniuses, innovators and experimenters' (Woods 1996). Teachers rarely describe themselves as 'geniuses', however, and it may be in the present educational climate that they are understandably averse to taking risks. To answer the question posed and enable the reader to present a new version of the lesson on materials that can claim to be creative, we will need to consider the possibilities open to a primary teacher.

In this chapter we shall discuss how teachers might take a few planned risks in their approach to teaching the science of materials, and in so doing hopefully make life and learning a little more interesting and satisfying.

Progressing from play to investigations

An aspect of teaching in the Foundation Stage is to encourage children's learning through exploratory play activities. Providing a range of stimulating resources and settings promotes understanding that is centred on the child's enquiries. The direction the activity will take is uncertain at its beginning, and the outcomes will be as many as there are children who engage in it. Truly this is teaching for creativity; teaching which encourages creative learning. From play-based activities there is a clear progression to more formal ways of applying science enquiry skills to answer questions. This progression usually happens through the primary school where children progress from *unstructured exploration* to more *systematic investigation* of a question using everyday language to using scientific vocabulary and symbols (DfEE/QCA 1998: 69). Let's not restrict exploratory play to only the Foundation Stage, however. This progression could occur during a single KS1 or 2 lesson or unit of work, where children would begin with exploratory play with materials and move on, when they are ready, to consider more formal scientific enquiry.

Examples of exploratory play include:

- Provide decorator's paintbrushes, hot and cold water. Invite the children to paint large-scale pictures on a concrete wall or patio. Take some digital photos of their work and observe what happens to them over the next 10 minutes. This could be tried in a shady area and a sunny one, or horizontal and vertical surfaces.

- A balloon or rubber glove filled with water, as large as possible, and frozen will immediately focus attention and give rise to questions: 'What will happen if we leave it in the classroom?', 'How long will it take to melt?', 'How can we make it melt more slowly?' Put the ice-balloons or sculptures on a plastic sheet or tray – what happens next?

- Let children play with a magnetic construction kit that has been supplemented with other bits and pieces – some metal, some not. Can they incorporate the other items into their models or structures?

- Provide brown and white sugar, flour, salt and water and clean cooking utensils. Ask one group to make a mixture or solution. Ask another group to use all their senses to identify the ingredients used.

- Allow children to explore a collection of inflatable objects, e.g. balloons, balls, beach toys, airbed, tyres, even an inflatable dinghy, and the different equipment we use to inflate them. Some can be punctured, children comparing these with unpunctured objects.

The intention of providing open-ended opportunities such as these is firstly to allow children to gain further first-hand experiences with the materials that will form part of the investigation. Secondly, by taking part in an open-ended activity there will be thinking time and freedom for some question raising and creative thinking during the activity. It is now recognised that we do need to give children more time to think rather than rush them into doing without thought (Claxton 2002). Observations and questions can be collected as children talk and think – by jotting them down on post-it notes as the play develops or having a 'feedback' or review session at an appropriate moment. As we get older we can think more abstractly and play with ideas, rather than materials, but even many adults need some material resources to get them started.

Planning for creativity: big ideas about materials

At the heart of our plans for teaching should be the notion that we are contributing to children's learning in a way that allows them to gain an understanding of the big ideas in science. By so doing teachers may feel some sense of the importance of the

Table 8.1 The big ideas about materials

Key idea from the National Curriculum	Big science idea	How Key Stage 1 and 2 can contribute to children's understanding
Changing materials	**Conservation of matter** Stuff can change, but matter isn't created or destroyed.	Pupils get a range of experiences of physical and chemical changes. Commonly chemical change is studied in the context of cooking but may also include burning, rusting and decay of organic matter (Millar and Osborne 1998). Physical change is studied by melting, solidifying, evaporating and condensing a range of substances, often water.
Classifying materials and separating mixtures of materials	**Particle theory** Things are made of tiny particles.	Through activities that involve separating materials, pupils begin to develop ideas about the small size of particles of substances which can pass through filters and sieves.
Grouping and classifying materials	**Particle theory** The properties of materials can be explained by the kind of particles that make it up and how they are joined together.	Initially, sorting and classifying games can introduce children to the wide variety of materials that exist, and they will build up a vocabulary for talking about properties. They will apply this to discussing differences between solids, liquids and gases, and can use kinaesthetic models to understand the behaviour of particles.

subject, and children will be gaining relevant experiences, which satisfy their curiosity and equip them for life. Throughout this chapter many approaches to teaching materials will be discussed, and these will draw on the ideas outlined in Table 8.1.

Planning for creativity: creative connections

A productive definition of creativity is 'making connections between previously unconnected ideas' (Koestler 1964). 'Connection making' can occur at a number of levels in learning and teaching:

- curriculum subjects;
- topics of study within a subject;

- pupils' lives and experiences in and out of school;
- the school and the community.

Connecting curriculum subjects

One effective way to achieve a connection between subjects is to base planning around a theme, which also gives children's learning a meaningful context. Cooking is one such theme which links well with many aspects of the primary curriculum for materials, and provides many opportunities for connections to be made to other areas of the curriculum such as recipe texts in literacy, measuring volumes and time in numeracy, and festivals and special events such as Pancake Day in RE.

Topics of study within a subject

The daily classroom experience of many primary teachers is a science curriculum divided into topics (Howe *et al.* 2005). However, these divisions are somewhat artificial, which makes it all the more important to develop meaningful links between topics. As the study of materials is fundamental to just about every facet of science, it is not hard to forge these links across the whole science curriculum. Even so, there are some topics which seem to lend themselves particularly to a cross-topic approach. For example, discovering what happens to light when it meets another material teaches children about transparency, translucency and opaqueness, plus reflection, shadow formation and colour. Also, investigating the breakdown of foods as they pass down the body's digestive system allows children to explore the idea of materials being broken down by mechanical action (teeth) then by chemical action (digestive juices). Some parts of our food cannot be broken down and digested, and this is also worth considering.

Connecting pupils' lives and experiences in and out of school

Teachers can make learning motivating and meaningful by choosing contexts that are relevant to children's lives outside school. Food is of course something that most children find relevant and motivating. In planning to use such contexts, it is all too easy to get 'carried away' with lots of ideas which, rather than becoming connected, become disjointed. A way to ensure that does not happen is to bear in mind the key concept that the activities planned are intended to develop. Table 8.2 shows one way how key concepts and contexts can be linked.

The school and the community

The study of materials provides many opportunities to focus on citizenship and sustainability issues. A visit from a waste recycling education officer or a visit to a recycling site allows children to explore what happens to their waste. Experiments

Table 8.2 Links to the theme of food

Key concept	Links to the theme of food
Substances can exist as solids, liquids or gases.	It is easy to find examples of foods that are solids and liquids, but harder to make connections with gases. However, fizzy drinks are a good starting point, as is the action of yeast during baking, the dough expanding as gas produced by the yeast is trapped within it. Gas production by yeast can also be demonstrated by mixing it in a bottle with sugar and warm water then tightly fixing a balloon over the neck of the bottle. Left in a warm place, the carbon dioxide produced as the yeast feeds on the sugar will cause the balloon to inflate.
Freezing and melting are reversible changes.	Making ice-lollies or ice cream has clear links with this concept. Other items can be frozen and defrosted too – ask children what they think would happen to milk, butter, sugar and air (in a balloon) in a freezer. What happens when things that are solid at room temperature are gently heated?
Evaporation and condensation are reversible changes.	At the same time as boiling an egg, an informative discussion can be based around the steamed-up windows. Where has all the extra water come from?
Dissolving is a reversible change.	Given a range of sugars (muscovado, demerara, icing sugar, granulated, cubes etc.), which one dissolves the fastest, and what does each look like once the process is reversed by evaporating off the liquid into which each dissolved?
Mixtures and solutions can be separated.	Separating materials lends itself to a problem-solving type of scientific enquiry, e.g. an accident in the kitchen has mixed up the rice with lentils and coffee; how might we sort each from the others?
Chemical changes are not reversible.	Much of cooking changes food in a way that cannot be reversed. How slices of bread change in relation to the temperature and length of time they are exposed to heat can be displayed by creating a toast colour chart. For a spectacular change, make popcorn.

can be set up that investigate which materials break down and which are not biodegradable. Bury a selection of waste packaging, and then examine their decay over a series of weeks.

Planning for creativity: adapting the QCA Scheme of Work

In other chapters we advocate adapting the National Scheme of Work for Science at Key Stages 1 and 2 (DfEE/QCA 1998) so it offers more opportunities for children's creativity to thrive. Changes to the scheme are prompted by a wish for the children to learn in a 'creative ecosystem' (Harrington 1990) which we note in Chapter 9 has some of these characteristics:

- stimulation (motivating starting points);
- opportunities for 'play' (exploring before investigating);
- easy access to resources (together with a degree of choice over resources);
- mentors and role models (opportunities for children to collaborate);
- information (scientific skills and concepts directly taught);
- open-ended assignments (fewer predetermined outcomes).

Many of the ways these characteristics could be developed by teaching the study of materials creatively will be considered by other parts of this chapter. Here we will show how the QCA Scheme of Work could be adapted so that it provides children with motivating starting points.

Children's interest will be captured by carefully choosing collections which have a theme relevant to them. We need to give careful consideration to liquids and gases, as well as solid objects. Examples of the collections that could be used at the start of Unit 1C *Sorting and using materials* or Unit 2D *Grouping and changing materials* include:

- parts of a bicycle – inner tube, tyre, saddle, handlebar grips, oily chain, wheel, spokes, reflectors;
- foods and their packaging – drinks in plastic bottles, paper wrappers, cardboard cartons, metal tea and coffee caddies;
- bath time – sponge, soap, towel, toys, shampoo, bubble makers, shower gels, perfumes and aftershave ('smellies');
- contents of the teacher's bag – including maybe a bottle of water, and hair spray;
- smelly balloons – when an essence is put in a balloon, some of it seeps through. Choose smells with which children may be familiar.

An alternative way to start Unit 3C *Characteristics of materials* is by presenting collections that illustrate how an object can be made out of a range of materials but fit the same purpose. For example, a collection of 'drinking vessels' (an eclectic collection is usually to be found in the staffroom) can be used to encourage children to look closely at the variation in terms of transparency, thickness, shiny-ness, hardness, flexibility and thermal insulation properties.

Teaching creatively in Materials and their Properties

In Chapter 2, it was suggested that there are ten approaches to teaching creatively. Each of these points is now considered in the area of materials.

1. Turning predictable outcomes into something better

Knowing what will happen at the start of a scientific enquiry is bound to limit its appeal. However, by carefully adapting such investigations, the seemingly mundane becomes far more interesting.

As an example, consider the learning outcome, 'children will recognise that objects that are attracted to magnets are made of metal'. It is quite possible the activity to support this outcome may involve providing children with a range of magnets, and they can sort a number of objects using their magnet. However, with a bit of forethought, the means by which children arrive at this outcome can be made into an opportunity for creative learning.

One approach is to develop children's understanding by making them apply their knowledge to developing a game. In the example above, children could make a racing game with a track to follow using magnets, or a fishing game with rods and magnets. Alternatively, children may be challenged to make a device for picking up a spillage of paper clips, paper fasteners, staples and ball bearings. Can children separate them by their choice of magnet and the way they use it?

Another approach is to pay attention to children's alternative ideas in science. For example, we know that children may think that all metals are attracted to magnets. By carefully selecting a range of metals for testing (iron and steel are magnetic but most metals e.g. aluminium are not), the teacher can promote some conflict in the learner's mind and encourage them to restructure their ideas. Even if objects look the same they can behave differently – some one- and two-pence coins are magnetic while others are not. The reason some coins are magnetic is because they are made of steel, which is magnetic, rather than bronze, which is not. In 1992, the Royal Mint started to produce pennies and twopences made of copper-plated steel instead of bronze.

2. Making the ordinary fascinating

Just how amazing the materials are which surround us is often lost on us, and it serves us well to be reminded of how fascinating they can be. One approach is to concentrate on one material and study its complexity and beauty in more detail. Alternatively, we could study the processes that alter the property and nature of materials.

Glass is something which we take for granted, yet it is incredible stuff. Is it a solid or a liquid, a question which still troubles material scientists? Does it really flow at room temperature so that ancient panes of glass are thicker at the bottom than the top? Probably not, but the research into this goes on (see www.cmog.org). As we discussed in the chapter on early years, scientists tend to be interested in things we don't yet understand. Realising we don't know everything about what we take for granted illustrates how we continue to learn more about the world and how new discoveries are there to be made.

We want to convey a sense of fascination in the ordinary by valuing children's explorations of commonplace materials and also give children a feeling that they are finding out things that interest them. We want them to create their own curriculum within the narrow range of materials provided, so the teacher places children's ideas at the heart of planning.

But first we need to stimulate their interest. A starting point is to make a collection of glass objects, possibly as a table-top display so that the variety and splendour of it are revealed. Paperweights, magnifying lenses, tumblers, mirrors, opaque glass, coloured glass and objects with fibre optics as part of them will serve as a reminder of glass's versatility to the teacher and a stimulus for children, although we will need to be careful to follow correct health and safety procedures. We may wish to include objects that are transparent but are made from other materials. Changing the lighting of the display, maybe by altering its colour or direction, stimulates further interest. Children could be encouraged to bring in their own objects to add to the collection (carefully and with the help of an adult), and question boards will serve as a starting point for further work. Questions raised by children can be investigated further, an approach which acknowledges children's ideas and allows them to create their own focus for further learning.

Some materials such as glass need only a little help to stimulate children's interest, others such as soil seem less promising, yet even a scoop of this can be fascinating if stirred into water in a large, clear jar and allowed to settle over the space of a few hours. Magically the variety and colour of different grain sizes are revealed as the soil sinks to form graded beds. Maybe some parts of the soil will float. Again, a table-top display with children being encouraged to bring in their own soil samples and ask their own questions forms the spark for future work.

Just as seemingly prosaic materials can be made to inspire wonder, everyday processes can also be marvelled at. Many of the processes which form part of the science curriculum's strand on materials and their properties can inspire wonder. A few examples include:

- Evaporation – watching water vapour rise from a body of hot water becomes fascinating when illuminated from the front. On a cold day, clothes drying on a washing line beautifully illustrate the process in action and an interesting comparison can be made between light- and dark-coloured clothes, and between those washed in hot water and cold water.

- Freezing – time-lapse photography of frost forming on the branch of a tree showing ice crystals forming in minute detail. Easier to observe might be the reverse process as a severe overnight frost thaws during the morning. Are there any areas that thaw more quickly than others?

- Burning – detailed observation of a lit candle, encouraging children to study the changes in the flame, wick and wax. Do different sized or coloured candles produce different flames? What happens when the candle is extinguished?

Another approach is to study the processes that have manufactured materials which we take for granted. It may be possible to re-create some of these processes in the classroom; for others, it may be necessary to refer to secondary sources of information. For example, to study the process of paper manufacturing from raw materials, secondary sources of information are needed, but making paper from recycled materials can be done in the classroom.

3. Sharing a sense of wonder

Advances in scientific research have led us to comprehend in greater depth the nature of matter and the way materials behave. There are many examples we could consider that help us appreciate the scientific ingenuity that led to us a more complete understanding of the nature of materials and the way they behave. We could review the significant advances that have been made in a particular aspect of material science, and at the same time we could study the work of famous material scientists.

If we look at how human understanding of matter has changed through time, it provides a powerful way of teaching about states of matter. Beginning with the knowledge shown in classical times in ancient Greece, discussions could develop about children's understanding of the nature of matter. The Greeks' view that all things are made from the four basic elements, fire, earth, air and water, can be compared with our understanding of solids (earth), liquids (water) and gases (air), leading to a discussion on the nature of fire.

As a successor to the earlier classical theories on the nature of matter, the scientific periodic table of elements could be studied through the work of Dmitri Mendeleyev, who created its first version. Children in the primary school classroom do not need to go into great detail, but the important aspect of his work and the one most relevant to them refers back to their own sorting and classifying activities. They could begin to make their own simple 'periodic' tables by first of all sorting a range of objects into two categories, such as metallic and non-metallic, progressing to Carroll diagrams. Further work on classification on the basis of properties with a range of values leads to more sophisticated sorting diagrams. Where would Coca-cola, thick shake, tomato sauce, honey and sweet and sour sauce be placed in a table which sorted for sweetness on one axis and viscosity on the other?

Of course, there are many, many other important scientific pieces of work that have led to advances in our understanding of the material. One difficulty for teachers is making these accessible for children, but this may be done by considering the work of famous scientists that have helped mankind. For example, and with sensitivity to children's feelings, we can discuss what happens at hospital if we are admitted with a broken arm or leg, leading to a class discussion about X-ray machines. An activity that might extend children's appreciation of X-rays is to make a collage picture that can only be seen when held up to the light.

4. Seeing differently

Once children's initial interest has been stimulated, maybe by an imaginative display, or by being given an opportunity to study an interesting object or process, the creative teacher considers how to maintain this curiosity by carefully selecting additional resources that encourage detailed observation and questioning. For example, with a little forethought, a range of candles of different colours and sizes will further encourage detailed observation. Modern technology can be made available to help children's study, by capturing on video and reviewing frame-by-frame a candle being extinguished.

A digital camera is another ICT application which supports children to look further, especially when it is used in conjunction with magnifying aids. When comparing the properties of a range of jumpers, children may discover that there are differences in the way each feels and looks. Capturing a digital image through a magnifying lens will reveal how the weave of fabrics can vary enormously, and begin to explain why each fabric has different qualities. Having an electronic image of their observations allows children to present their findings to others, which helps them share the way they look at things, providing an opportunity for children to learn new ways of observing from each other.

5. Maximising opportune moments

It is a challenge to primary teachers in all areas of learning to make their teaching relevant to children. Earlier we considered how we could relate advances in scientific understanding in such a way as to allow children to see how they have benefited from the work of scientists. Another way of making our teaching relevant to children is responding to current events, one obvious example being what is happening in the news and another being the weather. One requirement of this style of teaching is having the flexibility to alter short-term plans at short notice, in response to events such as the weather or the news. Another is having ready access to resources.

After a fall of snow overnight, why not consider how humans keep warm, and the thermal insulation properties of cold-weather clothing? When the early morning dew on the playground is being 'burnt off' by the sun, it would be an appropriate time to discuss the way water changes from liquid to gas. On a bright, spring afternoon as the sun streams through the classroom windows it would seem the ideal time to discuss the most suitable fabric for making a blind. In the depths of winter when it is almost dark at the time children go home, consider studying the reflective properties of materials. A day of heavy rain lends itself to studying waterproof properties of a range of materials used to make umbrellas. After a very cold night there are opportunities to discuss why some roofs keep their covering of frost while on others it has disappeared. Is it something to do with the direction these houses face, or do some houses keep the heat in better than others?

When responding to events in the news, one problem faced by teachers is finding items that primary children might find accessible. A possible way to begin is to listen to news reports that are intended for children, such as the BBC television programme *Newsround* or its website (see www.bbc.co.uk/cbbcnews). Often the main issues that are making the news and that also draw on parts of the materials curriculum are the environment and sustainability. It may be the case that by studying these news items children 'begin to think about the positive and negative effects of scientific and technological developments on the environment and in other contexts' (DfEE/QCA 1999: 21).

6. Humanising science

One approach that can help children understand how science has had an impact on their lives is to consider the nature of everyday materials. This could be developed so that consideration is given to how knowledge of materials is required in a variety of occupations that are not immediately thought of as scientific.

Waterproof clothing

A problem-solving enquiry that is commonly carried out in the primary school classroom is to make a coat for a teddy bear. This can be a good starting point for further study of the way manufacturers design and make waterproof clothing. With research of secondary sources of information, children may consider in more detail why a particular fabric or fabrics need to be chosen. Does the coat keep water out, and does it keep teddy warm? Can both of these be achieved with only one fabric or will teddy need a layered coat, and if so, which material goes on the outside? Finally, if the coat is going to sell, its look needs to be considered. Can materials be chosen which are attractive as well as functional?

Wood

Wood is relatively strong, hard and aesthetically pleasing to look at, feel and smell, qualities which are appreciated by those who work with it; wood-carvers, furniture makers and builders among others. Comparing wood from different trees by studying their structure in close-up reveals a range of textures. Softwoods from coniferous trees have far less prominent pores compared to the wood from some hardwood trees such as oak and ash. There are also differences in the hardness of wood, and its strength. Taking all of these into consideration, children can start to select wood fit for a purpose. Which would make the best furniture, or which would be good for making kindling, or a chopping board, or a shove ha-penny board? Inviting people who use wood in their job into the classroom to talk about their work is an opportunity for children to make the connection between the property of a material and its use.

Fire

When studying fire, a starting point is to discuss what is needed for it to begin: combustible matter such as paper, wood and gasoline; a combustive agent such as oxygen in air; an activation agent such as a spark or heat. Then the work of fire fighters can be introduced. They extinguish fires by suppressing the availability of combustible matter, asphyxiating the fire or cooling it by spraying it with water. It may be that the local fire brigade have an education officer who can visit the classroom to talk about their work and fire safety in general.

First-hand experience of fire can be gained in the primary classroom by close observation of a lit candle in a sand tray stimulating a range of questions, e.g. Why does the nightlight go out after all the wax is used up? What happens to the flame when it is covered by a snuffer?

Ice cream

Before the advent of refrigeration systems ice cream was something of a luxury. In the winter large blocks of ice were cut from lakes and stored in holes in the ground, insulated with straw. Ice cream was made in a large bowl surrounded by the ice. Today we use refrigerators which are usually powered by electricity. Studying the change of liquid to solid in the context of ice cream is particularly motivating, maybe by discovering the quality of ice cream produced when the liquid is undisturbed compared to when it is stirred at frequent intervals. More challenging is to consider why a fridge warms the air around it yet cools objects within it. Even noticing that this is happening is important for primary school children.

7. Valuing questions

Being able to raise questions is an important scientific skill recognised by the National Curriculum. By organising games that challenge children to sort and classify materials, many opportunities are provided for children to practise this skill. A collection of games that can be played are shown in Table 8.3.

8. Modelling explanations

One way that the differences between solids, liquids and gases can be modelled is by drama. During the activity pupils represent the atoms in a substance and their arrangement and behaviour change as the state of the substance changes. The teacher could tell the children how they should be arranged to show the structure of solids, liquids and gases but it may create a more interesting and stimulating activity if the starting point is children being told how a solid behaves and then they choose to represent it in their own way. So, at first they show a solid, which has particles vibrating about a fixed position and in such a way that they cannot move around. An important feature of their model will be the way they show that solids have a fixed shape and volume.

Table 8.3   Sorting and classifying games that support question raising

Guess which object
Present children with a collection of objects, and choose one of these, but do not reveal which it is. Children ask questions based on various criteria to try to discover which object it is, e.g. is it made from metal? If the answer is yes, remove all objects which are not metallic and ask further questions on those that are left. Only allow yes or no answers. Choose a child to select the object while others try to find out which one has been selected.

Mystery object
Place one object from the collection into a box or bag without the children seeing which it is. Pass the box around, encouraging the children to feel, shake, listen or smell it, and give them an opportunity to ask a question about the box's contents. Continue until the object is identified.

Spot the criterion
Split the class into groups and give each group a small collection, a sheet of sugar paper and a felt-tip pen. Ask each group to to devise three questions which could be used to sort the collection and record these on the paper. They then sort the group using a fourth question but without recording it this time. Each group moves to the next collection and tries to guess the final question thought of by the previous group. They record their own question and find another way of sorting the objects and leave it for the next group.

Making a key
Children work in small groups with a collection of objects, a piece of sugar paper and a coloured pencil. Ask them to develop an identification key using yes/no questions. Groups evaluate each other's keys by moving around, trying each one out.

(Adapted from Howe *et al.* 2005: 37)

Next, the solid is heated by an imaginary heat source and it melts. Children now need to represent a liquid. Particles vibrate faster so that particles are still closely bonded but are able to slide around each other. They need to show that liquids fit the shape of the container they are in, even when they are poured from one container to another. However, the volume of the liquid remains unaltered.

As further imaginary heat is applied, the particles of the liquid move around so quickly that they escape from its surface. At this point children are modelling the process of evaporation, which changes the substance into a gas. They are challenged to show particles of gas moving very quickly, filling all the space of the container, and, as they have no fixed shape or volume, they are further challenged to show what happens to them when they are squeezed into a smaller space.

After discussing the reversible nature of the physical processes they have acted out (melting/solidifying, evaporating/condensing), children can develop their understanding of the behaviour of particles by being asked to apply their knowledge to a series of activities (see Table 8.4). Children try out the activity first, consider the questions, and explain their ideas through drama, with one child acting as narrator.

Table 8.4 Activities for exploring particles

Activity	Questions
Observation of an air freshener	What do you notice when the cover of the air freshener is opened?
Put ice cubes into a screw-top jar. Dry the outside of the jar and leave for 15 minutes. Observe the water vapour (condensation) which forms on the outside of the jar.	Why do you think this has happened?
Observe jelly cubes inside a sealed plastic bag placed in a dish of hot water.	What is happening to the jelly? What will happen to it if it is left to cool?
Seal three plastic syringes, one containing air, the second water and the third sand.	What happens when you press down the plunger of each syringe? What are your explanations?

(Adapted from Johnson and Scott 1990 and reproduced in Howe *et al.* 2005: 46)

9. Encouraging autonomy

What might the creative teacher do to encourage children to explore autonomously? One approach is to allow children freedom to begin their enquiries with exploratory play-type activities. Maybe some resources will be provided by the teacher but others may be available for children to select if required. From this starting point children can follow their own lines of enquiry. Resources need to be chosen carefully by the teacher so they stimulate children's curiosity.

At the outset, the direction an activity is going to take may not be at all obvious. Consequently this style of teaching will place demands on a teacher's subject knowledge, but there are ways to cope with this. Maybe the activity can be used solely to raise questions that can be investigated further in subsequent sessions once the teacher has done more research. Alternatively, good secondary sources of information can be on hand, and children can be encouraged to find out more for themselves.

Below are some ways that children may be encouraged to develop their own lines of enquiry.

Water tray

At the start of exploratory play a range of containers of different shapes and sizes are provided in the water tray, along with a measuring beaker. Children's play could follow a number of routes, generating a great number of ideas for future investigation: What happens to light when it passes through a column of water? Why does the empty bottle pop back up to the surface when I let go of it under water? When I blow on the end of the bottle, why does the sound change as I alter the amount of water in the bottle? The creative teacher acknowledges all these questions, and could challenge the child to find out more to do with light, forces and sound. Likewise, when a child questions if there is the same amount of water when it is transferred from a tall, thin bottle to a short, fat one, the teacher has the resources available for the child to explore this further.

Shadow puppets

Given a range of shadow puppets, a screen and a source of light, children will soon be exploring the properties of materials. Some allow light to pass through, others only allow some light to pass through, casting grey or coloured shadows, and some materials will block all light Supplying a range of materials (transparent, translucent and opaque) will encourage them to go further, maybe by making their own shadow puppet. As the activity progresses the teacher may want to intervene with questions such as:

> Why have you chosen this material for your puppet?
>
> Can you explain why you are colouring in your puppet?
>
> What materials make a really good shadow puppet?

Soils

While playing with water and soil, children may be raising a number of questions:

> Where did the water disappear to when it was poured on the dry soil?
>
> What happens as I add more water?
>
> What sort of things float and which sink?

By investigating these further, children will start to build up simple theoretical models of soil that start to explain their observations. The teacher may ask questions which encourage children to reflect on their thoughts and help them make further sense of their findings. By asking the right questions, which stems from having a sound knowledge of the subject, the teacher is able to extend a child's learning.

10. Allowing for flexible beginnings

We have already mentioned the need for beginnings which allow children to explore their own ideas, and how we need to take advantage of unplanned opportunities. By doing both of these, we will be teaching materials from many different starting points. It may also be advantageous to look for opportunities to explore aspects of the curriculum on materials in other subject areas.

Summary of main points

Teaching the topic of materials in a way that engages children draws on a teacher's creativity because it can end up as a study of collections of rather dull, uninteresting objects. Yet we have seen that we can bring the topic to life in a number of ways, such as making the starting point of the lesson memorable. We could consider the work of great material scientists, or the material science that underpins the work of people in everyday occupations. Maybe most important of all is to think about the objects and phenomena we find interesting, since it is likely this interest will be shared by children too.

Issues for reflection

- It is suggested by Feasey (2005: 30) that 'critical thinking underpins creativity'. Have you seen examples of reasons and evidence being used to support conclusions by children in the primary classroom?

- What experience do you have of children being given the freedom to set up their own tasks? Did practical considerations in some way restrict the degree of freedom children were allowed?

Discussion points

- To what extent does the National Curriculum stimulate creative teaching in this topic, and in what ways does it inhibit it?

- Are there aspects of good practice in Foundation Stage teaching which could influence the way the topic of materials is taught in Key Stage 2?

Recommended reading

Chapter 2 in Howe *et al.* (2005) *Science 5–11: A Guide for Teachers*. London: David Fulton

References

Bryson, B. (2003) *A Short History of Nearly Everything*. London: Doubleday

Claxton, G. (2002) *Building Learning Power: Helping Young People Become Better Learners*. London: TLO

Department for Education and Employment (DfEE)/Qualifications and Curriculum Authority (QCA) (1998) *A Scheme of Work for Key Stages 1 and 2 Science*. London: QCA Publications

Department for Education and Employment (DfEE)/Qualifications and Curriculum Authority (QCA) (1999) *The National Curriculum for England: Science*. London: DfEE/QCA

Feasey, R. (2005) *Creative Science: Achieving the WOW factor with 5–11 year olds*. London: David Fulton

Harrington, D. (1990) 'The ecology of human creativity: a psychological perspective', in M. Runco and R. Albert (eds) *Theories of Creativity*. London: Sage Publications

Howe, A. (2004) *Play Using Natural Materials*. London: David Fulton

Howe, A., Davies, D., McMahon, K., Towler, L. and Scott, T. (2005) *Science 5–11: A Guide for Teachers.* London: David Fulton

Johnson, K. and Scott, P. (1990) *Children's Learning in Science Projects: Interactive Teaching in Science – Workshops for Training Courses.* Hatfield: ASE

Koestler, A. (1964) *The Act of Creation.* London: Hutchinson

Millar, R and Osborne, J. (eds) (1998) *Beyond 2000: Science Education for the Future.* London: King's College

Woods, P. (1996) 'The good times, creative teaching in primary school', *Education 3–13*, June

Yeomans, M. (1996) 'Creativity in art and science: a personal view', *Journal of Art and Design Education*, 15 (3), 241–50

Websites

www.bbc.co.uk/cbbcnews – newsround
www.cmog.org – the Corning Museum of Glass

Creative teaching and learning in 'Physical Processes'

Dan Davies

The secret to creativity is knowing how to hide your sources.

(Albert Einstein)

More than 15 years since primary science curricula were first introduced into all four home nations, what is now needed is a greater focus on sparking children's interest and enthusiasm, developing their skills and understanding, and giving them a sense of the relevance of science to their everyday lives.

(Wellcome Trust 2005)

Introduction

Recent research suggests that children in their last year of primary school are not enjoying science lessons as much as they did a decade ago (Ruddock *et al.* 2004). This is a sad indictment of a science curriculum at upper primary level driven by external assessment – Key Stage 2 Statutory Attainment Tests (SATS) were introduced in 1996. If children are not enjoying science they are much less likely to engage with it as an area of study and reach that totally absorbed state Csikszentmihalyi (2002) refers to as 'being in the flow'; a key characteristic of creativity. So to re-energise children's creativity in scientific learning, we as teachers need to inspire them with some creativity of our own. Physical processes – forces, electricity, sound, light and space – despite being associated with our 'fear of physics', offer us the opportunity of putting some of the 'Wow! factor' back into our teaching. The seemingly magical behaviour of magnets and light, the spectacular flight of 'stomp rockets' and the harmonious movement of the celestial spheres can all be harnessed to promote more exciting and engaging lessons. This chapter sets out to suggest a few ways of bringing familiar elements together in unfamiliar ways to stimulate children's creativity in their developing understanding of physical processes. Einstein's own work on the Special Theory of Relativity, celebrating its hundredth birthday in 2005, demonstrates this exquisitely. Faced with the conundrum that the speed of light is the same wherever it is measured – on a speeding train or standing 'still' – Einstein postulated that it is actually time and space (previously regarded as separate and immutable qualities of the universe) that are really part of the same essence and must change, depending on where you look at them from (your 'frame of reference'). Whilst as teachers of science we may not always demonstrate such exceptional creativity, we need to remember that teaching is one of the 'creative professions' (Howe *et al.* 2001), and that to teach for creativity we need firstly to teach creatively (NACCCE 1999). The first two-thirds of this chapter focuses on teaching for children's creativity, whilst the final section considers how we might teach physical processes creatively.

Time, space and resources

(Johnston 2005: 96) claims that 'creative science educational experiences have three essential elements: they should be practical, memorable and interactive'. In order to create such experiences within the limitations of the school timetable and teachers' levels of confidence and energy requires thoughtful use of time, space and resources. Let us start with time; science curriculum time in English primary schools reduced from around 20 per cent to 10 per cent over the 1990s (OfSTED 1999) and the introduction of National Literacy and Numeracy Strategies further relegated it to an 'afternoon' subject in many schools. Recently, primary teachers have been encouraged to think more flexibly with the curriculum (OfSTED 2002, 2003; DfES 2003), including a return to more cross-curricular approaches. In a recent survey (Wellcome Trust 2005) 40 per cent of primary teachers said they often integrated science with other subjects, and 54 per cent did so occasionally.

Use of time: cross-curricular approaches

For example, in the topic of sound, obvious links can be made with both music and literacy. There is a lot of scope for having fun with sounds when putting sound effects and background noises to a story or play. Children enjoy exploring the qualities of sound to create a certain atmosphere or to describe the movement of an animal or character. A good starting point for this might be to listen to a recording of Prokofiev's 'Peter and the Wolf', in which every character has a different theme tune, or to watch an episode of *Scooby Doo* in which sound effects are used to create atmospheres of fear or suspense. Children could discuss the choice of sounds for each effect – why do we associate certain sounds (e.g. 'creaking') with particular emotions? We can also link sound with PE, perhaps by 'being' air particles oscillating backwards and forwards to show sound travelling, or in the unusual context of a swimming lesson, listening to the differences between sounds above and below water level.

Another link with PE and dance is provided by the topic of forces. A theme where children are using their own bodies can lend itself to a performance as the mode of communication for their findings. They might develop a dance or sequence that involves 'two pushes', 'a push and a pull', 'everything balanced', 'twists and rolls' or 'hard and soft pushes'. Some children will be able to record their observations – noting everyone's 'personal best' at standing long jump, or the difference between a jump off one leg or two can be noted. Simple predicted correlations could be discussed, e.g. 'Will the oldest person jump the furthest?' This introduces a further link with mathematics; not normally considered a creative subject yet with plenty of scope for children to become excited by number patterns and trends. In the topic of Earth and Beyond, children in upper Key Stage 2 can explore number patterns by making a table of the relative sizes and distances of planets from the Sun, then modelling them with different sized beads, marbles and balls which can offer a mathematical challenge and provide a graphic illustration of the sheer scale of the Solar System. If you want to introduce more mathematics, you could position the orbits at roughly the correct relative distances from each other (if Sun to Mercury is one unit, Sun to Venus is roughly two, Sun to Earth three, Sun to Mars five – the Fibonacci series, though this breaks down at Jupiter).

The topic of light enables us to link science with art and design. Activities such as colour mixing, making spinning colour wheels, and using paint colour charts to stimulate colour hunts outside can stimulate children's imagination and promote a sense of 'awe and wonder' – a reminder of light's extensive links with religious education (RE). At a higher level, children can explore the difference between mixing coloured paints (subtractive mixing) and coloured lights (additive mixing – try using red, green and blue torches to make white). Light can also be mixed 'in the eye' – artists such as Seurat made use of this phenomenon by painting coloured dots (pointillism) that merge together when viewed from a distance, so an orange hat is in fact created by a juxtaposition of red and yellow dots. A similar effect can be created using 'spray' functions on Microsoft 'Paint'. If a computer screen is viewed with a magnifying lens, images can clearly be seen as made from dots of colours. The white page of a 'Word' document is actually made from dots of light and the words are created by an absence of light. There are also links to be made with other areas of science, such as camouflage, the use of colours for warnings and signals in the animal kingdom.

Use of space

Going outside the classroom to look at colour in the environment is an example of another key ingredient at our disposal as creative teachers – the use of space. One of the factors underlying the decline in pupil enjoyment in science referred to above may be the predominance of sitting at a table writing in many science lessons, especially towards the SATs revision period in Year 6. Children need the opportunity to clear the tables out of the way and work on the floor, perhaps when testing their aerodynamic alterations to a standard vehicle when rolling down a slope and measuring distance travelled. They also need to stand on tables (health and safety restrictions permitting) to release their designs for parachutes, spinners or gliders. They may need to work in the corridor to investigate the use of different types of twine or cups in string telephones, and can make good use of the hall to simulate the movement of planets in the Solar System. The school playground provides opportunities for launching 'stomp rockets' or observing the difference between the speeds of light and sound, for example by watching and hearing the beat of a drum at a distance. A 'sound walk' in local streets can provide opportunities for high-level scientific discussion, perhaps about children's ideas concerning the Doppler effect heard when the siren of a passing emergency vehicle appears to drop in pitch.

Use of resources

The final ingredient in our quest to make our science lessons practical, memorable and interactive is our choice and use of resources. Unfortunately, many primary schools devote a far smaller proportion of their resources budgets to science than to literacy or numeracy, but this should not deter us from inviting children to bring in objects of interest from home, or from making out of everyday materials many of the simple science toys which so fascinate children. If you are blessed with a budget, Feasey (2005: 45) suggests a set of criteria for choosing resources to support creativity in science, including 'Will it motivate staff to try different approaches to teaching and learning in science?' and 'Will it provide a "Wow!" factor in the classroom?' She suggests the use of a 'surprise box' containing a mystery object each week – perhaps linked to the science topic for the term, such as a prism, a kaleidoscope or a hologram – of which the class has to ask questions to identify its contents. To this advice I would add the following: do not be limited by the current primary science curriculum in your choice of resources; many of the most engaging science 'toys' exemplify some pretty tricky principles but we can engage children's own creativity and information retrieval skills in addressing these challenges to their current thinking.

Some resources which can be purchased fairly cheaply and promote plenty of discussion and 'conjecture thinking' (Craft 2000) include a dynamo torch, lit by pumping a handle. If possible, buy a transparent version which enables children to see the mechanism and flywheel within; other small battery see-through torches can really help with their understanding of switches and circuits. For the topic of light (or forces) an 'air cannon' shows vividly how a compression travels through the air, producing a disconcerting blast for anyone standing in its path. Children are fascinated by the time lag between releasing the flexible membrane of the cannon and observing, say, the leaves on a plant flutter. The force provided by air can also be dramatically demonstrated by a 'stomp rocket' which fires a foam dart a considerable distance at a pre-set angle when its air sack is stamped on (or has a brick dropped on it from a measured height if we wish to try to control this variable). Stomp rockets can supposedly be used indoors, but usually travel too far for an average classroom. An alternative is a smaller 'squeeze' rocket operated by hand. It is well worth purchasing some 'super' bubble solution containing glycerine for the 'wow' factor of enormous bubbles which can be caught and stuck together without popping. Children's philosophical enquiry can be directed at questions such as 'Why are bubbles spherical whatever shape the frame used to blow them?' and 'Why can we see rainbow colours in bubbles when the bubble solution is only one colour?' Playing with a handful of magnetic marbles can provide further enjoyable experience of how spheres stack together when they have forces of attraction and repulsion between them, offering the opportunity of making links between previously unrelated ideas (bubbles and marbles).

Other memorable resources which do not need to be purchased specially include the 'Bernoulli ball' (a ping-pong ball or balloon with a weight hanging from it which appears suspended in the air flow from a hairdryer). The science behind this is quite difficult – all about air pressure when it flows over curved surfaces – but that need not preclude discussion and speculation over what is a fascinating phenomenon. The same applies to the static electricity effects of rubbing a balloon on a synthetic jumper and using it to attract hair, scraps of paper, the ceiling or a trickle of water from the tap – a real 'wow' factor as the stream bends towards the balloon. Simple explanations can be provided in terms of pushes and pulls, though many children will want more and can be encouraged to find fuller explanations from secondary sources. For the topic of light, buying a large pack of small rectangular plastic mirrors can form the basis of making our own simple kaleidoscopes (three mirrors arranged as a triangular prism) or periscopes (mirrors placed parallel at 45-degree angles at either end of a cardboard tube). In this case, explaining how the kaleidoscope or periscope works with the aid of annotated drawings can provide much of the scientific learning from the activity. To explore forces in water, making a 'Cartesian diver' out of the bulb from a water dropper with a paperclip to weight its open end, suspended in a full 2-litre drinks bottle, will fascinate children as they squeeze the bottle to make the diver sink and release to let it rise. Again, the concepts involved (compressibility of air, change in density) are somewhat beyond Key Stage 2 level, but discussing it should challenge the 'conjecture thinking' of higher attainers. A fun illustration of balanced forces and centre of gravity can be provided by making a 'balancing toy' from a cork with two forks inserted on either side to slope downwards and a pin in the bottom – commercial versions including birds and butterflies can also fascinate and challenge. Likewise, making an electromagnet out of a 4.5 V bicycle lamp battery and a loop of insulated wire coiled round a steel nail may prompt some children to make the first tentative conceptual links between electricity and magnetism.

Assessing children's creativity in Physical Processes

In the report from a national research project on creativity in the classroom – *Creativity: Find it, Promote it* – the Qualifications and Curriculum Authority (2003) suggest that before we can begin to develop children's creativity, as teachers we need to learn to spot it in the classroom. With such a nebulous and individual quality as creativity, this form of assessment for learning (Black and Wiliam 1998) is easier said than done. When asked to identify children with creative potential for an out-of-school design experience, we found that teachers tended to choose children they viewed as 'quirky' or who found social interaction difficult – a deficit model that was a far cry from the 'gifted and talented' agenda we were expecting (Davies *et al.* 2004). Rogers *et al.* (2005), in a survey of primary trainee teachers, found that many took the view that since creativity is seen as a desirable personality trait to have, the idea of making a judgement about the child's personality is anathema, for 'what was a creative act for me, may be mundane for you'. Nevertheless, QCA (2003) assert that it is possible to identify when pupils are thinking and behaving creatively in the classroom by noting occurrence of the following behaviours:

- questioning and challenging;
- making connections and seeing relationships (echoing Koestler (1964));
- envisaging what might be (like Craft's (2000) 'conjecture thinking');
- exploring ideas; keeping options open;
- reflecting critically on ideas, actions and outcomes.

Interestingly, this list bears a strong resemblance to Harlen's (2000) set of scientific attitudes – curiosity, respect for evidence, willingness to change ideas, critical reflection – perhaps to be scientific is also to be creative? Let us examine what each of these might look like in the context of physical processes. Anyone who has asked a class of children to come up with a list of *questions* to start off an investigation into, say, magnets may be disappointed in the outcomes. Children simply do not ask neat, investigable questions such as 'How do we test which is the strongest?', or if they do these are hidden amongst an odd collection of what Goldsworthy *et al.* (2000a) classified as questions asking for an opinion, e.g. 'Which is the best magnet?', or those which are unanswerable, e.g. 'Why do magnets exist?' It is these latter questions, often discarded in science lessons but prized by devotees of philosophy for children (Matthews 1994), which some would argue offer the greatest indications of creativity. Unfortunately, after repeated experiences of suppression of such questions since they do not meet current learning objectives, children may stop asking them. Another alternative is to use a 'What if . . .?' approach drawn from the genre of science fiction (Feasey 2005). Turn a philosophical question such as that above into: 'What if there was no such thing as magnets?' or 'What if everything was magnetic?' This can lead to fruitful discussion and conjecture thinking, possibly leading into some rich writing during literacy hour.

Creative thought may be exhibited when children *make connections* between two different aspects of science using analogy, for example the 'push' of a battery in driving electricity around a circuit. Feasey (2005) reports on a lesson in which the teacher introduced two cans of cola, one diet and one ordinary, asking for the children's predictions as to what would happen when they were placed in a tank of water. To their surprise, the diet cola floated higher in the water than the other, promoting a great deal of speculative hypothesis, e.g. 'There are more bubbles inside the diet cola so it will be lighter and float higher. Diet cola is always fizzier.' Regardless of whether they were 'right' or not, children here were drawing upon previous experience and *seeing relationships* between, say, gas and density.

This is perhaps a dilemma for the teacher who wants to promote greater creativity in science; many of the statements we categorise as misconceptions or alternative frameworks may be children's creative and individual ways of expressing scientific ideas. For example, many young children's ideas about a phenomenon such as day and night are extremely creative in terms of envisaging what might be, e.g: 'Night happens because we need to sleep', or 'The Sun goes down and down ... under the hills and you can't see the Sun and then the Sun pops back up when it's morning' (an anthropomorphic idea of the Sun 'hiding' from us). Such ideas may need further *exploration*, with children keeping their options open so that they are prepared to change their ideas if presented with contradictory evidence. For example, some children may suggest that sound travels only if there is nothing to get in the way: 'Tunes are very small and they can get through gaps in the doors.' Listening to sounds through open and shut doors could further explore this idea – how does shutting the door change the sound and how can some sound still get through? The ability here to *reflect critically* on their ideas will stand children in good stead. The physicist Stephen Hawking has recently had to admit that his most controversial – perhaps his most 'creative' – theory was wrong. Willingness to take risks, tolerate uncertainty and accept failure as part of the learning process are key attributes of successful learners in science.

We cannot leave this discussion without a brief mention of progression in children's creativity. Whilst many (e.g. Hollings and Whitby 1998) have outlined clear lines of progression in children's scientific concepts and process skills, little thought has yet been given to how they might progress in terms of creative thinking in science. Rosenblatt and Winner (1988) distinguish three phases of children's creativity: the *pre-conventional phase* (up to the age of about 6–8 years), the *conventional phase* (from age 6–8 to about 10–12) and the *post-conventional phase* (from about 12 years of age and extending into adulthood). The assumption that post-conventionality is inherently superior to pre-conventionality (since it involves awareness of constraints and the ability to transcend them) could be regarded as deriving from a deficit model of childhood – casual observation might lead one to a view of children as *more* creative than adults. This appearance, argues Root-Bernstein (1989), may be due to the 'novice effect' – creative adults are often characterised by shifting fields or focuses of attention at regular intervals in their careers, avoiding 'staleness' by putting themselves in the role of novices. Most children are relative novices by comparison with adults – hence the frequent 'freshness' of their responses. At a neurological level this may correspond to greater plasticity and capacity for making connections between neurons in a child's brain by comparison with 'creatively exhausted' adults.

The framework above could be taken to suggest that young children will become *less* creative as they move into the conventional phase during Key Stage 2. Some children, however, having attained a degree of confidence in their scientific skills and knowledge, may begin to *challenge* us as teachers from a *post-conventional* level of development. It can be profoundly uncomfortable as a teacher to respond to statements beginning, 'But I thought you said . . .' when a child has discovered that light passing through glass or water doesn't always travel in straight lines. These challenges are qualitatively different from those of a pre-conventional child whose reluctance to accept evidence is rooted in their own highly imaginative take on the world.

Planning for creativity in Physical Processes

Planning for creativity sounds like a contradiction in terms. However, if we want to avoid the much-criticised 'laissez-faire' 1970s approach to allowing children's creativity to develop through serendipity (Alexander *et al.* 1992), we need to sequence the types of experience we offer them carefully. In medium-term planning this could mean adapting existing published or school schemes and units of work so they offer the following characteristics adapted from what Harrington (1990) described as a 'creative ecosystem' – a vibrant classroom environment in which children's creativity can flourish:

- stimulation (motivating starting points);
- opportunities for 'play' (exploring before investigating);
- easy access to resources (together with a degree of choice over resources);
- mentors and role models (opportunities for children to collaborate);
- information (scientific skills and concepts directly taught);
- open-ended assignments (fewer predetermined outcomes).

We suggest a few adaptations to the *National Scheme of Work for Science at Key Stages 1 and 2* (QCA 1998) in the light of the above framework. For example, to provide a *stimulating starting point* to Unit 1F *Sound and hearing* children could enjoy identifying a range of 'mystery' household sounds from a tape, e.g. filling a kettle, shutting a door, and cleaning teeth. The story *Peace At Last* by Jill Murphy (1980) or the poem 'The Sound Collector' by Roger McGough (1987) are good starting points when working on this topic with young children. Children can explore how far the sound of a clock, a telephone or an alarm will travel. An alternative way to start Unit 3F *Light and shadows* is to show the children posters or satellite images of the world at night, asking the following questions:

- Where is the most light?
- Why is this?
- How would we manage without electric light?
- Is it a good thing to make so much light?

This discussion could be revisited later in the school (e.g. in Year 6) when it can be developed more as education for sustainable development. To start Unit 6F *How we see things*, why not start with careful observation of the pupil of the eye in a mirror, revealing that it gets smaller when the observer moves towards a sunny window. Children may not realise the pupil is in fact an opening that allows light into the eyeball. They might measure the amount of time it takes for the pupil to widen as the iris dilates when the classroom lights are dimmed and notice it is more difficult to see clearly until the pupil has adjusted. These experiences can be used as starting points to develop understanding of how our eyes respond to light.

Introducing an element of *play or exploration* into the beginning of each planned unit of work will often encourage children to try things out, whilst also providing a degree of orientation (Ollerenshaw and Ritchie 1997) towards the topic concerned. For example, Unit 2E *Forces and movement* suggests using malleable materials and toys to classify forces. We could alternatively start this unit by encouraging children to play with these materials and talk about what they are doing, perhaps with the following additions to promote discussion: blowing up a balloon and letting it go, building a house of cards, blowing bubbles, bouncing a ball or playing a mini-pinball game. To start any of the forces units, children can experience different types of forces in a kinaesthetic 'whole body' way through play. Many schools have on-site play equipment, or are likely to be located near a play park with access to a slide, swings, a roundabout, see-saw and climbing frame (don't forget to undertake a risk assessment first). A pre-visit discussion will help children to think in terms of pushes, pulls, starting, stopping, speeding up, slowing down and changing direction when they are on the equipment. Perhaps organise one group to play while another group watches – and get the children to describe what is happening: 'Karla is pushing the roundabout', 'Drew is sliding down', 'Nathan will fall down when he lets go'. Take some digital photos or movies of the children and discuss these afterwards. Ask questions such as: Can we see anyone pushing? Why did the seesaw go up and down? What did it feel like on the swing? Who had the most friction on the slide?

Bring a greater degree of choice into the *resources*, materials or examples recommended in the scheme. For example, in Unit 3E *Magnets and springs*, provide a wide range of magnetic games and toys such as a fishing game, a racing game in which the racers are controlled by magnets under the board, fridge magnets, 'Antz' (in which players have to capture stacks of opponents' magnetic 'ants' which disconcertingly flip over if the poles are similar), Brio trains with magnetic couplings etc. Some of these could be made or brought in by children, not only demonstrating the huge range of applications for magnets but providing starting points for children to design their own toys or games using magnetic principles. For Unit 3F *Light and shadows* why not introduce torches with coloured filters to produce coloured shadows and links with drama through theatre lighting. Include a range of translucent coloured materials (cellophane) to produce coloured shadows when making shadow puppets (see above).

Mentors and role models are vital, as it is increasingly argued that creativity actually belongs in 'communities', residing in the 'spaces' between individual minds, rather than being sited entirely in the individual (Craft 2000: 149). In our own work (Davies *et al.* 2004) we have observed children who seem to exhibit their creativity only when working in collaboration with others, and Siraj-Blatchford (1996) writes about the importance of 'design collectives' in the classroom to make the most of everyone's ideas. We as teachers can act as role models by exemplifying Harlen's scientific attitudes (see above) which, as we have already noted, bear strong resemblances to QCA's (2003) creative behaviours. For example, we could demonstrate *curiosity* by showing an interest in new things, particularly those children have brought in from home. We can tell children about times when we have *changed our ideas* about a scientific principle, e.g. 'I used to think it would be easier to swim in the deep end because the water holds you up more, but when I saw that things float just the same in shallow or deep water I had to think again.' Another way in which we as teachers can promote a *social* approach to creativity is through the use of more 'dialogic' interactions – those which involve genuine discussion and reasoning by children rather than simple question–answer sequences. For example, as part of a whole-class demonstration, we could ask them to discuss with a partner then make a prediction by writing upon and holding up a mini-whiteboard. Older children could make a prediction in graph form to a question such as 'If we plotted "surface area of parachute" against "time taken to fall", what would the graph look like?' (Unit 6E: *Forces in action*).

The need for *information* reminds us that teaching for creativity is not some vague or laissez-faire approach to science education, but actually demands that we develop a degree of expertise in children so that they can exhibit *post-conventional* creativity (see above). For example, whilst investigating the rate of fall of different objects as part of Unit 6E: *Forces in action*, we can provide some background information about Galileo's fabled experiment to drop cannon balls of different masses from the leaning tower of Pisa, and visit the National Aeronautics and Space Administration (NASA) website to download the video clip of the famous 'hammer and feather' demonstration by Apollo astronauts on the moon. Children could debate these ideas and factor them into their design of investigations into parachutes, spinners and falling film canisters with or without plasticine filling. Information in science is not restricted to conceptual knowledge, however; it is just as important to provide children with *procedural* information to enable them to enquire creatively. By using some of the resources from the ASE–King's College Science Investigations in Schools (AKSIS) project, for example *Getting to Grips with Graphs* (Goldsworthy *et al.* 2000b), we can help children to record, present and interpret their findings in mathematically appropriate yet imaginative ways, such as a scattergram of parachute diameter against time of fall.

Finally, our approach to planning for a creative ecosystem requires that we build in *open-ended assignments* without the kinds of predetermined outcomes often anticipated in standard science investigations. For example, in working through the three units on electricity: 2F, 4F and 6G, we can construct a whole-school teaching and learning sequence for electricity around a series of 'challenges' requiring children to use creative problem-solving strategies such as those studied by Roden (1999: 23). These include *personalisation*, in which 'children sought to relate the task to themselves and make links with past personal experiences of a similar nature. This appeared to aid concept building and helped them bridge the gap between personal and school knowledge.' Another useful strategy was *negotiation and reposing the task*, meaning that 'children tested the boundaries of the task and what was "allowed" within the classroom culture.' The challenges we suggest for electricity include:

Unit 2F – Using electricity

- Challenge 1 – can you make the bulb light/buzzer sound?
- Challenge 2 – can you find the fault in the circuit? (Can you make a fault?)
- Challenge 3 – can you make something with your circuit?

Unit 4F – Circuits and conductors

- Challenge 4 – can you predict which of these circuits will work?
- Challenge 5 – can you make a circuit to test whether materials conduct electricity?
- Challenge 6 – can you make a working switch?

Unit 6G – Changing circuits

- Challenge 7 – how many ways can you find to change the brightness of a lamp/speed of a motor?
- Challenge 8 – can you find two different ways of lighting two lamps in one circuit?
- Challenge 9 – investigating resistance. What will be the effect on current of changing thickness, length or material of wire?
- Challenge 10 – can you control two lamps each with its own switch? What about one lamp using either of two switches? Any other combinations?

Another way of looking at planning for physical processes is to look at the 'big ideas' offered by the topic concerned (see Chapter 7). For example, in relation to a topic on Earth and Beyond, the ways in which the Earth, Sun and moon move in relation to each other to give us day and night, seasons and lunar phases are the 'big idea' in this topic. It might help to humanise the scientific process behind this idea if we plan our teaching around telling an 'explanatory story' (Millar and Osborne 1998), introducing new characters and ideas as the weeks progress. Most people believed that the Earth was flat and at the centre of the universe until the end of the 16th century when Magellan's global circumnavigation and Nicholas Copernicus' observations of planetary motion challenged science and Church teaching. Copernicus suggested that the Sun is at the centre of the universe, and that all the planets including Earth move around it. A few decades later, Galileo famously got into trouble with the Pope for suggesting that his telescope observations supported Copernicus' model. We now know that the Sun itself orbits the Milky Way galaxy, but our understanding of the movements of Earth and moon are still based on this big idea. In planning a science lesson which offers scope for children's creativity, NACCCE (1999) remind us of the need to appreciate phases in a creative activity and the ways in which time away from a problem may facilitate its solution; what Dust (1999) terms the 'incubation' period in a creative process. We need also to remember that our prime intention is actually to teach children some science; this can lead to tensions in the planning process:

> For many practitioners the problem is how to incorporate the features of effective creative science education, but maintain the rigour and focus on key objectives for development and learning.
>
> (Johnston 2005: 99)

One possible resolution of this tension is to be as explicit as possible about the creative behaviours we expect as learning outcomes from a lesson, in addition to the knowledge and skills. For example, in a lesson about night and day, as part of Unit 5E: *Earth, Sun and Moon*, one of our objectives could be for children to use 'conjecture thinking' in relation to their explanations, as in this comment: 'It's morning in a different place when it's night-time here. Because it's a different country and the sun can't go everywhere.' Later, we could be expecting them to draw ideas from as wide a spectrum as possible as part of a debate on 'the evidence for a spherical world'.

Using ICT to promote children's creativity

Whilst planning, we need to remember the huge potential of information and communications technologies (ICT) for promoting children's creativity in science. For example, using a computer simulation of, say, a bungee jumper (*Science Explorer II* – Granada Learning) '. . . provides conditions with a number of the advantages offered by play . . . an opportunity to produce novelty without risk since a simulation can be reversed at will' (Cropley 2001: 172). Loveless (2002) has noted a close correspondence between the features of ICT (provisionality, interactivity, capacity, range and speed) and the framework for creativity suggested by NACCCE. In relation to physical processes, data logging is a fruitful application for encouraging children to demonstrate creativity in designing investigations. For example, during Unit 5F *Changing sounds*, data logging could be used to answer the question: 'Which material would be the best sound insulator for a pair of ear defenders?' Children can think of a good way to make a 'standard' sound (perhaps a simple circuit including a buzzer, though this can become rather irritating!) and set up the sensor and material being tested in the same place each time to make the test 'fair'. Similarly, comparing how reflective different materials are is greatly enhanced for older children if they use a data logger to measure the amount of light that is being reflected. When children are making kaleidoscopes and periscopes (see above), they can make use of an art program such as Fresco, which has the facility to draw pictures with a simultaneous mirror image.

Case study: Animating forces

Liz Ireland, science co-ordinator at Redfield Edge Primary School, South Gloucestershire, wanted to find a way of helping her after-school science club – 21 pupils aged 8–11 – understand forces in real-life situations. She decided to involve the children in using stop-frame animation, using a digital camera and plasticine models (like the 'Wallace and Grommit' films). Her aim was to learn to use the digital camera and animation software alongside the children, as part of an action research project for her Master's degree dissertation. The children, working in groups of two or three, were asked to tell a story with their short animations that would involve everyday examples of forces in use. For example, one group of three girls shot a simple story of two boys having a fight: 'pushing each other over' and a dog jumping on top of them. One child described the process: 'Each picture you move it a bit but you have to keep your hand out of the way.' Next they loaded all of the frames on to Animation Shop and selected the period of time that each would be displayed. They then annotated the resulting short movie on the computer with 'push', 'pull', 'gravity' or 'air resistance'. One child commented: 'It's good being able to make it, and to put it all together, and to see what you've done.' Another added: 'You can be more creative when you do animation, because you can design what you're going to do, and you get to think things through, like what forces you're going to use and how the forces work.'

Not only had this experience helped reinforce children's understanding of the tricky and abstract conceptual area of forces, it had also enabled them to exercise choice, make links with other curriculum areas and engage in critical reflection as they viewed their results – an important component of QCA's creative behaviour cited above, which also mirrored the review process Liz undertook at the end of her first cycle of action research. She concluded that the project was an example of teaching for creativity in science because, 'You're wanting them to think outwardly. A lot of the time science uses left brain thinking – quantitative, sequential enquiry methods. The other side is about making things link, making leaps of understanding. Often we stifle this kind of learning in science, but the story element helps get both sides going and provides a kinaesthetic experience.' For the next cycle in the research, she decided to focus more on children's explanation of ideas about forces – specifically gravity, air resistance and friction – whilst seeking to help them annotate their cartoons with arrows showing the size and direction of the forces. Since by now children had gained familiarity and confidence with the animation process, many of these second-generation films were more ambitious; for example, involving people falling from aeroplanes, with and without parachutes!

Teaching creatively in Physical Processes

The discussion here necessarily overlaps to an extent with the planning section above, since creative classroom approaches need to be planned for. These teacherly behaviours may be influenced by all kinds of factors – gender, for example. A study for the Wellcome Trust (2005: 20) found that: 'female teachers tended to use creative contexts such as role-playing and drama in science teaching more often than male teachers'. Creative teachers need to engage children's visual, auditory and kinaes-thetic learning in this way. Feasey (2005: 37) suggests a checklist of activities linked to multi-sensory approaches to learning in science, including visualisation, phonetic clapping-out of sounds and use of sorting activities and puppets. The following suggestions draw on the ten points introduced in Chapter 2.

1. Turning predictable outcomes into something better

Predictable outcome from Unit 6F *How we see things* might be a diagram of the human eye, showing how rays of light pass through the pupil and form an image on the retina. However, since this rather passive activity is unlikely to challenge children's ideas about how we see, we could alternatively involve the children in making pinhole cameras. A pinhole camera works in a similar way to the eyeball and can be made using a cereal box – make a pinhole in the front, cut a window in the back and replace with a tracing paper 'screen'. Shield the screen with a 'visor' of black paper. With some experimentation, an upside-down image will be visible. If you're feeling particularly adventurous, why not replace the tracing paper with a piece of photo-graphic paper. This has to be done in dark conditions, then the camera held in place looking at a strong light source such as the window for a period of five minutes, before developing. If this is too technical, simple 'sun prints' can be made using sugar paper. Place objects with strong shapes onto the paper and leave on a surface in strong light for up to a week. The exposed paper will fade leaving a silhouette of the object. Children could experiment with different papers and discuss how this idea is used in photography and to bleach clothes in some countries. Similarly, when investigating shadows we can ask children to draw a picture showing how an object stops the light from travelling, but why not actually draw round their own shadows with chalk on the playground on a sunny day and explore making different shadow shapes. Alternatively, make silhouette pictures by drawing round shadows that are formed when a child's profile or object is in front of the overhead projector light. Can you identify the owner of the shadow?

2. Making the ordinary fascinating

The way that our eardrums vibrate in response to incoming sound waves in the air and transmit this movement – amplified by the bones of the middle ear – to the cochlea is an extraordinary phenomenon, yet completely invisible to us. However, by modelling the process in a larger scale we can make the invisible visible and increase that sense of wonder at the way in which sound waves travel. The idea of the eardrum picking up sound can be demonstrated by placing a sheet of tissue paper, or a burst balloon, across one end of a cardboard tube with a rubber band. By placing a finger gently against the tissue paper and shouting or singing down the tube, the children should be able to feel the vibrations in the 'eardrum' caused by sound travelling down the tube ('outer ear'). Another dramatic way of making vibrations visible is to hold a table-tennis ball on a thread up to a vibrating tuning fork; children become fascinated with the distance the ball travels from unseen vibrations.

3. Sharing a sense of wonder

The topic of light lends itself to 'awe and wonder' particularly well. Spectra or rainbows can be created in the classroom using a strong light source and a prism – a glass bowl of water can work, as can water mist and some plastics. The 'playing surface' of a CD makes a particularly effective spectrum. Light can be 'mixed' by making colour wheels divided into the six primary and secondary colours and spinning them quickly by mounting them on a motor, for example. If you have access to coloured lights such as stage lights, discoveries to be made include the fact that shadows will be the complementary colour to the light source (e.g. red light creates a green shadow) and some objects lit with coloured light will appear to change colour.

4. Seeing differently

Children enjoy looking at optical illusions and these are a good way of demonstrating how the brain decodes what we see. As teachers we can share our own perceptions of these images; children may be able to decode them better than adults. If you can, bring in a 'Magic Eye' book to see whether anyone can defocus their eyes sufficiently to see the hidden three-dimensional images hidden in the pictures; it's quite spectacular when you suddenly see in the 'right' way.

Children often see the world very differently from adults, and trying to 'gain understanding of their understandings' (von Glasersfeld 1978) can help us as teachers to plan the next step in their learning. For example, modelling the Earth, Sun and moon with plasticine is an effective strategy for eliciting children's ideas about the shapes of these bodies. The Earth may well be represented as a sphere, whereas some children may model the Sun as a flat disc (as it appears in the sky) or the moon as a 'banana' shape (deriving from standardised depictions of a crescent moon in story books). If you then introduce small model figures (e.g. Lego) and ask children to place them in two different locations on the Earth's surface, you can begin to find out their ideas about gravitational attraction and the concept of 'down'.

5. Maximising opportune moments

'Much of the artistry in being a successful teacher involves holding on to the notion of possibility in what may seem to be adverse situations' (Craft 2000: 3). When an investigation 'goes wrong' or throws up unexpected phenomena, such as the discovery that in a circuit containing a lamp and buzzer wired in series the buzzer will sound but the lamp won't light, it's tempting to blame faulty equipment or seek to sweep the inconvenient science under the proverbial carpet. However, the creative teacher of science will use such moments to spark new ideas for enquiry, demonstrating along the way some of the scientific attitudes referred to above. We could respond as follows: 'Wow! That's interesting. I wonder if any other combinations of two different components in a circuit will do the same thing? What if we put a buzzer and motor together? Anyone got any other ideas?' This should spark children's creativity to come up with new investigations, and novel explanations of the surprising result (it's actually the high internal resistance of the buzzer which reduces the current all around the circuit to such a low level that, although it flows through the lamp, it doesn't make the filament hot enough to glow).

6. Humanising science

Liz Ireland's animation project, described above, is an excellent example of relating a scientific concept to a series of everyday situations involving a range of fictional characters. Because these characters get pushed over, stuck in mud or fall out of aeroplanes as the result of forces acting on them, children can engage with them in a much more human way than with abstract ideas. This also links well with our earlier suggestion of using a visit to the playground to explore forces in 'real life'.

7. Valuing questions

In science education we claim to value questions more than answers, but this is sometimes belied by our actions as teachers! Building an exploration or orientation phase into our classroom practice is more likely to generate children's questions than diving straight into investigation. For example, whilst exploring a collection of toys, children might initially ask 'Which toy is the best?', which could, with guidance, become 'Which toy goes the furthest?' With further guidance an *investigable* question such as 'Does the size of wheels (or weight of vehicle, or shape of vehicle) affect the distance a toy rolls?' can be developed. Rolling two or three different toy cars down a slope seems a straightforward way to answer the question but is fraught with problems as the cars may differ in all sorts of ways – weight, diameter of wheel, width of wheel, length, shape, etc. To help children control variables a construction kit can be used, such as Lego, where test vehicles can be constructed that are near identical, apart from the factor under investigation. Keeping the slope fairly short will ensure more manageable measurements either in centimetres or non-standard units, although very short or shallow ramps will not give enough variation in the data to compare and contrast. For older children, the question 'Which trainer provides most grip on the school hall floor?' might be more relevant. The challenge arising with this investigation is that each shoe tested will vary in a number of ways. This will give children the opportunity to think creatively about how to control factors such as the size of the shoe, its mass and how a push or pull is applied and measured.

8. Modelling explanations

To engage children's visual (and ideally kinaesthetic) learning it is always useful to have physical resources with which to explain difficult concepts. For example, a lovely simple way of showing the relationship between pitch of sound and length of a vibrating object is to make a paper straw 'clarinet' by cutting one end into a 'v', flattening it and blowing through. It takes a bit of practice to get the lip position and force of breath right, but children should soon be able to produce a 'toot', a little like the sound some people can make by blowing over a blade of grass held between thumbs. Making 'clarinets' of different lengths, or even cutting pieces off the other end of the straw as they blow, very clearly demonstrates pitch rising as the length shortens. A clear demonstration of friction as a force between surfaces can be given by pulling the bristles of two hairbrushes against each other. The interlocking bristles *model* the microscopic unevenness of any two surfaces acting against each other. You might let children put sand, water, talc, hand-cream or cooking oil on their hands to experience the reduction of friction by lubricants. Lubricants act by filling in those uneven surfaces – so small particles which don't soak in or evaporate as the surfaces get hotter tend to work better, though even large objects such as marbles, rollers and wheels can be effective since they reduce the area of contact between the surfaces.

To model the flow of electric current in a circuit, join two ends of a piece of rope to make a loop large enough for your class (or a group) to hold whilst standing in a circle. This represents the 'electricity' (strictly speaking, the electric charge carried by electrons) that is already present within the wire, and which starts to flow once the circuit is connected up to a source of energy. Most children hold the rope loosely, palm up, allowing it to slip through their fingers. One child (representing the 'cell' – you could have more than one representing a battery) passes the rope through their hands so that it moves around the circuit. This makes the point that the cell/battery gives the 'electricity that's already there' a 'push/pull' to get it moving around the circuit (strictly speaking, it gives energy to the electric charge to produce a current or flow). One or more children can now grip the rope lightly (avoid rope burns!) to represent components that place a 'load' on the circuit (e.g. lamps, buzzers, motors). They don't 'use up' the electric current – there's still just as much rope after it's passed through their fingers as before – but they do take energy from it (represented by the warming of their hands) because they 'resist' the flow.

9. Encouraging autonomy

If our scientific enquiry is too tightly controlled – for example by pre-specifying the question to be investigated, variables to be changed, resources to be used, or format for communicating findings – we limit children's opportunity for demonstrating their creativity. In an atmosphere of tightly specified learning outcomes (see above) it can feel a bit risky to let children take the decisions, but the outcomes are usually of a higher order (if less predictable). For example, Feasey (2005: 31) reports on a class of 6- and 7-year-olds who were given a selection of magnets and different materials, their open-ended instructions being to find out as much about the magnets as they could and also to think about what they would like to find out about them; their result was a rich floor book of ideas. Older children studying the Earth and Beyond could be invited to find a way of modelling the impact of a meteorite (lump of rock) colliding with a planet or moon. Any observation of the moon's surface will reveal craters caused by such impacts, so this activity can be linked to work on the moon's shape (see above). One starting point could be to drop a marble into a tray of sand – this will make a crater and a little exploration will reveal that the higher the drop, the bigger the crater. At this point children need to be asked to plan the investigation, deciding on the independent variable (e.g. height of drop, mass or diameter of marble) and dependent variable (diameter or depth of crater). They should make a prediction (e.g. which mass will form the largest diameter crater) and consider some of the practical issues involved in testing this. For example, how can they change the mass without changing size (different materials?). How will they measure the diameter or depth of crater accurately? Will they need to make repeat measurements? Once they start the practical part of the investigation further issues will no doubt arise, which children could reflect upon in their evaluation of the experience.

10. Allowing for flexible beginnings

We have already recognised the need for practical, memorable and interactive starting points. For example, within the topic of forces the theme of 'projectiles' might begin in a sports context, with children exploring what happens when a ball or 'soft javelin' is thrown. They will observe that the angle of throw and the strength of the push will determine the distance the object travels. They experience gravity and air resistance thwarting their attempts to create a new school record. A digital video can be made to study the trajectory of the projectiles in slow motion. Investigations such as 'What is the best angle to throw a ball?', 'Why do some balls swerve more than others?', 'Does a shuttlecock always land "nose-down"?' can be carried out. For younger children, creating a dark area such as a cave can give children first-hand experience of darkness and how the introduction of light enables them to see objects. Stories such as *Can't You Sleep, Little Bear?* by Martin Waddell (2004) or *A Dark, Dark Tale* by Ruth Brown (1998) can be used to set the context for young children. The cave could have curtains to open and let in the light from the classroom or children could use torches to help them find objects in the cave.

Summary of main points

The topic area of physical processes in science lends itself particularly well to a creative approach, since:

- many of the starting points, resources and activities are intrinsically practical, memorable and interactive;
- work on all topics but particularly light and sound lends itself well to cross-curricular links;
- ICT, in the form of simulations, data logging and animation, can be integrated to give children opportunities to move from left-brain to right-brain thinking;
- medium-term plans can easily be adapted to offer stimulation, opportunities for 'play', easy access to resources, mentors and role models, information and open-ended assignments;
- classroom approaches in this area lend themselves well to the ten characteristics of creative teaching outlined in Chapter 2.

Although some teachers and children may fear the difficulty of topics such as forces and electricity, their very conceptual challenge raises points for discussion requiring flexibility of thinking and willingness to change ideas, two characteristics of creative physicists.

Issues for reflection

● How do you use time, space and resources creatively in your teaching of forces, electricity, sound, light and the Earth and Beyond?

● How does your planning for physical processes put in place the elements of Harrington's 'creative ecosystem' referred to on page 168?

● How could you make your teaching in this area more practical, memorable and interactive?

Discussion points

● How do you see progression in children's creativity in physical science? Is the notion of 'pre-conventional' and 'post-conventional' creativity useful in this area?

● How far can medium-term planning stray outside the confines of the National Curriculum and QCA Scheme of Work in this area?

Recommended reading

Davies, D. and Howe, A. (2003) *Teaching Science and Design and Technology in the Early Years*. London: David Fulton

Feasey, R. (2005) *Creativity in Science*. London: David Fulton

Howe, A., Davies, D., McMahon, K., Towler, L. and Scott, T. (2005) *Science 5–11: A Guide for Teachers*. London: David Fulton

Johnston, J. (2005) 'What is creativity in science education?', in A. Wilson (ed.) *Creativity in Primary Education*. Exeter: Learning Matters

References

Alexander, R., Rose, J. and Woodhead, C. (1992) *Curriculum Organisation and Classroom Practice in Primary Schools – A Discussion Paper*. London: Department of Education and Science

Black, P. and Wiliam, D. (1998) *Inside the Black Box: Raising the Standards through Classroom Assessment*. London: King's College School of Education

Brown, R. (1998) *A Dark, Dark Tale*. London: Anderson

Craft, A. (2000) *Creativity across the Primary Curriculum: Framing and Developing Practice*. London: Routledge

Cropley, A.J. (2001) *Creativity in Education and Learning*. London: Kogan Page

Csikszentmihalyi, M. (2002) *Flow*. London: Rider

Davies, D., Howe, A. and Haywood, S. (2004) 'Building a creative ecosystem – The Young Designers on Location Project', *International Journal of Art and Design Education*, 23 (3): 278–89

Department for Education and Skills (DfES) (2003) *Excellence and Enjoyment: The National Primary Strategy*. London: DfES

Dust, K. (1999) *Motive, Means and Opportunity: Creativity Research Review*. London: NESTA

Feasey, R. (2005) *Creativity in Science*. London: David Fulton

Goldsworthy, A., Watson, R. and Wood Robinson, V. (2000a) *Investigations: Developing Understanding*. Hatfield: ASE

Goldsworthy, A., Watson, R. and Wood Robinson, V. (2000b) *Investigations: Getting to Grips with Graphs.* Hatfield: ASE

Harlen, W. (2000) *The Teaching of Science in Primary Schools* (3rd edn). London: David Fulton

Harrington, D.M. (1990) 'The ecology of human creativity: a psychological perspective', in M.A. Runco and R.S. Albert (eds) *Theories of Creativity.* London: Sage Publications

Hollings, M. and Whitby, V. (1998) *Progression in Primary Science.* London: David Fulton

Howe, A., Davies, D. and Ritchie, R. (2001) *Primary Design and Technology for the Future: Creativity, Culture and Citizenship in the Curriculum.* London: David Fulton

Johnston, J. (2005) 'What is creativity in science education?', in A. Wilson (ed.) *Creativity in Primary Education.* Exeter: Learning Matters

Koestler, A. (1964) *The Act of Creation.* London: Hutchinson

Loveless, A. (2002) *Literature Review in Creativity, New Technologies and Learning.* Bristol: Futurelab. http://www.nestafuturelab.org/research/reviews/cr01.htm

Matthews, G. (1994) *The Philosophy of Childhood.* Cambridge, MA: Harvard University Press

McGough, R. (1987) *Nailing the Shadow.* London: Viking/Kestrel

Millar, R. and Osborne, J. (1998) *Beyond 2000 – Science Education for the Future.* London: King's College School of Education

Murphy, J. (1980) *Peace at Last.* London: Macmillan

National Advisory Committee on Creative and Cultural Education (NACCCE) (1999) *All Our Futures: Creativity, Culture and Education.* Suffolk: DfEE

Office for Standards in Education (OfSTED) (1999) *A Review of Primary Schools in England, 1994–1998.* London: The Stationery Office

Office for Standards in Education (OfSTED) (2002) *The Curriculum in Successful Primary Schools.* London: OfSTED

OfSTED (2003) *Expecting the Unexpected: Developing Creativity in Primary and Secondary Schools.* London: OfSTED

Ollerenshaw, C. and Ritchie, R. (1997) *Primary Science: Making it Work* (2nd edn). London: David Fulton

Qualifications and Curriculum Authority (QCA)/Department for Education and Employment (DfEE) (1998) *Science – A Scheme of Work for Key Stages 1 and 2.* London: QCA

Qualifications and Curriculum Authority (QCA) (2003) *Creativity: Find it, Promote it.* London; QCA

Rogers, M., Fasciato, M., Davies, D. and Howe, A. (2005) 'Trainee primary teachers' understanding of the assessment of creativity', unpublished paper given at *BERA 2005*, University of Glamorgan, 14–17 September

Roden, C. (1999) 'How children's problem solving strategies develop at Key Stage 1', *Journal of Design and Technology Education,* 4 (1): 21–27

Root-Bernstein, R. (1989) *Discovery.* Cambridge, MA: Cambridge University Press

Rosenblatt, E. and Winner, E. (1988) 'The art of children's drawing', *Journal of Aesthetic Education,* 22: 3–15

Ruddock, G. *et al.* (2004) 'Where England stands in the Trends in International Mathematics and Science Study (TIMSS) 2003', in National Foundation for Educational Research (NFER) *National Report for England.* Slough: NFER

Siraj-Blatchford, J. (1996) *Learning Technology, Science and Social Justice.* Nottingham: Education Now Publishing

von Glasersfeld, E. (1978) 'Radical constructivism and Piaget's concept of knowledge', in F.B. Murray (ed.) *The Impact of Piagetian Theory.* Baltimore: University Park Press

Waddell, M. (2004) *Can't You Sleep, Little Bear?* London: Walker Books

Wellcome Trust (2005) *Primary Horizons – Starting Out in Science.* London: Wellcome Trust

CHAPTER 10

Enjoying assessment

It ain't what you know that causes the trouble. It's what you know that ain't so.

(Mark Twain 1885)

Assessing science

Speculation and facts are a strange combination to assess in science. This makes assessment a special activity needing judgement far removed from a tick-box mentality. The process of doing practical science and applying knowledge equally support the child in developing scientific rigour and understanding. Consequently, assessment in science is not just concerned with outcomes. Scientific understanding is about processes rooted in planning, teaching and learning. This does not make for an easy life. Instead the teacher identifies and reflects critically on evidence of scientific understanding and knowledge. This is a creative activity in itself, requiring practice and several examples to show how this might be done.

Assessment of selected outcomes in any subject puts boundaries on creativity. Summative tests only give a 'snapshot' of a child's scientific understanding when far more is possible. Meanwhile, the value placed on crude 'snapshot' testing from many parties, including parents, is hard to ignore. Tempting though it is to teach to the test, there are clearly better ways. Meaningful assessment is more justly based on formative methods, to include professional teacher-judgement of what has actually been understood. Professional judgements are made to support more flexible routes to further learning. These add a creative dimension to the assessment itself, rather than relying on summative assessment alone. Problem solving, selection of knowledge, exploring authentic aspects of science and having the opportunity 'to be scientists' can make assessment a dynamic feature of science teaching. Children can use their imagination to consider the implications of what they discover. Ritzer (1993) has pointed out that assessment, as a simple technical activity, often misrepresents the true extent of a child's understanding. By contrast, many teachers who are prepared to accept the assessment challenge take a stance against 'snapshot' testing. They put the child at the centre of the process, trying out a range of approaches to inspire motivating assessment opportunities.

How much of a risk is this? Much scientific thinking and discovery already results from rejection as well as acceptance of theories and initiatives. This means that a degree of irrelevance in following children's ideas must be accepted if their creative thinking is to be valued. There is little doubt that an expected result in a science lesson is easier to manage. With clear instructions to follow and certain information to understand, children will follow a direct path. Unfortunately, they will also lose the chance to be spontaneous or consider wider possibilities. How much more exciting, creative and informative it is to be brave and say, 'Let's find out, I don't know what will happen but let's see.' Justifying decisions to help children be creative and know where they are going takes a little practice, but it is certainly rewarding.

If asking the right question to challenge thinking and assess understanding requires good subject knowledge, then understanding how to make assessment relevant takes professionalism. There is no formula with an easy answer when a creative science teacher involves the learner in assessing their progress. There is no doubt that care needs to be taken to understand children's thinking beyond the answers they give. Often they will not have the language capability to explain their ideas. Other methods such as 'concept mapping' (Briggs *et al.* 2003; SPACE Reports, 1990–1996) can be used, but whatever the methods, this is never going to be a predictable journey. Children's ideas are changeable and sometimes accidental. The challenge of assessment in science is to better relate assessment to each child. To do this effectively, construction of individual understanding needs to be built, taking into account a child's understanding through discussion.

Finding significant starting points

Before planning a block of work, Joanne, who taught 10-year-olds, decided to spend time asking them for their ideas about Earth and Beyond. The main reason for this was to gauge children's understanding without making them feel that 'getting the right answer' was the expected outcome. Qualter (1996: Ch. 3) discusses identification of starting points. She claims that finding significant starting points is crucial in understanding how to progress with teaching and learning. Joanne recognised the value of this approach and incorporated it with the rationale of 'encounter, interaction and dialogue' put forward by Elstgeest (1985a). She did this as a means of gathering information about children's understanding of difficult concepts such as planetary relationships, day and night, the seasons, phases of the moon and the influence of gravity. She began by drawing a representation of the Earth and asked the children to draw what they thought they might see from a spaceship orbiting the Earth. She started discussions about space, climate, seasons and gravity, often getting the children to draw pictures, share ideas and sometimes write down what they thought using both words and pictures. No reference materials were available. The final question Joanne posed simply asked, 'How would you describe space?' The following responses from Conor and Robert, both aged 10, are astoundingly different, indicating the vast disparity in perception and modes of learning, subject understanding and knowledge base between the two boys:

Conor's response was brief, just three words conjuring up a very poetic picture: 'Polar silver soot.'

Robert's response was more lengthy, focusing on random facts, some at a high level:

A vacuum of space where galaxies and such as NGC 68222 magelanic and cloud and Fomax and Andromeda and Leo 1, Leo11, NGC148, NGC205 and stars; Redgiant, Yellow dwarfs, White dwarf, Neutron Star, Black holes too (although light cannot escape). When a star collapses then it is very gravitational, the furthest can see is 15000000km light speed is 330000km/hr and cannot be separated. The sun has many layers, such as chromosphere, chemosphere? Photosphere convective zone and solar interior. The sun burns on Hydrogen, Helium Nitrogen and Oxygen. Arrangements of stars are called galaxies. There are millions of known and unknown galaxies. The nearest star (Centain Proxima) would at the speed of light take 9 earth years (although if you travel the speed of light you will be in a time continuum).

It might be intimidating for a teacher to receive a response such as Robert's, especially as Robert had no access to research material or prior indication of the particular question. But what must be remembered is that one-off assessments can be misleading. No true assessment can be made on a single piece of work. In this case, although Robert could recite facts and figures at a level higher than his peers, the teacher discovered that he found it difficult to visualise models. For example, 'the movement of the Earth in relation to the Sun and moon,' or 'the tilt of the Earth and received sunlight resulting in seasonal change,' caused him concern. His spatial awareness and ability to visualise was not so advanced as Conor's. Work set for Conor (and the majority of the class) would not be appropriate for Robert but in this case the teacher decided to include Robert in aspects of teaching where simulations, e.g. phases of the moon, were modelled.

In addition, through negotiation with his teacher, he was set the task of designing a space suit and researching and reviewing a text, 'Space Physics' (Fogden 1989). The summative assessment task for Robert was individual to him and focused on setting a multiple choice quiz for teachers. He used a computer package to present this. An example was 'Which electromagnetic waves have the shorter wavelength?' A) radio waves, B) microwaves, C) X-rays, D) infra red. Many of the questions set had a mathematical base, as would be expected. He was able to explain the answers, an ability which fits in with high-level thinking.

Assessment of the modelling aspect of the phases of the moon was carried out in a design technology (DT) lesson in which the children in pairs made a model using a selection of black and white paper to design a picture book for young children. Conor and Robert worked together on this project. Although their thinking was very different, the teacher had identified aspects of understanding in which they could support each other by doing different yet collaborative tasks.

Interpreting pupils' work

In Cockburn (2001), Fig. 13.1 depicts a drawing of a Year 4 child's theory about the Sun and the planets. The Sun and the nine named planets are placed in a row. What is unique in this representation is that each planet has a line drawn to join it to the Sun. Mercury has the shortest line and Pluto the longest, each neatly placed in order. Various logical suggestions as to what the lines joining the individual planets to the Sun represented were given by trainee teachers e.g. 'The lines represent the orbit of each planet', 'The planets are kept from flying off into space', 'The line means it is sunny in the daytime'. This last answer is the closest to the child's thinking. Remarkably, not one of the 167 trainee teachers who studied the drawing accurately predicted her explanation, 'The planets go to the sun each day. When one goes then the next one goes. They all have a go so the world is light in the day.'

This is an example of idiosyncratic construction of data to make sense of a scientific phenomenon. It is an excellent use of the imagination, but why is children's understanding so different from a trainee teacher's? When the trainees analysed what had happened they started the process of interpretation from an 'expert' view. Understandably, young children are not proficient in deciding what is useful information so instead they rely on fragments of knowledge. This is of limited reliability in supporting their imaginative and intuitive ideas. Sense construction is different for each child and should be analysed and interpreted in collaboration with the owner, otherwise it will be inaccurate and partial. Teaching creatively to counter pupils' plausible but incorrect thinking is only possible with understanding of their personal construction of sense. It would, however, be counter-productive to reject such imaginative explanations. They are the foundations of scientific understanding.

In adopting a creative approach to assessing understanding it is worth remembering that science operates through investigation, exploration and questioning. Key investigative questions for discussion are 'What might be?' or 'What might happen?' Valuing more than one possibility, acting as devil's advocate, and taking ideas seriously

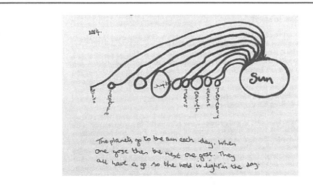

Figure 10.1 Rosie's theory about the Sun and planets

will support creativity. So will promoting imaginative speculation by not stamping on it as wrong. Scientists make choices from all possibilities, some of which are stepping stones to verify theories. Using discussion as a strategy for assessment will open up creative opportunities to ascertain understanding. Discussion should not be devalued as a process; quite the opposite is true. Often ephemeral 'wow moments' of understanding when the 'light goes on' are not recorded but these give teachers a real sense of purpose. They know that, for them, this is what teaching and learning is really about. Doing and discussion of the doing informs the teacher of the thinking behind the process. It informs the reasons for holding particular ideas.

However naïve children's existing ideas are, they enable teachers to construct further learning experiences at a level appropriate for the individual. School assessment procedures often seem to have greater value if evidence is visible in the written form, drawing or electronic recording. Assessment (of what amounts to discussion of discoveries) will not produce instant 'hard copy' and immediate written records. It is different in that it leads to written records, but these are a summary of a child's understanding and development of conceptual understanding. The delayed prize of achievement is to be had. Recording it in a form that is appropriate for others may involve some translation of the experience into a recognised assessment scale. That can wait, because it depends not on simple tests of understanding, but professional judgement of the level of understanding achieved. The question is never 'Does the child understand?' but 'How well does the child understand?'

Using naïve ideas

All children hold naïve ideas in science which go beyond the learning of information to include beliefs which do not match accepted understanding of scientific theories. Research in this area (Driver 1985; Keogh and Naylor 1997; Nussbaum 1976; SPACE Reports 1990–1996) have all identified common misconceptions often based on logical thinking and experience. For example, it is perfectly reasonable to believe from experience that 'the Sun travels round the Earth'. It is not so acceptable to hear a trainee teacher (2004) say, 'We have leap years because of the Olympic games.' This misconception relates to connections being made in childhood which have not been challenged. Another trainee teacher (2005) was astounded to be told about 'upthrust' in a workshop on 'floating and sinking'. She considered her science subject knowledge to be good:

I have pieces of paper (A levels) which tell me that I have a good understanding of the subject, I have a B for physics but none of my teachers has ever mentioned 'upthrust'. I can't believe it. I never really thought about 'why' things float before. I only ever thought about sinking and gravity, density, displacement and buoyancy. I can recite Archimedes' principle but I didn't know upthrust existed!

For both trainees a change in belief was a palpable experience, both shocking and amazing. It was mentioned for some time afterwards. To build on partial or misplaced knowledge and help the learner make sense of limited experience by challenging naïve ideas is the starting point of effective assessment. But it must be based on a thorough understanding of those ideas.

A discussion tool for assessment

'Concept Cartoons', http://www.conceptcartoons.com/concise.html (INSET 2005), are available as an excellent creative discussion tool to help teachers recognise starting points for assessment of understanding. Cartoon characters offer different explanations for scientific concepts. For example, in finding out pupils' understanding of how light travels, in 'Concept Cartoon' (12.9 Torches) four cartoon characters hold shining torches and state different explanations to include, 'The big torch shines further than the little torch.' 'They both shine the same distance.' 'The bigger torch lights up a bigger area.' 'They both shine the same distance but the big torch shines more brightly.' A common misconception is that the distance the light travels depends on the brightness of the light source. There is well-documented evidence in SPACE Research Reports (1990–1996) to substantiate and support this misconception and many others used in Concept Cartoons.

There is a clear link that much scientific understanding is based on conceptual development. For example, research from SPACE (1990–1996) shows that most primary-aged children believe that 'light travels from the eye to an object and that is how we see'. One trainee teacher found this hard to believe so she asked her class (9–10 years old) to put a direction arrow on a line drawn to represent a beam of light between an eye and a candle. To her amazement 28 pupils marked the direction of the arrow from the person's face to the candle, verifying findings of the SPACE project. This simple exercise prompted her to revise her plans and spend more time giving children practical tasks to question their thinking and ascertain useful ways of teaching the class.

Assessment to support creativity

An assessment system which is thorough in supporting creativity must be more concerned with assessment *for* learning rather than assessment *of* learning. More bluntly, formative assessment has more value in creative science teaching than snapshot summative assessment. That is not to say that assessment of learning cannot be achieved through creative summative methods such as role play. 'Script an interview of what it was like to be a spider and a fly' or 'Write instructions for a seed packet' can be summatively assessed. But this will probably relate to what the teacher wants to find out, rather than being open-ended. To recognise when pupils are thinking and behaving creatively demands close observation and study of particular traits through interpretation and explanation. Traits such as those listed by QCA (2003) complement a creative stance and need to be embedded in assessment strategies. The nature of science as a process and science as a bank of knowledge fits well with the identified criteria.

- Questioning and challenging . . . 'What are seeds?' 'Are they same as pips?' 'What is inside them?' 'How many ways can you make a rainbow?' 'Can you make a shadow story from digital pictures?'

- Making connections and seeing relationships . . . 'Which seed matches which fruit?' 'Why do some puddles dry up faster?' 'Can you make a shadow clock?' 'Why do some animals eat other animals?' 'Comment on a journey through a rainforest.'

- Envisaging what might be . . . 'Which seed will germinate first?' 'How could people survive on the moon?' 'What would life be like without electricity?' 'To anticipate the effect of pollution on a stream.'

- Exploring ideas; keeping options open . . . 'Some magnets are stronger than others.' 'How does a compass work?' 'Can you make the toy car travel more slowly?' 'Windmills have changed over the years and in different countries, why is this?' 'Making glue using flour and water.'

- Reflecting critically on ideas, actions and outcomes . . . 'Why is it important to eat fruit and vegetables?' 'Which boat can carry the most cargo?' 'Why do some things float?'

Encouraging the flow of ideas by sharing what is found and working towards a common understanding is an approach which would support the above. Whatever route is taken, certain questions remain important and imperative for the teacher to ask in assessing pupils' progress and understanding. Consider the implications of the following checklist.

Questions to guide assessment
- What is it that I want to understand?
- Why do I need to know this?
- How will verification of scientific understanding be evident?
- How can I use this information to support teaching and learning?
- Does this alter what I want to know?

The second question, 'Why do I need to know this?', is concerned with the moral and philosophical rather than the organisational and pedagogical implications. This is a question not so often asked but evident in teachers' frustration when they ask themselves 'Why am I doing this?'

It may be that the very activity that makes creative teachers fight back is the experience of 'teaching to the test'. Testing understanding can be a disempowering experience for any teacher, and many would prefer to change practice to find another, more exciting way. This is because believing in creativity is not concerned with being attached to fixed ideas or methods. The hurdle many teachers have to stride is being able to value differences and varied outcomes as the norm. Creativity in assessment is not about simple mechanistic operations or ticking boxes. Creativity is about celebrating differences, recognising the lone voice and applauding the courage of the individual. As Malaguzzi (in Edwards *et al.* 1998: 77) comments, 'Creativity becomes more visible when adults try to be more attentive to the cognitive processes of children than to the results they achieve in various fields of doing and understanding.' This fits well with the notion that to be an effective assessor the teacher must listen, watch and see what is going on and examine critically the impact that ideas, thoughts and knowledge have on developing scientific understanding. At the same time, it is important to appreciate that any assessment is always partial, tentative, imperfect and provisional. Assessing effectively is about the intellectual willingness to add to, rather than oppose, ideas. There are many ways of finding out what children know, but one of the best is to build a picture of children's understanding. This is done through observation, communication and the critical importance of the child–teacher dialogue. Within such dialogue, providing conditions for learning and assessing learning will be greatly influenced by the professional choice of questions raised and questions asked.

Creating appropriate dialogue

A creative teacher will probably ask interesting questions, such as 'Does an earthquake make a noise under the sea?', 'Why do you have to shout to be heard when it is windy?', 'Is it easy to hear in a greenhouse?', and 'Does something make a sound if it is still?' Such questions encourage discussion and speculation compared with 'How does sound travel?' or even, 'Does sound travel through a liquid?' Dull questions do not demand a personal view or offer a chance for a child to speculate. Creating a 'science dialogue' in which ideas are teased out, discussed, negotiated and explored is crucial for the verification of understanding but it is never going to be a straightforward process. There is a fine line to tread between intervention that informs assessment and intervention that stifles discussion. For example, a teacher on playground duty noticed a group of 6-year-old children watching a spider at the edge of a web. One child gently touched the web with a twig to try to make it move but the spider stayed still. The teacher listened to the following conversation but did not join in.

> Child A.   'It won't move. It's stuck.'
>
> Child B.   'I wonder why it keeps still, why doesn't it run away?'
>
> Child A.   'It's stuck.'
>
> Child C.   'It's waiting for us to go, it's frightened.'
>
> Child A.   'No, it can't see us, it hasn't got eyes.'
>
> Child B.   'It knows we are here, it can feel the stick, it made the bits (web) wobble.'
>
> Child D.   'Why won't it move?'
>
> Child A.   'It's asleep.'
>
> Child C.   'It's scared.'

The children were obviously inquisitive and tried to give explanations for the spider's inactivity. The teacher saw this as an opportunity to use her knowledge of the pupils' experience to adapt her plans to accommodate their interest. There were several aspects of the curriculum which could be addressed in response to the overheard conversation.

She decided to focus on spiders as predators, their anatomy and survival habits. This is a creative approach because in identifying and responding to a particular situation learning is put in context. Such opportunities are often wasted because it is impossible for teachers to respond to every observation, comment or dialogue. It is important, however, to listen carefully to conversations to gain evidence of thinking. Children will often be motivated to talk about things they have been doing in school. In this case they had been on a mini-beast hunt in the previous week. Their attention during break times had been focused on looking for mini-beasts and they were pleased to tell the teacher that they had seen a worm or ladybird or that they could not find a snail. This information shows a high level of interest but the overheard conversation tells the teacher much more about misconceptions and gaps in knowledge. Often evidence of children's science learning presents itself at a time when science is not being taught. Primary school teachers have an advantage of being with their pupils for most of the day and teach several, if not all, areas of the curriculum. This gives them the opportunity to create unplanned questions, deal with misconceptions and assess scientific understanding in a variety of situations.

Opportune moments to assess science

Example 1

Vicky, a teacher on playground duty, noticed some of her class kicking autumn leaves about, breaking up the swirling heaps positioned by the wind mostly near the bike sheds. She went over to where they were playing and began a conversation. With her 'science hat on' Vicky asked questions such as 'Why do you think there are so many leaves just here?', 'Wow, look at this red one, it's so bright, can you see how many different colours there are?', 'Have you noticed that not all the trees have lost their leaves?', and 'Why do you think leaves change colour and fall in the autumn?' She interspersed questions with general statements such as 'You seem to be having fun,' 'I can't believe how many leaves have fallen this weekend,' 'Don't they look pretty?', and 'Most of them seem to be near the bike sheds, there aren't too many on the playground.' In this way she felt that the children did not feel pressurised to answer specific questions but could join in as they wanted. Even so, Vicky was surprised by the information she gleaned in the dialogue.

> Last year it was colder earlier so the leaves fell off sooner. They go red because it's nearly Christmas . . . well that's what my mum says . . . and when they are all gone it will be Christmas. But Christmas trees stay green, don't they, miss? (Pause) Well, they do outside here but if you take them indoors they go brown and fall off, don't they? Is that the same as autumn, 'cause it's hotter not colder indoors?

Initial comments indicated a reasonable understanding but, as with most conversations, partial understanding and mismatched connections often of a logical nature emerged. Scientific questions and responses to them raise further questions, which are also assessment answers of a kind.

Example 2

A group of 6-year-olds came back into the classroom after a games lesson to change their clothes. It was a bright sunny day and several of them complained that they couldn't see very well. One boy said it was difficult to find his navy blue socks. They were on his black trousers. As the children were getting changed, Vicky again decided to use this opportunity to find out what they thought was happening. She asked questions to prompt them to think about how they see and what conditions might affect their ability to see. She spontaneously created an opportunity to assess understanding by using questions centred on linking experience to thinking about how we see. Vicky asked 'Have you found it difficult before to see when you have come indoors on a sunny day?', 'How long is it until you can see clearly again?', 'What does it feel like when your eyes are getting back to normal?', 'Is it more difficult to see dark things?' and 'Is it difficult to see when you come in on a cloudy day?' She followed this with 'What do you think is happening to your eyes when you come into the classroom from the sunshine outside?'

Using questions at opportune and unplanned moments to assess scientific understanding provides the potential for relating experience to complex scientific ideas. It follows that collecting information from interactions such as the examples shown is a non-stop process. It is worth undertaking if it is used to add to the picture of what the child knows and challenges thinking. Vicky planned a series of lessons to explore how we see, why we see colours, what affects our vision and how light behaves. She called the block of work 'the blue sock investigation'.

In both examples children's thinking was not constrained by the need for expected outcomes and took a direction not planned by the teacher. Teachers will relate to the comment 'Children say the most unpredictable things, they go off at a tangent and I'm thinking hang on a moment, I didn't want you to go down that route' (class teacher 2005). Ultimately it is this information that strengthens understanding of thinking and helps unravel partial understanding and misconceptions.

> If teaching is monodirectional and rigidly structured according to some 'science' it becomes intolerable, prejudicial and damaging to the dignity of both the teacher and learner.
>
> (Malaguzzi in Edwards *et al.* 1998 : 83) indicating the value placed on exploring thinking.

Tangents explored

When children are introduced to new experiences they do not compartmentalise their thoughts in the way we often do as adults. New experiences make them think in individual and unpredictable ways, not always what the teacher expects or wants. This is exemplified in the following lesson. Debbie, a KS2 teacher, organised a palette of activities for her 6-year-old class to introduce the concept of force. She set the agenda of tasks to give children the experience of observing the effect of forces using many well-known objects and contexts. Her planned assessment of understanding focused on the National Curriculum Sc4, Physical processes (2a 2b 2c), the main teaching points being, 'forces are pushes and pulls, they can't be seen only what they do to slow things down, cause movement and change direction'. The environment was child friendly, using toys and situations familiar to the children. For example, a group of boys were exploring the movement of air and how it can be altered with a fan, hairdryer and straw. They had fun with identifying pushes and pulls with a game of moving dried peas from one container to another. Space was used freely and one group of boys and girls spilled out into the corridor and began pushing toy cars on different surfaces and watching what happened and then had another go with a different car. One boy started pushing cars really hard against the wall to make them 'crash'. This behaviour might not be acceptable in some circumstances but Debbie observed carefully without comment. The boy then started behaving differently and instead of 'crashing' the cars with a great force he started to control the 'crash' by moving the cars at different speeds, some very slowly. Debbie heard him tell another child, 'If the car hits against the wall then it bounces back.' This was enough information for the teacher to intervene and direct thinking.

Debbie stood close to the boy and placed both hands against the wall and pushed hard then walked away saying, 'Have you tried that?' After a few moments she returned to find a line of children pushing against the wall and finding out how far away they could stand and push. When the teacher asked if it made a difference how hard they pushed, the answers came thick and fast: 'Yes, if you push hard you nearly fall over', 'It's hard to stop falling', 'You can't stand still' and 'The wall wants to push you back.' A few minutes later a small boy was seen pushing against the wall and letting go; another joined in but with his feet nearer to the wall and said, 'I'm being pushed back more.' The boys started to experiment with how close they could get to the wall. Soon the whole class wanted to join in so the teacher took them outside to the playground so that they could carry on trying out this new 'game'.

Previously, teacher-led demonstrations had interspersed the activity. One such demonstration involved pupils taking turns to hold a house brick at arm's length, the purpose being to help them realise the force needed to hold the brick in a stationary position. This is a well-used demonstration and indicates physically the push needed to stop movement but it does reinforce the misconception that people are needed to create force. However, as a result of discussion focused on 'pushing against the wall' one boy commented, 'The wall was pushing us just like when we had to push to keep the brick in the air,' and another boy added, 'The ball jumped out of the water when we let go like it was pushed by a wall.'

It is very rare to hear young children talking about a wall pushing; it is something that normally would not be considered at this stage. Because the teacher observed a tangential action and encouraged divergent thinking, formative assessment became part of the teaching process, providing a good example of assessment for learning. Pupils were tackling concepts considered appropriate for Key Stage 2 Sc4, 2d 'that when objects for example a spring, a table are pushed or pulled, an opposing pull or push can be felt'. Debbie placed value on application and analysis of thinking and by placing evaluation of responses at the heart of her teaching she took a reactive approach to accommodate information received.

Assessing what we value

Assessing what is of value can be very different from valuing what is assessed. This is a tricky business, especially in ascertaining science knowledge; hitting the right level is difficult. The teacher in the above example clearly has good science knowledge, enabling her to ask relevant questions and pursue useful lines of inquiry. Nonetheless, what teachers perceive as value in science will obviously have an impact on how they go about assessing. Enjoying assessment from the teacher's perspective will hinge on purpose and belief in the process as well as methods used. From the child's perspective there will not be such a clear understanding of the purpose and engagement in the process will be affected by personal experience. For example, imagine you are a child sitting with your class and the teacher asks, 'Why is it colder in winter in England?' or 'Why do heavy lorries take longer to stop?' or 'What is the hardest material?' You might want to answer the question but are not sure of the answer. You look for clues on the teacher's face, and know if you wait a minute she will probably give you a clue, but Yasmin answers, and your moment is gone. The opportunity to tell the teacher what you understand has passed.

Why do we ask 30 children these questions? If the answer is that we want to find out what they know, then other questions need to be considered. If we want to evaluate formative assessment of this kind, there are self-critical questions to ask, such as 'Is it usually Yasmin who gives the correct response?', 'Will every child be able to participate?', 'How many pupils will be able to answer the question?', 'Will pupils feel comfortable expressing their views in this way?', 'How much information will I have gleaned to assess understanding?', 'Do I value what I have found out?' and 'Did the pupils benefit from the experience?'

Pupils' prior experience

Not only do children develop conceptual understanding at different rates, they also have very different life experience. Out-of-school learning influences starting points and indicates clearly that every child's knowledge is affected by other influences. There will be a common understanding of classroom practice and shared lessons but each child will begin at a different level. Assisting learning by being aware of prior experience is a well-established concept, not least as formulated by Vygotsky (1978), expounding the advantages of the 'zone of proximal development'. The creative process here is to see things that we do not expect and be ready to adapt teaching to make formative assessment work as a result of what is seen.

Example 1

Holly (age 5) could use the word 'oesophagus' in context, and could explain that food in the mouth went down it to the stomach. She could point to it and when singing 'head, shoulders, knees and toes' added this and other body parts to the rhyme, pointing to the correct area for sternum, anus and lungs. She also told me that when you swallowed, food went down the oesophagus 'like a wriggling snake 'cause it's got muscles and if they work the other way (waving hands in an upward, rolling motion from stomach to throat and mouth and pretending to gag) you are sick'. Holly's father is a medic and a lot of conversations are concerned with the human body and physiology.

Example 2

Charles (age 7) started talking about the orbit of planets whilst looking at the night sky. When Pluto was mentioned as the furthest planet from the Sun, he interrupted, 'Only some of the time because its orbit crosses over with Neptune and sometimes like now it's Neptune which is furthest.' Neither of his parents is a physicist but his father has a telescope which Charles has been used to using for some time.

In each example, experience had given the children insights and knowledge not commonly shared with their peers. Understandably, learning from experience will be partial and not necessarily correct but to teach without consideration of individual experience will do nothing to challenge or advance learning. To observe closely, teachers need to hear what pupils say and see what they do. Creative use of observations promotes a culture of subjective possibilities individual to the learner. To find out what a child understands begins with observation, as Craft (2002: 17) so succinctly says, 'fostering the agency of the individual'.

Observing learning

In a creative lesson a wide range of interactions will provide a palette of information to use to interpret progress and achievement. Achievement is difficult to measure but without observation to build a picture of the child's thinking and progress it is a worthless exercise. The singular observational experience will do little to guide purposeful assessment. For example, how children set up and use equipment. A teacher might say, 'You need to look at the water at eye level to measure it' and *predict outcomes* such as, 'When water freezes it expands, so as the ice melts, the volume of water will decrease,' and 'As the ice melts the chunk of ice will reduce in size and the water level will get a little higher.' Children might *make sense of data*, as in 'The shadow was fuzzy because someone opened the blinds.' There are questions to be asked, such as 'If you live in Australia do you see the same stars as us?' and these will all add to the bank of knowledge needed to assess progress in learning. The child and the child's work need to be viewed, discussed and reflected upon through interaction with experience. Qualter (1996: Ch. 3) supports this view, describing theory as explanations, driven by 'talk and chalk', and justification without practical interaction as poor openings to observing progress. Understandably, if observation of understanding is limited solely to teacher-directed tasks then a great deal of information known by the child will be missed. By design certain responses will be pre-empted but others will be as a result of observing children at work and identifying individual understanding.

Making sense through observation

Children often have a running dialogue which evolves as they try to make sense of explanations, as these thoughts about seed growth show. 'The seed has a tiny plant inside (I think), then it grows into a little tiny plant, then it gets bigger. It only gets bigger if it has water but if you break it you can't see the tiny plant but if you give it water you can,' says Simon, and 'Seeds don't grow in the dark, they need light to grow but some grow in the dark in the cupboard,' says Yasmin. These conversations are common in primary science lessons and necessarily based on partial knowledge. Within the scope of limited understanding the child is trying to justify reasons for certain beliefs and contradictions. In the seed and growth investigation, bullet-point information given to explain conditions needed for growth had already been shared with the class. The 'what is needed' was put in simple words i.e. water, warmth and air. Why certain conditions aid growth and what can affect growth had not been discussed. Consequently the child contradicted 'seeds need light to grow' with 'seeds don't grow in the dark' and 'but some do in the cupboard' after observing growth of cress in various situations. If sense is to be made through observations, then teacher intervention is needed to discuss observations and explain the science. The teacher needs to be clear about assumptions made and the thinking that supports reasoning. A mapped evolution, from the simple intuitive description to more complex ideas based on research, will help teachers to match understanding to cognitive development. For example, Phases of the Moon: 'Clouds cover part of the Moon; full Moon in Summer,' 'Shadow of Sun falls on Moon; no pattern observed,' 'Shadow of Earth falls on Moon; some regularity,' 'Part of Moon illuminated by the Sun and part visible on Earth; pattern explained' (Hollins and Whitby 1998: 138).

Teaching methods

Person-centred questions (Elstgeest 1985b) offer a way of avoiding the restrictions and pressure of a 'right answer' which can deter an atmosphere conducive to inquiry and speculation. Open questions of this type include, 'What has happened to *your* bean since you planted it?', 'What do *you* notice about the size of all the beans?', 'What can *you* tell me about the colour of *your* bean?' or 'What do *you* think helps *your* bean to grow?' Person-centred questions ask for ideas about the subject matter, but emphasise 'you' as the central responder. Subject-centred questions ask directly about the subject matter and include, 'Why did your bean grow more quickly in the cupboard?' and 'Did it need water to grow?' Not only can pupils answer these questions, they can do it without understanding, as Littledyke and Huxford (1998) so aptly describe. In the gobbledegook example, Ross asks, 'Brenda, what happens to the orbal when it passes through a dovern mern?' and receives the following information: '*When an orbal of quant undual to the markobine bosal passes through a dovern mern it is deranted so as to cosat to a bart on the bosal called a markobine gando*' (Littledyke and Huxford, 1998: 69).

There needs to be a progression of understanding linked to science knowledge not only in assessment practices but also in the nature of tasks set. Tasks set must check understanding otherwise credence will be given to an answer such as 'It is deranted so as to cosat to a bart on the bosal.' For example, if the teacher wants to check pupils' ability to identify symbols used to represent components used in electric circuit diagrams and draw representations of simple circuits then they need to know that pupils recognise symbols and can use them to communicate understanding. Using circuit diagrams to set actual components to match drawings will test understanding. If they are asked to make a selection of circuits and then represent them diagrammatically, understanding can be assessed with even more accuracy. This progression of expectation is a common method of checking understanding but nowhere does it take into account pupil explanation.

Example 1

Three girls (age 10) set up a simple circuit with one bulb and one cell. They were explaining that 'the battery hasn't got electricity in it but when the circuit is connected then it gives a push to the electricity which makes the bulb light'. They explained that 'the electricity moved like a bicycle chain wherever it was in the circuit and the pedal gave a push like the battery'. Anyone listening to their conversation and assessing their progress would be forgiven for presuming that they had quite good understanding of how electricity moves in a circuit and that they had certainly remembered the analogy given in a previous lesson as to how electric circuits operate. However, once they were given a new challenge of adding another bulb to the simple circuit explanations were not so certain and questions were raised. Andy, their teacher, set progressively more difficult tasks to check understanding and was surprised by the results as he initially thought that this particular group had a very good understanding of how circuits work.

To begin with, the teacher felt that understanding was good.

Girl A.   'The battery hasn't got electricity in it.'

Girl B.   'No, it gives the electricity a push.'

Girl A.   'Yeah, but only when it's connected.'

Girl B.   'That's why the bulb lights up.'

Girl C.   'Then the electricity can get round.'

Girl A.   'It needs the battery to push it otherwise it doesn't work.'

As the lesson progressed they were asked to add another bulb and predict what would happen:

B.   'It will still work, they will both light up.'

C.   'It might take longer.'

A.   'No, they will both light up.'

When they observed that both bulbs lit but more dimly they put forward suggestions as to why they were dimmer.

A.   'Well, the electricity comes from here (pointing to the cell) and goes round to each bulb (positioning index fingers on either end of the cell and following the wires to each bulb) so it is shared out and so they are dimmer.'

B.   'Yeah, that's it.'

C.   'Yes, it does.'

They were asked to explain what happened in the wire between the bulbs.

A.   'Nothing, 'cause it doesn't get through.'

When Andy challenged them to explain what would happen if a third bulb was added to the circuit they realised that this explanation would not easily fit with their ideas. Although one girl attempted an explanation, they did not feel confident with their response.

A.   'Well, some will get through from this end but some will get through from that end.'

B.   'No, it all goes the same way so it must get through.'

C.   'Yeah.'

A.   'I'm not sure, it's a puzzle.'

Their initial description concerning the function of the battery appeared sophisticated and reasonably accurate. The idea that a current was produced once the circuit was complete added credibility to the explanation. The analogy indicating a push from the battery fits with a naïve yet accepted description of how an electric current moves. It would be easy to assume that they had a good understanding of the function of a series circuit. However, on closer scrutiny subsequent questions revealed a mismatch between their original explanations and well-held beliefs. Although they could explain the function of the battery, they could not apply this knowledge in another context. When posed the question, 'If another bulb is added to the circuit, why are both bulbs dimmer?' they readily reverted to the naïve view that electricity comes from the battery and it is shared between the bulbs. The need to justify explanations is a way of verifying knowledge but because it is based on present understanding it is flawed. If the original explanation had been taken at face value and accepted without question, assessment of understanding would not be accurate. It is easy to see from this example how much assessment can be concerned with accepting knowledge without checking understanding. Left to their own devices children will only go so far in developing understanding and there is a danger of recycling naïve ideas. What a creative teacher will be concerned about is teaching to check understanding, with the opportunity to encourage exploration and possibilities through play as well as structured scenarios.

Checking understanding

When deciphering pupils' understanding it is sometimes helpful to design specific tasks that check understanding. By gradually increasing the level of expertise needed to successfully complete the task, levels of understanding can be assessed, as with the previous example. Staying with the topic of electricity, this can be done in conjunction with Design Technology (DT) and Information and Communication Technology (ICT) by making models of lighthouses, houses and buildings in which children set up circuits to control lights or buzzers. Tasks can easily be differentiated to assess progression and development of competence. Each task, (T), will be followed by an assessment focus, (AF).

- (T) Making a downstairs light come on when the door is closed. (AF) Ability to use components to complete a simple circuit and use a switch (door) to break the circuit.
- (T) Making the light upstairs dimmer than the light downstairs. (AF) Recognise wire of differing thickness will affect electrical resistance.
- (T) Making lights come on upstairs but not downstairs. (AF) Ability to set up a parallel circuit and use switches to control different parts of the circuit.
- (T) Operating a door bell when the lights are on. (AF) Ability to increase the voltage in a simple circuit.

Not only will the pupils act as problem solvers, they will learn as they are being assessed, trial and error being part of the process. The perseverance and confidence displayed will offer information about the child's ability to cope with problems. If tasks are successfully completed without help then observable evidence will eradicate the need for discussion to assess understanding. If help is needed then discussion and dialogue initiated by the teacher will support analysis of understanding. The information received need refer only to the question asked or the problem posed. This is a neat, tidy package of planned assessment and should be viewed as such. But in the primary classroom it is possible to set up scenarios and situations to check progress which are much more adventurous, far reaching and collaborative.

Creating conditions for meaningful assessment

If we are to accept that assessment can be a creative process then we need to understand conditions which are appropriate for assessing not only subject knowledge but also the practice of doing science. Opportunities for children to work at a pace without interruption where decisions can be followed and resources are chosen independently will encourage creative endeavour. Spontaneity is essential. Children can become excited about surprises such as a mixture of yeast, sugar and warm water blowing up a balloon or an eggshell dissolving in vinegar. Events can be used to trigger discussion, such as on a clear day observing both the full moon and Sun visible in the morning sky or the contents of a lost lunch box in which the apple had not gone mouldy. The key to creative assessment is in recognising opportunities and providing conditions which enable children to work with teacher support in:

- considering possibilities;
- using a range of situations and locations;
- sharing thinking;
- speculating on outcomes;
- monitoring progress;
- discussing problems;
- identifying new connections.

For example, children may be asked to help detectives gather evidence to solve a crime with instructions:

Detectives need to eliminate some of the evidence they have collected to build a profile/picture of the criminal. They have found fingerprints and lipstick on a glass. In the glass there is some liquid. They have a scrap of paper with some writing on it, two footprints, some fibres and an apple core found near the footprints. Several work stations are set up to help you test each piece of evidence. Tests including chromatography, using an Intel microscope to compare fibres, taking fingerprints and Ph test for acids will help you decide which evidence is important.

What can you find out? All evidence is important but some of the evidence will be eliminated from your inquiry. Discuss reasons for eliminating evidence with your team. When you have completed all the tests, write a report for the detectives telling them what you have found out. Bullet-point the facts. Bullet-point evidence rejected.

In teaching science it is important to help children make the distinction between fact and inference. For example, a simple chromatography test will identify black ink by colour separation but it will not identify the writer. This approach will raise debate as well as covering several science skills and subject knowledge. Although there is a tight structure to the instructions, opportunities for assessment have been created to fit in with the checklist above. If pupils devise their own 'forensic science' scenarios for fellow pupils to explore then assessment becomes less predictable but more informative. This happened with a class of children working at the university. The pupils planned a 'who dun it' scene similar to one found in a game of Cluedo. They set the scene by drawing a chalk outline of a body, laid out a murder weapon, candle, food and drink on a table, and put blood (food colouring) on a handkerchief with the instruction to 'Find the time of the murder.' This was a neat twist as the assessment focus was on recognising physical and chemical changes.

If instead pupils were given multiple choice questions on physical and chemical change as an assessment exercise then their experience of exploring the subject would be limited to giving answers. This in turn would emphasise the need to be 'right' which in turn will limit children's confidence in asking questions for fear of 'being wrong'. In this case the teacher will discover only what is asked for. Children are innate theory builders; they try to make sense of what they see and give explanations which indicate understanding, just like adults, by the knowledge they have. Consequently, meaningful assessment must focus on opportunities to involve the child and not be reduced to a set of procedures.

Summary of main points

- Creative assessment must be concerned with gaining evidence from a variety of sources and settings. It must be seen as a journey in which children's understanding is supported as part of the process.

- Setting the scene for discovery, problem solving, collaborative challenges and unknown outcomes will provide a wider spectrum of evidence on which to base judgements.

- Teachers' professional judgement builds a picture of the child's understanding of science. This judgement will be influenced by assessment strategies chosen:

  - There are better and more creative ways of assessing understanding than merely assessing selected outcomes. 'Teaching to the test' puts boundaries on creativity.

  - Creative assessment relies on a degree of speculation. Irrelevance must be accepted if creative thinking is to be valued.

  - Assessment works best if it goes beyond specified recall to include confirmation of understanding and is part of teaching and not a separate add-on activity.

  - To make assessment enjoyable it should be useful, interactive and practical.

Issues for reflection

- What would be the arguments for and against abolishing statutory assessment tests?

- Have you experienced a 'wow' moment when you observed a child or children make a leap of understanding? How did you recognise the learning? From your experience of teaching primary-aged children, identify some examples of creative assessment opportunities.

- What would you want to see included in a school's assessment policy for science?

- Can you identify opportunities to assess science understanding in other areas of the curriculum? For example, in art or PE.

Discussion points

- Assessment is a process with clearly defined and separate stages to include the collection of evidence, critical analysis of evidence to include judgements and outcomes which support learning. In which ways could creativity enhance each stage?

- Adopting a creative approach to assessment which puts the child at the heart of the process is not possible in a primary classroom. Discuss.

Recommended reading

Clarke, S. (2001) *Unlocking Formative Assessment*. London: Hodder & Stoughton

Conner, C. (1999) *Assessment in Action in Primary School*. London: Falmer Press

Drummond, M.J. (1993) *Assessing Children's Learning*. London: David Fulton

Hall, K. and Burke, W.M. (2003) *Making Formative Assessment Work*. Maidenhead: Open University Press

Torrance, H. and Pryor, J. (2002) *Investigating Formative Assessment*. Maidenhead: Open University Press

References

Briggs, M., Woodfield, A., Martin, C. and Swatton, P. (2003) *Assessment for Learning and Teaching in Primary Schools*. Exeter: Learning Matters Ltd

Cockburn, A. (2001) *Teaching Children 3 – 11: A Student's Guide*. London: Paul Chapman

Craft, A. (2002) *Creativity across the Primary Curriculum: Framing and Developing Practice*. London: Routledge Falmer

Driver, R. (1985) *The Pupil as Scientist*. Buckingham: Open University Press

Edwards, C., Gandini, L. and Forman, G. (eds) *The Hundred Languages of Children: The Reggio Emilia Approach – Advanced Reflections* (2nd edn). London: ABLEX

Elstgeest, J. (1985a) 'Encounter, interaction and dialogue', in W. Harlen (ed.) *Primary Science: Taking the Plunge*. London: Heinemann

Elstgeest, J. (1985b) *The Right Question at the Right Time*. London: Heinemann

Fogden, E. (1989) *Science Now! Space Physics*. Cheltenham: Stanley Thornes

Hollins, M. and Whitby, V. (1998) *Progression in Primary Science*. London: David Fulton

INSET (2005) *Concept Cartoons*. Available: http://www.conceptcartoons.com/concise.html [2005, 28/09/2005]

Keogh, B. and Naylor, S. (1997) *Starting Points for Science*. Sandbach: Millgate House Publishers

Littledyke, M. and Huxford, L. (1998) *Teaching the Primary Curriculum for Constructive Learning*. London: David Fulton

Nussbaum, J. (1976) 'An assessment of children's concepts of the earth utilizing structured interviews', *Science Education*, 60: 535–50

Qualifications and Curriculum Authority (2003) *Creativity: Find it, Promote it*. London: HMSO

Qualter, A. (1996) *Differentiated Primary Science*. Buckingham: Open University Press

Ritzer, G. (1993) *The McDonaldization of Society: an Investigation into the Changing Character of Contemporary Social Life*. Pine Forge: Sage Publications

SPACE Reports, P. S. P. R. R. (1990–1996). Liverpool: Liverpool University Press

Vygotsky, L.S. (1978) *Mind in Society: The Development of Higher Psychological Processes*. Cambridge, MA: Harvard University Press

CHAPTER 11

Conclusion

The ways of creativity are infinite: the ways of formal learning are numbered.

(Robert Grudin)

I wrote this book after talking to a group of teachers at a science workshop in 2003. They conveyed to me a palpable sense of frustration. They experienced a tension between how they wanted to teach science and what they actually found themselves doing. They wanted to have more autonomy, be creative and take risks but felt restricted by schemes of work and expected outcomes. It would be reasonable to assume that because the National Curriculum is a statutory document and the curriculum is laid out for them, their concerns were about content. This was not the case. They did not so much question the content as methods of teaching and learning. They said:

> I cannot teach science how I want to teach it, I try hard to keep my negative feelings from influencing the enjoyment of the lesson. I try to make it interesting in some small way.
>
> Science is a minefield. On the one hand it claims to be the last bastion of absolute knowledge, answers and explanations, yet many changes have/are occurring in that knowledge which makes the whole thing fluid. We all need to look with seeing eyes and not be restrained by political dictates. Politicians are interested in results, so are teachers but the criteria are somewhat different.
>
> I can't teach the Earth and Beyond in 3 hrs, that is what I have been given. It's ridiculous. It's just coverage and will turn children off science. It's such an interesting subject. What message are we giving them? Science has such potential but this is immoral.
>
> In the spring term all Year 6 do are revision classes for SATs and it is a case of making sure they know the answers. They do past papers and booster classes and revision guidance. They are told key words and phrases to use and practise doing this. It is a school management decision. I don't agree with it but I am told to do it. The children groan when I say we are doing science, they hate it too. I feel that children learn best if they are

doing something active rather than passive, if they are curious and enthusiastic and can get pleasure from their involvement.

There is too much written and recorded work for Year 2, it is too regimented.

(Primary science teachers 2003)

I hope after reading this book that you will agree that teaching science can be about creative endeavour within the statutory science requirements and limitations. Teaching is not just a job to be done. Some of the best lessons are created by teachers becoming aware of problems, thinking up solutions and testing them on a daily basis. If a teacher believes that creativity enhances learning and is the best opportunity for the child then purpose is identified and nothing else will do. The question, 'Why am I teaching science in this way?' must then be asked and an answer found. In a fast-changing world, many teachers agree that, for them, creative teaching is the answer. If methods go against beliefs then teachers can lose the motivation to teach well. To be creative is no easy option, but the rewards are worth having. This raises its own question, 'What is so good about creative learning?'

Asked to describe their best science lesson, what might the response be? It is unlikely that a teacher's response would be, 'The children learnt that plants get their food through a process called photosynthesis. It was great because each child could draw the diagram, explain the process and passed the test' or 'It was wonderful, they all drew a rainbow and could identify the colours. They recognised that red light has a longer wave length and that blue is shorter. They wrote a mnemonic and memorised the order of colours.' This of course is an over-simplification to make a point, but such replies are not commonly heard from creative teachers.

A far more likely description would match that given by Dawn:

It was fantastic. The children got really involved. They were working out how to make the strongest glue, just using different types of flour and amounts of water. They tested their samples, devised a fair test and some used a hairdryer to speed up the process. Others said that wasn't fair. Then they tried to suspend larger and larger masses to see how strong their glue was. Some slipped but other samples were so strong. They were amazed at the force needed to separate the paper and in some cases that the paper broke first. They made Christmas decorations, paper chains, with their own glue. They knew exactly how to replicate the strongest glue as they wrote recipes on their test samples. I just watched them working for most of the time.

(Primary teacher 2003)

If children are asked to describe their best science lesson, similar indications regarding autonomy, involvement, participation and choice are evident in their responses:

We were allowed to make a lighthouse and to make a flashing message, we ended up doing Morse code because we couldn't work out how to make the light flash by itself. Damien's group did, they used a computer. It was brilliant. We made up messages and sent them across to other groups.

(Maya age 9)

I like drawing things and the best science was when the teacher cut open a melon and a pomegranate and a star fruit and I could see all the seeds. Some children counted them but I didn't, there were hundreds, all squishy. I dried some in the oven and made a pattern in clay, my Mum's put it on the windowsill. I like looking at seeds. I looked at a tomato and lemon and orange at home. I tried to cut a mango but I couldn't. I made a necklace from seeds but it broke.

(Toni age 7)

My group had to guess who had stolen some jewels. We had footprints to investigate and a load of shoes to look at and try to match in wet sand. The thief might have worn someone else's shoes. The teacher wanted facts so it was difficult. We also had a silhouette on the CCTV to match. Fingerprints and lipstick on a glass and a bite from an apple and threads to look at. When we found the match we knew it was Miss Moore the dinner lady, 'cause her apron matched the threads and we took her fingerprints. We thought it was our teacher but her fingerprints did not match.

(Sam age 11)

The relationship between the child learner and adult teacher is the fundamental focus implicit in the answers. Creative relationships are driven by a creative approach to learning, by responding to individual needs, recognising a sense of purpose, and offering a rich variety of experience from which to make choices. All this depends on allowing freedom to explore ideas with the premise of 'Why not?' instead of 'Why?' so that creative thinking can be encouraged.

The many practical examples in this book show that creative teachers encourage learning opportunities which are fuelled by a wide variety of possibilities. Immersion in the process is key to developing creative ideas. Following children's ideas is crucial. To support originality and imagination the teacher needs to provide the resources and openings to encourage divergent thinking. Moving away from expected responses, encouraging children to elaborate and redefine ideas is a powerful tool in the creative process.

Teachers can agonise about taking risks. One problem teachers will encounter is that creative activities cannot always be measured, in terms of achievement, against set criteria. Understandably, they want to know where their pupils will be at the end of a session. If you are a teacher who feels teaching science with an unknown outcome is too scary, then I would urge you to be brave. The remedy is simple. Go on small expeditions of adventure. You might fear that creative ways of teaching and learning can be unsettling, challenging and at times utterly disheartening but try it out. It will not be a cosy, predictable or easy ride. It may be chaotic, but it is worth the risk. As your confidence grows you will realise that there is more than one route to follow to a desired outcome. And more importantly, it is not always the easy option that is the most satisfying learning experience. The important decisions made by the teacher about possibility thinking, seen as a core process to creativity, and a child-centred approach to learning science cannot be underestimated. Learning science is not a one-way street. Pupils' views, problems and questions need to be listened to and supported in a secure and empathetic manner.

Children are not inhibited by constraints in the way that adults are. Boundaries and barriers have not become part of their psyche. They have not yet become programmed to compartmentalise their thinking. Making connections, to them, is a random process based on curiosity. Children see the world subjectively, and for them the here and now has meaning. Creativity goes beyond this, and playing with ideas is only a starting point. Sharing ideas and valuing different viewpoints, accepting and rejecting understanding is a high priority. Creative curiosity is unpredictable but goes beyond low-level instruction. Science cannot be taught well or received well without feeling a sense of wonder. The joy of 'fooling about' and creating happy learning cannot be underestimated. Even boring topics in the hands of creative teachers are turned into animated activities. Openness to experience and awareness of what might be alerts the observant teacher to opportune moments and happy accidents. Learning science must be thought of as a journey involving detours, dead ends and bumpy tracks as well as smooth rides. The time spent on the journey must be seen as a process of discovery full of surprises, transformations and growth.

Science education is an enjoyable end in itself and not just a preparation for adult life. As Douse (2005: 3–4) states, 'We do our students a serious disservice if we treat them predominantly as future adults. It is what they "are" rather than what they may "become" that is significant. Stimulate them, stretch them, encourage them, inspire them, promote their potential, advance their individuality, cultivate their community spirit, foster their natural curiosity, underwrite their divergent enthusiasms, in other words, educate them. But do so with their present pleasure rather than their future fulfilment as the primary objective. Let there be laughter as their inalienable right.' He goes on to say that, 'Half of the UK adult population has studied science for at least four years and yet very few can analyse a contemporary scientific issue such as GM foods, homeopathy, or MMR vaccination.' Teachers' attitudes, confidence and ability in providing creative, fun and enjoyable lessons is fundamental to sustaining interest in science. Teacher participation and knowledge of the creative process will be enhanced by a clear understanding that science can be creative and that dispositions to cultivate creativity are in place.

This includes:

- choice in decision making;
- immersion in ideas;
- recognition of possibilities;

- rewarding failure;
- original ideas and solutions;
- pupil's interpretation;
- questions;
- democratic negotiation;
- lack of targets or prescribed outcomes;
- ethical courage;
- imaginary scenarios;
- collaborative discussion;
- purpose;
- risk taking.

My final thoughts acknowledge that science is about technical competence as well as creativity in teaching and learning. Technical competence is the mechanism which supports theories, ideas and knowledge. Creative thinking is the mechanism which challenges ideas, theories and knowledge by considering possibilities and seeking the truth. We can have technical competence in science teaching without creativity, but rarely can we have scientific creativity without technical competence. Science teaching based solely on technical competence is a trip down memory lane, touring only what is known and never taking another path to see where it leads. The playwright Alan Bennett described his own education as one of being taught to pass examinations by learning strategies. He met inspiring teachers who seemed to teach a strategy, then digress into inspirational chatter about their subject. It was as if their inspiration had nothing to do with the real business of passing examinations, or it emerged once the tedious business of a strategy was out of the way. Even at Oxford, Bennett learned to pass examinations, reproducing what he had learned. Fortunately he had the courage to write for a career, but he still sees his education as something of a lost opportunity, but for the inspiration of one or two rebel teachers. Examinations often bring out the worst and are a necessary way of testing only the testable. If children are taught just technical competence they will be able to reproduce the skills used by scientists. That may be fine, but if they can go beyond this, they can realise the joy and wonder of discovering something for themselves.

Reference
Douse, M. (2005, 13–15 September) 'Learning and laughter – and let livelihood come after', paper presented at the UKFIET International Conference on Education and Development Learning and Livelihood, Oxford, UK

Index